Playing It by Ear

Playing It by Ear

Literary Essays Ear *and Reviews*

William H. Pritchard

University of Massachusetts Press   Amherst

Copyright © 1994 by
The University of Massachusetts Press

All rights reserved

Printed in the United States of America

LC 94-12255

ISBN 0-87023-947-3 (cloth); 948-1 (pbk.)

Designed by David Ford

Set in Adobe Minion by Keystone Typesetting, Inc.

Printed and bound by Thomson-Shore, Inc.

Library of Congress Cataloging-in-Publication Data

    Pritchard, William H.
      Playing it by ear : literary essays and
    reviews / William H. Pritchard
        p.   cm.
      Includes index.
      ISBN 0-87023-947-3 (alk. paper). —
    ISBN 0-87023-948-1 (pbk. : alk. paper)
      1. English literature—20th century—
    History and criticism.   2. American
    literature—20th century—History and
    criticism.   3. Books—Reviews.   I. Title.
    PR473.P75   1994
    820.9—dc20   94-12255
                                     CIP

British Library Cataloguing in Publication data are available.

For Bill Youngren, my oldest critic

Contents

Contents

Acknowledgments

Earlier versions of the present collection were read and usefully commented on by Francis Murphy, David Sofield, and Brad Leithauser. Christopher Benfey advised me about what to include in and leave out of *Playing It by Ear* and also suggested the title. Bruce Wilcox was a responsive editor and Pamela Wilkinson a scrupulous reader of the manuscript. Doris Troy assiduously read proof.

I owe an immense debt to Frederick Morgan who twenty-seven years ago opened the pages of the *Hudson Review* to me and has unfailingly continued to support and encourage my work as a critic.

Preface

Many years ago, after I had just accepted an appointment to teach English at Amherst College, my mentor at Harvard, Reuben Brower—who had taught at Amherst for many years—gave me a piece of advice. Amherst was a small college in a small town, he said, and I had better find something to do besides my teaching. There was peril in too exclusive a commitment to designing courses, reading student papers, and participating in the world of departmental and college politics; he, Brower, had found gardening to be a good alternative when the academic world was too much with him. Although the notion of creative outdoor work did nothing to make my heart beat faster, I filed away the warning.

At that time I hadn't the vaguest notion that writing essays and reviews would turn out to be my substitute for cultivating a garden and my alternative to an exclusively academic and collegial life. I got into reviewing books almost accidentally when the editor of Amherst College's alumni magazine asked me for eight hundred words about a critical study of Henry James by an alumnus. I wrote the words for free, but got to keep the book: that was the beginning, and I was hooked. A few years later the editor of the *Hudson Review*, Frederick Morgan, invited me to do a critical roundup of poetry published during the previous three months. In due course forty or so slim volumes arrived, were stacked on the mantelpiece or piano top, and made me feel intensely professional—after all, this time I would be paid. One thing led to another, and I soon found myself writing for various quarterlies and weeklies. This involved real mail (sometimes containing real checks) and real phone calls about subjects that had nothing to do with Amherst College; it began to feel as if my spiritual fitness depended on confronting a book or a writer and composing the occasion into a critical statement someone might be interested in reading.

The effect of all this activity was to make me feel less like a proper American academic. I directed admiration rather toward the prodigious talents of book critics like V. S. Pritchett, Geoffrey Grigson, and Julian Symons—all English, none of them university-educated—whose many-sided virtuosity could be emulated if not attained. I avoided conventions of the Modern Language

Association, "our" professional body, and missed symposia of various sorts on current hot topics. I had my teaching and a few books to write; in between there was always what Irving Howe once termed the "steady work" of reviewing.

Most of the hundreds of essays and reviews I've written—more reviews than essays, though sometimes it's hard to draw the line—are ephemeral, as should be the case. But I've gathered together thirty-three items that deserve perhaps a slightly longer life. In making this sampling I looked for instances in which I managed to say something about the novelist or poet or critic (all of them American or English, almost all from this century) that still seems to me of interest. I've excluded "straight" reviews of new fiction or poetry, whether omnibus chronicles for magazines like *Hudson Review* and *Poetry,* or responses to a single work. And I've also excluded anything that overlaps with or duplicates material from my books about modern writers.

The selection contains a few polemically inclined treatments of contemporary voices, mostly within the academy, that seemed to me overrated or pretentious, at any rate in need of deflation. I have tried not to pick on the obscure, only on those who had been to one degree or another well rewarded with praise. And I have been at pains to meet solemnity with ironic humor, remembering Robert Frost's remark that he was never more serious than when joking. The only principle consistently observed is to quote liberally from the book or writer under consideration: you don't have to admire the words, but you should let them speak. The pieces have been grouped into simple categories ("Poets," "Novelists," "Critics," "Polemics") with a concluding section titled "Personal Disclosures" made up of "lighter" efforts about Frost-watching, soap-opera watching, and the writing of hostile reviews. Aside from minor corrections, they are unrevised, but I've provided some retrospective words about origin or motive.

Randall Jarrell says in "The Age of Criticism" that the first demand made upon any real critic is that he stick his neck out, just as the artist does, and risk making a complete fool of himself. I concur, believing also that criticism can only be as incisive as it is playful, and that the critic must read with his ears as well as his eyes. The introductory essay to this book describes my style and practice as a teacher of literature who likes to play it by ear; the pieces that follow it enact, I hope, the kind of reading described in that credo.

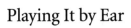

Playing It by Ear

Credo

"Ear Training" was written for a collection of essays by members of
the Amherst College faculty titled *Teaching What We Do* (1991),
and reprinted in the *South Atlantic Quarterly* (Summer 1992). The
essays—by, among others, a physicist, a painter, a political scientist,
a psychologist—attempted to describe what it was, individually, we
thought we were up to in the classroom, the presumption being
that such matters would be of much interest to alumni. Three
years later, the sales figure of twelve hundred copies suggests something less than overwhelming curiosity on their part.

Ear Training

The critic William Empson once said that he did not know how much of his mind T. S. Eliot had invented. In setting out to write about myself as a teacher in Amherst classrooms, the only proper place to begin is with an earlier self in those same classrooms, forty or so years ago, when my mind—such as it is— was invented. The inventors were essentially three in number—Theodore Baird and G. Armour Craig, both professors of English at the college, and their colleague Reuben Brower who had an effect on me at Amherst but even more when he became a teacher and I a graduate student at Harvard. I encountered Armour Craig in the fall of freshman year when I took the required Composition course, conceived by Theodore Baird some years previously and—by 1949—having come fully into its own as a brilliantly original approach to writing as an activity. That activity, performed by us three times each week—in short responses to difficult, sometimes impossible questions about thinking, meaning, knowing, and other essential human pastimes—was my introduction to serious intellectual inquiry. Having graduated from high school, I had already become an expert in solemnity, but the Amherst English inquiry, as it was conducted in the questions asked us and in the professor's response to our papers, was invariably playful, therefore puzzling to us. By the end of the term if not earlier, we began to suspect that language was something other than the mirror of reality; that—in a phrase of Joseph Conrad's I would come to later on—words are, among other things, "the great foes of reality"; and that the way we went about marshaling our words into sentences, "composing" reality, could be a matter both for despair and for hopefulness, but was nothing less than central to what we did every day.

Freshman Composition was valuable to me partly as a deterrent to flatulence. Since among other things the course was an elementary education in irony, it was salutary for a young achiever whose high school valedictory address three months previously was titled "Health" and stressed the importance of all of us staying healthy. In the extended activity of writing as practiced in English I (thirty-three times the first term) we—teacher and students—looked at what we had written, at what could or couldn't be said in a sentence. The

3

course took no notice of literature; that noticing occurred the following year in the sophomore "Introduction to Literature," another staff course, this one mainly the creation of Reuben Brower. English 21–22 had the effect, whether intended or not, of helping us regain some of the confidence we might have lost the previous year, since Brower and his staffmates had what looked to be a useful vocabulary for talking about what went on in poems and stories and novels. That vocabulary, which featured such terms as tone, attitude, dramatic situation, was derived from Brower's study with I. A. Richards, author of the extraordinarily influential *Practical Criticism.* In Sophomore English, and in the Humanities 6 course Brower subsequently introduced at Harvard (in which I did my first teaching), we engaged in collaborative reading carried on in both a leisurely and a sharply focused manner. Just as Freshman Composition consisted in examining the particular essays, paragraphs, and sentences we students had produced, so the literature course never wandered for long from its intent consideration of the words on the page—of the individual poem or stanza or line or word that momentarily engaged us.

The words on the page—well, yes; but what I remember most about my Amherst English teachers is the way they took words off the page and brought them to life through the speaking voice. Baird reading aloud a soliloquy from *Hamlet* in a rather self-consciously loud, deliberately unactorish way, yet one that was scrupulously observant of the syntax and sense of the lines; Craig beginning his consideration of Milton's poetry with an extended reading out of "Lycidas" ("Yet once more, O ye laurels, and once more / Ye myrtles brown, with ivy never sere"); Brower imitating the finicky, weary cadences of the lady in T. S. Eliot's "Portrait of a Lady":

> So intimate, this Chopin, that I think his soul
> Should be resurrected only among friends
> Some two or three, who will not touch the bloom
> That is rubbed and questioned in the concert room.

Behind such performances—the insistence that in the beginning, first of all, the poem needed to be *heard,* realized in the manner through which it was read aloud—was the example of Frost ("Now I'm gonna *say* a few poems for ya"). It was the same Frost who remembered hearing Brower, when he was a student at Amherst, read aloud in class a sixteenth-century poem by an otherwise forgotten poet, Richard Edwards, which began "In going to my naked bed as one that would have slept." "Goodness sake, the way his voice fell into those lines, the natural way he did that very difficult poem," said Frost years after the event.

This primacy of the speaking voice, this insistence on getting the tone right—of (in Frost's own words) seizing the special "posture" needed to deliver it correctly—informed, in ways I surely wasn't conscious of at the time, my "approach" to literature and eventually my dealings with it in the classroom. Nor was I conscious that Frost's discovery, so he truly thought it, of the primacy of voice in poetry was the cornerstone of what theorizing he did about the act and the art of reading. He put these thoughts powerfully and succinctly in a letter written home from England in February of 1914:

> *The ear does it.* The ear is the only true writer and the only true reader. I have known people who could read without hearing the sentence sounds and they were the fastest readers. Eye readers we call them. They can get the meaning by glances. But they are bad readers because they miss the best part of what a good writer puts into his work.

My education at Amherst—that part of it conducted within the English department, both in the composition and the literature course, and in their successors—was essentially a training in ear reading, whether the bit of writing under scrutiny was (as it often was) a lyric of Frost's, or the opening of Henry James's *Portrait of a Lady* ("Under certain circumstances there are few hours in life more agreeable than the hour dedicated to the ceremony known as afternoon tea"), or one of the unwittingly fatuous sentences I turned out in my papers. Do you want to sound like *that?* was the direct or implied question we were invited to put to our own prose, while practice in listening to Frost and James brought the awareness that other designs, other ways of sounding, were possible, at least within reach of our ears.

Despite my introduction to ear-reading, I graduated from Amherst a philosophy major, with the intention of becoming a teacher of that discipline. Accordingly, I spent a year listening to some very good eye-readers in the Columbia University department of philosophy. Unlike Frost's eye-readers, who speedily picked up the meaning by glances, these professors were hard-nosed teasers-out of the sense of passages in Locke or Kant or Whitehead. But outside of class I was reading Kenneth Burke's *A Grammar of Motives,* in which Burke performed "dramatistic" readings of and listenings to the philosophers, showing how their sentences talked to each other and made for a "life" in their words analogous to that found in poetry or fiction. Burke's subversive demonstrations of how philosophic meaning was as much a creation of language, of voice even, as was "literary" meaning, pushed me out of the formal study of philosophy and into literature. Subsequent work quickly showed me, however, that the academic study of literature could be every bit as "eye"-oriented as traditional academic philosophy. With the important exception of Brower, by then teaching at Harvard (the institution to which I transferred), professors of literature were either scholars or historians of ideas, English literature being conceived of as a matter of sources and influences, traditions and literary movements. Reading, it was assumed, was something people did on their own time and presumably were perfectly capable of doing. Were we not, after all, in graduate school and at Fair Harvard to boot?

Whether Harvard English was right or wrong in its procedures and assumptions, "we"—the Amherst people studying literature there, a substantial number—were up to something rather different. Insofar as we conceived of our purpose in criticizing and teaching literature, it was something clearly distinct from the way Harvard laid out the map of literature and placed individual figures and groups on that map. Most of us in the "Amherst contingent" (we were sometimes referred to as such) didn't think of ourselves as scholars, or even as potential writers of books. There was rather—and I think in contrast to many of our peers from other institutions—an eagerness to get into the classroom and instruct others about the kinds of literary discoveries we were making. While our peers were busily contriving to get a first article published (so it seemed to us, perhaps paranoically), we contrived to ignore the whole matter of publication, even though it might be necessary to move our professional careers into orbit.

If my own career didn't exactly get into orbit, it began to assume a direction when, suddenly and unforgettably, a call came in December of 1957 from the then chairman of the Amherst English department, Benjamin DeMott, asking me how I'd like to come down for an interview with the president and the department, with the likely outcome of an appointment at the college. For someone who had carried around with him since undergraduate days the notion of teaching at a small college like Amherst, this was a heady and risky invitation—for now it was to be not just "like" Amherst but the very thing itself. How fitting it was that, in preparation for my interview with President Charles W. Cole, the only piece of advice I received was a simple, memorable injunction from Theodore Baird: "Speak up!" I was, in other words, to announce myself at the outset as a young man with a voice, someone who was going to be heard. I must have spoken up at least enough to convince the department and president of my adequacy; later, when it came time for the tenure decision to be made, I was again smiled upon and became—in one colleague's word—a "keeper." Except for terms spent on sabbatical leave I've been teaching at this college since the fall of 1958.

So much, then, for autobiography: there follows an attempt to say what I've been doing in the classroom during the past three decades. Along with describing one or two pedagogical clarities or discoveries, I need also to name what I'm "against"—approaches to teaching, to literature, to students, that seem to me markedly unhelpful toward, sometimes destructive of, good reading and writing. My examples are taken from courses I've taught over the past few years: period ones in Romantic and Modern British poetry; seminars in literary criticism and in seventeenth-century poetry; larger lecture courses in Reading Fiction and Modern Satiric Fiction; and the introductory course, Writing About Reading, which I teach every fall.

Recently a secondary school teacher of English asked me what I expected or hoped my students would "know" about poetry, about literature, when they came to college as first-year students. My response was, after thinking about it for a while, that students need not necessarily know anything in particular— need own nothing except, in Yeats's phrase, their blind stupefied hearts. Less melodramatically, let them own an ear open to the soundings of words; let them also own feelings not wholly dedicated to immediate suppression in favor of preparing for law or medical school exams. What then do they need, to read with some success the following lines from Shakespeare's *Antony and Cleopatra* in which Cleopatra eulogizes her dead lover:

> For his bounty,
> There was no winter in't: an autumn 'twas
> That grew the more by reaping: his delights
> Were dolphin-like, they show'd his back above
> The elements they lived in: in his livery
> Walk'd crown and crownets: realms and islands were
> As plates dropp'd from his pocket.

In asking a class of first-year students what's going on in this sequence I don't expect they will immediately begin talking about the difference it makes that the lines are enjambed; that the sentence units run over the lines and create an impassioned—and vividly metaphorical—utterance quite different from, say, a speech in *Romeo and Juliet*. My main concern has to do rather with the quality of feeling these lines about Antony project or express through the extraordinary language Shakespeare gives Cleopatra. But of course that quality of feeling can be approached only by readers who listen to the pace and cadence of the verse instead of merely moving their eyes across the lines.

For a moment, suppose we forget that poetry is written in feet and lines, thereby presenting special challenges to the reader who is attempting to tune in. One of the hoariest prejudices or assumptions among my students is that it takes a special talent or faculty to read poetry well, whereas everybody is pretty much equal before prose. (My fiction courses are much more heavily enrolled in than the poetry ones.) In fact, as I try to show them, such is not the case. Consider the ending of one of Hemingway's early stories, "Indian Camp," in which the young Nick Adams witnesses his father-doctor's makeshift Caesarean operation on an Indian woman, the operation undertaken with "a jackknife and nine-foot, tapered gut leaders." During this operation the woman's husband slits his throat, and as Nick and his father return home in their boat the following dialogue between them concludes the story:

> "Why did he kill himself, Daddy?"
> "I don't know, Nick. He couldn't stand things, I guess."
> "Do many men kill themselves, Daddy?"
> "Not very many, Nick."
> "Is dying hard, Daddy?"
> "No, I think it's pretty easy, Nick. It all depends."
>
> They were seated in the boat, Nick in the stern, his father rowing. The sun was coming up over the hills. A bass jumped, making a circle in the water. Nick trailed his hand in the water. It felt warm in the sharp chill of the morning.
>
> In the early morning on the lake sitting in the stern of the boat with his father rowing he felt quite sure that he would never die.

This lovely moment in Hemingway's work is especially vulnerable, in its delicate poise, to unlovely attempts by interpreters of the story concerned to tell us what it Really Means: one of them has called "Indian Camp" "the story of a boy coming into contact with violence and evil," while another has informed us that, at the story's end, Nick has "rejected his father and retreated from reality."

With Shakespeare's figurative and tonal richness everywhere evident ("For his bounty, / There was no winter in't"), it would be a travesty to say that in praising Antony lavishly Cleopatra has "retreated from reality" or has exaggerated his virtues through the enlargements of metaphor. These would be unfortunate attempts to "understand" Shakespeare's language by reducing it to formula and pretending that the characters made up their own speeches. With Hemingway, who—unlike Shakespeare—leaves out rather than puts in, aggressive and all-too-confident ways of understanding (such as are offered by the critics above) get in the way of good reading. They do so by providing crude and hasty ways for us to avoid what we should be engaged in; namely, with *listening* to the rhythms and manner of presentation, the "feel" of the scene. "A bass jumped, making a circle in the water. . . . It felt warm in the sharp chill of the morning": how could anyone who really listens to those sentences want to go on and talk about rejection of the father or retreating from reality? Why would they not want instead to talk about the beautiful sequence Hemingway has created here, from the father rowing, to the sun coming up over the hills, to the jumping bass, to Nick trailing his hand in the water and feeling it "warm in the sharp chill of the morning." Why would they not want to engage with what Frost says all poetry is about—"Performance and prowess and feats of association." "Why don't critics talk about those things?" Frost went on to ask. "What a feat it was to turn that that way, and what a feat it was to remember that, to be reminded of that by this. Why don't they talk about that?"

"They" don't—and here I mean by "they" many secondary school and college teachers of literature, as well as professional critics—because they are looking for literature to provide kinds of stabilities, the moral and psychological certainties writers like Shakespeare and Hemingway are concerned to undermine, or at least to ignore. When students of mine begin sentences telling me that in such a poem Keats or Emily Dickinson says that . . . , or how, in "Sunday Morning," Wallace Stevens believes that . . . , or how Shakespeare thinks that . . .—such sentences are tip-offs to a conception of literature as the repository of messages, opinions, and beliefs about life held by the writer and conveyed (doubtless in excellent language) to readers ready to be instructed. And if the teacher or critic has a strong agenda, the poem or story may be enlisted as an ally in furthering the cause. Or perhaps it is simply that teachers confronting a class and critics trying to get their essay written are reluctant to live with the instabilities and fluidities that imaginative writing like Shakespeare's or Hemingway's presents us with. "Did Shakespeare think anything at all?" T. S. Eliot once asked somewhat mischievously. "He was preoccupied with turning human actions into poetry," added Eliot. And it was Eliot also who remarked that Henry James had a mind so fine "no idea could violate it." Such challenges were aimed at disconcerting readers eager to extract ideas or beliefs from the work of notable artists; Eliot reminds us that these artists will not be reduced to the pedagogical or analytical needs of those who talk and write about their art.

One of our best critics and teachers of poetry, Helen Vendler, wrote recently of her teacher at Harvard, I. A. Richards (who years previously had been Brower's teacher at Cambridge), that he was the only professor she encountered there who—as she put it to herself at the time—"taught poetry":

> My other teachers rarely talked in detail about poems they had assigned: they talked about history, or politics, or theology, or literary movements, or archetypes—but not about those radiant and annihilating complexes of words that seemed to me to be crying out for attention, so inexplicable was their power and so compelling their effect.

My experience at Harvard tallies with Vendler's, though with Brower's and other Amherst voices in my head I didn't feel the need, as she did, to seek out Richards. But Vendler's speaking of poetry's "complexes of words" as both "radiant and annihilating" should give us interesting pause. Annihilating of what? Perhaps Richards's own writing provides a clue, if we remember what he once said about the final moment from *Antony and Cleopatra* when Octavius Caesar gazes down at the dead Cleopatra and observes that

> She looks like sleep,
> As she would catch another Antony
> In her strong toil of grace.

After quoting once more the final line—"In her strong toil of grace"—Richards asked "Where in terms of what entries in what possible dictionary, do the meanings here of *toil* and *grace* come to rest?" This is a question not to be answered by neat measurement, and one provoked, I think, by the way a particular complex of words, used by a master of language, can be "annihilating" of boundaries and limits as defined by the dictionary, or by the teacher intent on fixing a character or the play within some "meaningful" scheme of his own.

Most Amherst students who elect to take a poetry course with me expect that we will be centrally concerned with "complexes of words" as they are laid into lines and stanzas. But when fiction rather than poetry is the subject, such an assumption about focus is less common. In Modern Satiric Fiction we read many books during the semester—about one a week—so that there isn't time to pay the kind of respectful and detailed attention to language one can afford a lyric by Hardy or Yeats. Does that mean that attention must, initially or ultimately, be turned somewhere else than toward language? There are different ways to view this issue, and one critic (Marvin Mudrick), whose major interest was in fiction rather than poetry, has warned us that "in the beginning of poetry is the word; in the beginning of fiction is the event." Mudrick argues that the words of a work of fiction needn't be so precise and special as the words of a poem, and that fiction's words should not arrogate to themselves too much precision or "radiance" (Vendler's word). Perhaps so; yet the characters and events in a novel are perceived—are constructed by the reader— only through language. If some novelists, Dreiser say, or Dostoyevsky, ask to be considered in terms other than for their "precise and special use of words," there are others, James or Proust or John Updike, who as far as I can see stake everything on their "verbal complexes," on their styles.

In any case, I find that students in my fiction class are often puzzled as to what, in their papers, they should be writing about. I remember vividly how one member of the class who had done poorly on his first essay came to talk to me about this matter: what did I, in the famous word, "want"? I may have been somewhat evasive, but finally he asked, point blank, "You mean you want us to write about the language?" Remaining calm, I said that this didn't seem a bad idea to me; sure, why not try writing about the writing, rather than about the truth, or American society, or male-female relationships. No doubt the student left my office figuring that he'd pegged me as one of those aesthetes interested in technique rather than substance. What he didn't know, and what I couldn't tell him at that point, was that "technique" is more mysterious and even "annihilating" of clearly marked boundaries and dictionary definitions than he might have thought. Once more Eliot provides the useful formulation: "We cannot say at what point technique begins or where it ends."

Writing well about writing—whether that writing is poetry, drama, or fiction—means that the student must be helped to listen well; so, in a recent term of Reading Fiction, I invited the class which had just completed works by Dickens, Trollope, and George Eliot (the latter two items were fairly short, and I assigned only half of Dickens's *Pickwick Papers*) to see what would happen if they practiced some of Frost's "ear-reading" with respect to a particular sequence from one of these writers. They were to select a passage, quote it at least in part (such focus localizes attention to individual sentences), and then—in a deliberately vague question I often resort to—try to describe their "interest" in the sequence or passage. One student quoted some sentences from Eliot's short novel, *Amos Barton,* in which the clergyman's wife Milly is introduced: "a lovely woman—Mrs. Amos Barton: a large, fair, gentle Madonna, with thick, close chestnut curls beside her well-rounded cheeks, and with large, tender, short-sighted eyes." The student felt, rightly, that such language contrasted rather sharply with Eliot's comic and satirical presentations of other characters—most notably, the Rev. Amos Barton himself—in previous chapters. Where on earth, asked the student, did "this gentle Madonna" with her "placid elegance and sense of distinction" come from?

> Is she perhaps instead a divine being descended directly from the heavens? Somehow it is too much to swallow without choking a bit. Are we to believe that the sly wit so skillfully exhibited on the preceding pages can perform such an abrupt about face?

He went on to quote more of Eliot's picture of Milly as possessing the "soothing, unspeakable charm of gentle womanhood; which supersedes all acquisitions, all accomplishments. . . . You would even perhaps have been rather scandalized if she had descended from the serene dignity of *being* to the assiduous unrest of *doing.*"

All this, the student felt, was too much. Was it possible, he wondered, that Eliot, "a highly intelligent and sensitive woman in a society dominated by the male sex," felt contempt for the "regard" in which women were held? Could indeed the description of Milly be understood as "a parody of the skewed, romantic, Christian notion of the 'ideal woman' current at the time"? Could Eliot, in going so far as to write the following sentence—"Happy the man, you would have thought, whose eye will rest on her in the pauses of his fireside reading"—be deliberately mocking the conception of woman as pure and sacrosanct, a conception given much currency by male poets and novelists?

Whether his speculations and inferences are wholly correct or need to be adjusted and qualified needn't concern us here, though they were of concern when we discussed his paper in class. The point is that the student gave us something to argue about and did so by beginning with George Eliot's "technique": with matters of voice, diction, and intonation—words brought off the page and to life in an imagined utterance. We can't say where technique begins or where it ends, proof of which statement is there in the student's move from small, local matters of hearing and noticing, to speculations about male and female in nineteenth-century England—large matters indeed. But the respect paid to Eliot's art is both evident and admirable. This is an "English" paper, a piece of literary criticism rather than a sociological or political argument.

One further example of how practice in listening to, in constructing and describing the "sound" of a particular novelistic moment may lead to results that couldn't otherwise have been achieved. The climactic chapter of Jane Austen's *Persuasion* is one in which the heroine, Anne Elliott, and her lover-husband to be, Captain Wentworth, become fully aware of their love for one another. Anne is engaged in conversation with a mutual friend of hers and Wentworth's, Captain Harville, while Wentworth sits nearby, writing a letter, but in fact eavesdropping on the conversation. Anne and Harville get into a friendly argument about the differences between men and women, and which sex has the stronger capacity for feeling, for "loving longest" especially "when existence or when hope has gone." (Anne and Wentworth, through her decision, were separated years previously and she has never ceased to grieve for him.) Anne claims the privilege for women, but Harville, somewhat teasingly reminds her that "all histories are against you, all stories, prose and verse." He tells her that

> "I do not think I ever opened a book in my life which had not something to say upon woman's inconstancy. Songs and proverbs, all talk of woman's fickleness. But perhaps you will say, these were all written by men."
> "Perhaps I shall.—Yes, yes, if you please no reference to examples in books. Men have had every advantage in telling their own story. . . . I will not allow books to prove any thing."

Since throughout this particular book Anne has been characterized as a very serious reader, exceptionally responsive to fiction and poetry, her forbidding any reference to books has a sharp ring to it. The discussion continues with her own voice gradually becoming firmer and more poignant as, without ever mentioning his name, she indirectly confesses to the ever more attentive Wentworth the faithfulness and durability of her love for him.

In the exercise I gave my students I said that this passage in *Persuasion* could be studied for what it might reveal about Jane Austen's attitude toward the sexes. But, I suggested, it might be studied—at least *read*—for something else, and I asked them to try to describe that something. I had in mind the way, as

Credo

Anne assumes the ascendancy and moves toward a quite glowing affirmation of her love, she responds to Harville's polite admission that, since the evidence he alludes to comes from books which were all written by men, she is justified in denying their authority as foolproof indication of female inconstancy: "But perhaps you will say, these were all written by men." Then, with no narrative indication of how Anne says them (vigorously, teasingly, scornfully, determinedly?) we are given her three words back at Harville: "Perhaps I shall—." My point was that in this wonderful moment Austen is inviting, indeed compelling individual readers to do something, to "hear" these three words in a particular way—or at least to entertain some different ways in which they might be spoken. Whether the reader opts for calm certainty on Anne's part or a sudden seizing of the reins as the opportunity presents itself; whether she makes a humorous, eye-twinkling riposte to Harville or settles into a righteous affirmation of her claim's virtue—the three words need to be heard as rendered other than in a monotone. It is a moment in a dramatic sequence, in a conversation that has a before and after; it is progressive; it issues in something beyond itself. Returning to Frost once more: "The ear does it; the ear is the only true writer and the only true reader." My mildly polemical point in the exercise was that a reader interested only in what Jane Austen "thinks" about the sexes (in fact she thinks lots of things, contradictory ones even) is engaged in eye-reading merely, and is losing the best part of the experience of art.

> "I'd no more set out in pursuit of the truth
> than I would in pursuit of a living unless
> mounted on my prejudices."
> —Robert Frost

Kingsley Amis, one of the most entertaining novelists currently at work, once said with regard to a question of English usage: "I sometimes feel I have shifted a good way to the right in this matter over the years, but I feel no less often that (as in other matters) I have stayed more or less where I was while nearly everybody else has shifted to the left." There are a number of matters involving teaching, colleagues, students, and curriculum, where Amis's observation strikes home to me. Some are trivial; others perhaps less so. For instance: I still call students by their last name (Miss Jones, Mr. Smith) in class; still give a two-hour final examination in my courses. I dislike catalog descriptions by colleagues that go on for too long, or use "critique" as a verb ("students will critique each other's papers") or show an over-fondness for words like "problematizing." I look with a wary eye on courses that appear to have a political agenda with a view to replacing presumably unexamined student prejudices with "correct" left-liberal ones—though sometimes I think the left-liberal ones are correct. (It will of course be pointed out to me that the claim to have no political agenda is but another sort of political agenda. My withers are unwrung.) Although my department offers serious courses in film, I would prefer that students chose to study Shakespeare or Romantic poetry first, just as I want them to read and study literature before they take a course in literary theory, if they ever do. And at a time when the cry is for "opening up" what is termed the literary "canon" so as to include within it (or substitute for it) works by recently discovered or rediscovered female and minority, non-Western, nonwhite male writers, my interest is in going deeper into the canon as currently perceived. Or rather, in exposing students to the canonical works few of them are even acquainted with.

Some years back I had occasion, in a required course for English majors, to ask the class what it thought of this notion of opening up the canon; to a man and woman they replied that it seemed like a fine idea. I then threw out some names of well-known works and authors from the unopened canon—Marvell's "Horatian Ode," Wordsworth's "Resolution and Independence," Samuel Johnson, John Henry Newman, Anthony Trollope, Bernard Shaw. Not just the majority but virtually the entire class of intelligent and articulate Amherst College students had no sense at all of these writers and their work. Admittedly this fact isn't about to impress teachers dedicated to opening things up. But it brought home to me that, in these days of "pluralistic" (to use the dignified word for it) approaches to the teaching of English—days in which, more or less, anything goes—that it might be adventurous to teach the canon. Accordingly over the past few years I have offered old-fashioned "period" courses in English poetry from Spenser to Pope, or Wordsworth to Tennyson, and I plan to offer further ones involving eighteenth- and nineteenth-century British novelists and prose writers. In an important sense this is a selfish act on my part, since I'm serving my own need to explore further an already established list of writers and to share my discoveries with an audience. (It is easy, by the way, to forget how important students are in providing ears—sometimes responsive ones—for talk about writers, Marvell or Wordsworth or

Credo

Samuel Johnson, on whom you'd have trouble focusing the conversation at a dinner or cocktail party.)

How much does my resistance to some of today's going concerns have to do with being one of the tiny number of Amherst graduates who currently teach on its faculty? (There are four extant, three of us in our late fifties.) I do know that I'm strongly prejudiced against the notion that education at Amherst has improved over the past few decades as a result of gradual liberation from a required curriculum—The New Curriculum. Those who delight in Amherst's current pluralism have been known to characterize the learning atmosphere of that old New Curriculum as an "intellectual boot camp." On the other hand, nobody has suggested that the U.S. Marines were not well trained, and there is a case to be made for the kind of learning that, sometimes, went on in Amherst between 1946 and 1966. Still, the teacher-alumnus must also distrust his own affection for an undergraduate experience he may well be idealizing. The last two lines of Randall Jarrell's "In Those Days" put the case with proper ambiguousness—"And yet after so long, one thinks / In those days everything was better." "One thinks" that everything was better back then, when in fact things were, perhaps not worse, but certainly different. And to a nostalgic eye like my own, the very fact of difference, of something that was once and is now retrievable only in memory and imagination, imperceptibly elides itself from "different" into "better."

An unskeptical eye may also view the profession of English studies in rather more glamorous colors than are appropriate to the case. A useful critic of such glamorizing, Richard Poirier, has written of what he calls the "illusions" under which many academics labor—

> the illusion, first, of the necessity, and second of the enormous importance of literary studies. These illusions, shared in some degree by anyone occupationally involved, are difficult but necessary to resist. They intrude themselves because the study is confused with the subject, and teaching confused with the thing taught, the teacher, very often, with the author, whom he is "making available" to the young and to himself. It's a heady experience, after all, to have a direct line to Shakespeare, especially when it's assumed there's only one.

The warning is worth heeding, and yet—as Poirier himself admits—anyone who teaches English has to share such illusions "in some degree." Who knows when a line of poetry, read aloud in the classroom or to oneself in one's dormitory room, may come home to roost? More than once I've received testimony from a student about how—fifteen, twenty years after the fact—something Yeats wrote in a poem (a poem read sophomore year at Amherst) suddenly made sense. There is a poignant moment in Saul Bellow's *Seize the Day* when its hapless protagonist, Tommy Wilhelm, on the edge of failure and disaster, recalls involuntarily some words from a Shakespeare sonnet—"love that well which thou must leave ere long." Wilhelm begins to think about his college days and "the one course that now made sense"—"Literature I":

> The textbook was Lieder and Lovett's *British Poetry and Prose,* a black heavy book with thin pages. Did I read that? he asked himself. Yes, he had read it and there was one accomplishment at least he could recall with pleasure. He had read "Yet once more O ye laurels." How pure this was to say! It was beautiful.
>
> Sunk though he be beneath the wat'ry floor . . .

For all his clunkishness, Wilhelm has got it right, and the rightness involves his listening to a voice—Shakespeare's or Milton's or his own buried one—that suddenly surfaces with something momentous. Here, it seems to me, "the enormous importance of literary studies" (Poirier's words) becomes not illusory, but real and inescapable.

"Teaching what we do"—my "doing" in this essay may well sound too simple and schematic in its dwelling rather exclusively on matters of voice and listening as my focus in the classroom and in the papers I ask students to write. I might have gone on at some length about the mutually enhancing relationship I feel between the teaching I do in class and the writing I do outside of it. Or, if it were not an impossibly self-regarding occupation, I could have written about my teaching style as a humorous one. "If it isn't any fun, don't do it," D. H. Lawrence once advised; as I grow older I grow less interested in classes where there's no laughter. "Humor is the most engaging form of cowardice," was Frost's inventive definition, and it's clear to me that, with the exception of one or two transcendent geniuses like Milton or Wordsworth, few poets and novelists live without engaging us in humorous ways (in fact the poetic behavior of both Milton and Wordsworth can be the occasion for a good deal of fun in the classroom). So the teacher—and the student as well—needs to speak back to the work in a comparably fresh and enlivening manner. The most awkward moment in any class term is that first meeting, in which any pronouncement, no matter how outrageous, is likely to be met with total, if not totally respectful, silence. To make that silence come to life is part of the fun and point of any academic term. One of my best recent students wrote me a note at the end of a semester, saying that her sister was planning to take a course of mine in the fall, and that she had advised her sister to read the books carefully, write honestly on the papers, and listen hard for my jokes. If it's true that "the ear really does it," then her final bit of advice was a particularly good one.

Teaching What We Do: Essays by Amherst College Faculty. Amherst College Press, 1991.

Poets

"Frost Revised" was an unfriendly review of *The Poetry of Robert Frost*, a volume of Frost's complete poems published in 1969 by Holt, Rinehart and Winston and edited by the then librarian of Dartmouth College, Edward Connery Lathem. Lathem's editorial procedure, especially his wholesale repunctuating of the poems, was attacked by the poets Donald Hall and Frank Bidart as well as by me. Without acknowledging any names, Lathem replied to the charges a few years later in the *Dartmouth Alumni Magazine*, absolving himself of every one. In October 1995 the Library of America will publish an edition of Frost in which the poems will be un-Lathemized (or re-Frosted).

"Epistolary Eliot" was a review of the first of four promised volumes of T. S. Eliot's correspondence. As of 1994, no further volume has appeared.

The occasion for "MacLeish Revisited" was the poet's death in 1982 and subsequent publication of his letters, edited by R. L. Winnick. A biography of MacLeish, begun by Winnick and completed by Scott Donaldson, appeared in 1992, but there is no evidence that the poet is finding his way back into anthologies of American poetry. If he ever does, it should be on the basis of poems other than those anthologized ones of the past.

"Big Spender," about the poet who in certain ways has been MacLeish's English counterpart, was not undertaken with an open mind, since I'd disliked Sir Stephen's poetry (especially "I think continually of those who were truly great") for many years. Since his reflections in prose seemed scarcely more credible, an invitation to review his *Collected Poems* (1928–1985) and *Journals* (1939–1983) was accepted with malice aforethought. Probably not too many assignments should be taken on in this spirit.

"Robert Lowell (1917–1977)" was written just after Lowell died when, in response to the college newspaper's request for some words about his work, I provided an impressionistic and informal account of how it had impinged on my life. The parodist "Robert Lowly" was in real life Ian Hamilton, who would become Lowell's biographer.

Two years after Philip Larkin died in 1985, I wrote "Larkin's Presence," an appreciation of his poetry. The "small" poetic output I refer to was seen, after the publication in 1988 of his *Collected Poems,* to be rather larger than we'd suspected, since Larkin refrained from publishing so many poems most poets would be proud to see in print. Recently he has been on view in his published letters and in Andrew Motion's biography. Whatever disillusioning revelations these are found to contain don't make me revise downward in the least my opinion of his poetry.

I have reviewed a number of Kingsley Amis's novels, always with enthusiasm, but decided to include here "Entertaining Amis," written on the occasion of his *Collected Poems* (1979). After collecting them Amis seems to have shut up shop as a poet. I was interested in making a case for a body of work most people didn't seem to know about.

"How to Open a Pigeon," on Ted Hughes's long poem *Gaudete,* is an exception to my rule of not including reviews of new novels or volumes of poetry. I include this one because it illustrates the way a reviewer can be provoked enough by the book he's adversely criticizing to be carried into an oddly spirited energy that leaves him exhilarated instead of depressed.

With Sylvia Plath ("An Interesting Minor Poet?") it was a case of trying to make up my mind about a difficult body of work, under the useful stimulus provided by a deadline. Irving Howe, referred to in the review's conclusion, dropped me a postcard after it appeared saying that he still was not convinced of Plath's merits but that he would give her poetry another chance. I don't know whether he ever changed his mind.

The reviews of collections by two poetic Johns, Ashbery and Updike, reflect my inclination to honor and value "reference" to the things of this world that I find in Updike and not in Ashbery. Like those of Kingsley Amis, Updike's poems have been overlooked because of his identity as a novelist (the *New York Times Book Review* hasn't bothered to review his *Collected Poems*). As for Ashbery, nothing I've read of his work since 1985, when *Selected Poems* appeared, causes me to modify my opinion that his high reputation is one of the most curious examples of contemporary critical fashion.

Frost Revised

If you've dropped in at the local bookstore lately you may have noticed that the familiar green *Complete Poems of Robert Frost, 1949* has been replaced by a new collected edition called *The Poetry of Robert Frost,* followed by, in smaller letters, "Edited by Edward Connery Lathem." Running through the titles of other collections of famous modern poets—*The Collected Poems of W. B. Yeats,* or *T. S. Eliot: Collected Poems,* or *The Collected Poems of Wallace Stevens*—you may recall that none of those collections (one of them made posthumously) was edited by anyone, and you may wonder, therefore, why it is that Frost's poetry was judged to stand in need of editing. A publisher's note at the beginning of this volume tells us that, although the time has not yet come for a variorum or a definitive edition, "the current need is for a convenient volume both for general readers and scholars, scrupulously edited for textual accuracy"; and that because of Holt's long association with Frost, the book is thus published with special pride.

How convenient is the volume, and should Holt, Rinehart and Winston be proud of it? Its major addition to the 1949 *Complete Poems* is Frost's last book of poems, *In the Clearing* (1962), hitherto available only separately. The new volume has 607 pages, where its predecessor had 666; it is priced at $10.95, a few dollars more than the collections of the poets mentioned above. It is sturdily double-bound, as was the 1949 edition, and the poems are line-numbered as they were not previously—an advantage to critics and teachers, especially when dealing with longer poems. But since almost 100 pages of the volume are taken up by an editor's statement and the textual apparatus which follows it, let us scan those pages for what they tell us about the spirit and principles brought to the presentation of Frost's poems.

As one would expect, the bibliographical and textual notes are occupied mainly with documenting divergent readings, citing variants from the different editions, providing place and date of first publication. The typographical character and organization of the individual volumes—some of which

The Poetry of Robert Frost, edited by Edward Connery Lathem. Holt, Rinehart and Winston, 1969.

were retained at least in part in *Complete Poems, 1949*—are now relegated to, and described in, the notes. In some cases this means that material absent from *Complete Poems, 1949*, but present in the individual volumes as they appeared, has now reappeared in the textual notes; in this connection it is particularly pleasant to have handy once more the original glosses to the poems from *A Boy's Will*—"The youth is persuaded that he will be rather more than less himself for having forsworn the world" etc. But a good deal is lost too: no longer are we permitted the luxury of no more than one poem to a page (as in the *Complete Poems* edition), so that if we open to pages 12–13 we come upon the last two lines of "To the Thawing Wind," immediately followed on the page by "A Prayer in Spring," which in turn is followed by the first five lines of the first stanza of "Flower-Gathering"; then on to page 13 and the remaining three lines and second stanza of that poem, which is then followed by "Rose Pogonias." In other words, the pages are crowded, the poems often broken up unattractively. And much of the pleasure of those very short poems (originally introduced as *Quantula* in *A Witness Tree*, and preserved within the text of *Complete Poems, 1949*) is now lost. Most of the fun of "The Secret Sits"—"We dance round in a ring and suppose, / But the Secret sits in the middle and knows"—was to come upon the poem sitting there on a big white page in gnomic isolation; the same goes for "An Answer"—"But Islands of the Blessed, bless you, son, / I never came upon a blessèd one." In the new edition these poems share two pages along with seven other poems, and quarters are cramped.

These inconveniences, losses of fine old ways of presenting Frost's poems, would probably be forgivable: one could sigh about publishing costs, though that sigh might be tempered by the guess that Holt, Rinehart and Winston has made a fair amount of money from their Frost sales. But the editing of the poems goes beyond a listing of variants or dates of publication: Mr. Lathem is also responsible for "changes introduced by the present editor that constitute departures from copy-texts." The main copy-text is *Complete Poems, 1949*, but departures from it have been made "both for the correction of errors and for achieving greater textual clarity." I'm not quite sure what "greater textual clarity" means in principle; but in fact it seems to mean that the editor has seen fit to correct or improve Frost's punctuation of his own poems when that punctuation for one reason or another is deemed inadequate or misleading or awkward or whatever.

Though he does not elucidate specifically, it is clear that the editor thinks one of the best ways to correct error or achieve textual clarity is to declare war on the hyphen; so "witch-hazel" or "sleigh-bells" or "window-pane" or "star-like" now become "witch hazel", "sleigh bells," "window pane" and "starlike." Aside from what seems to me the needless and presumptuous fiddling involved in such emendations, what happens when the amusing line from "Fire-flies in the Garden" about how though the fireflies aren't stars they "Achieve at times a very star-like start" now becomes "starlike"? Or when the humorous command in "Clear and Colder"—"Then take some left-over winter" becomes "leftover"? Or even more annoying in "Birches" where "As ice-storms do" now becomes "As ice storms do," a somewhat duller deed; or "snow-crust" becomes "snow crust" or where Truth used to break in "With all her matter-of-fact about the ice-storm" she now breaks in without the fine emphasis those hyphens provide? What has happened to all the hyphens? A friend of mine suggested that perhaps the editor was bequeathed some large basket in which to store hyphens, and that after picking them out of the poems, he has so stored them.

But he must own an equally large basket of commas—seasoned with more emphatic dashes—eager to find their way into some poem or other, because Mr. Lathem has been as lavish in his providing of them as he has been saving of hyphens. Here are three instances of small changes made in some of Frost's best and most familiar poems; the reader may judge how small the changes are. In "An Old Man's Winter Night" the lines describing the old man's preparation for sleep used to read this way:

> He consigned to the moon, such as she was,
> So late-arising, to the broken moon
> As better than the sun in any case
> For such a charge, his snow upon the roof,
> His icicles along the wall to keep;
> And slept. . . .

The editor emends the first two lines to read:

> He consigned to the moon—such as she was,
> So late-arising—to the broken moon

Evidently Frost's steady unbroken trail of commas was not emphatic enough for Mr. Lathem's taste which judged that "such as she was, / So late-arising" needed the more special treatment provided by surrounding dashes. A second example: the Oven Bird's message used to be delivered this way:

> He says the early petal-fall is past
> When pear and cherry bloom went down in showers
> On sunny days a moment overcast;

Now a comma has been placed after "past," supposedly to warn us against the strong enjambment that sustains our voice from one line to the next. Did Frost not know what he was doing when he "omitted" the comma? Finally the famous lines from "Stopping by Woods on a Snowy Evening"

> Whose woods these are I think I know.
> His house is in the village though;

now read

> Whose woods these are I think I know.
> His house is in the village, though;

while "The woods are lovely, dark and deep," now has an added comma after "dark." It is as if a prim schoolmaster were at work, showing his concern for Robert's getting the correct punctuation into the business or friendly letter so that his English will be Good and Understood By All, rather than "Under a spell so the wrong ones can't find it, / So can't get saved." Perhaps the absence of a comma can be a very positive presence in the spell cast by a poem. In the case of "Stopping by Woods" the substantive change in tone introduced by the editor's emendation of a comma before "though"—"His house is in the village, though"—turns the speaker into a coyly twinkling fellow with all too much of a clever tongue lodged in his cheek. Robert Frost was more impersonal than that, and his jokes were harder to catch.

One of his poems ended (and still ends) with the following lines: "For I am There, / And what I would not part with I have kept." On the evidence of this edition I'd have to say, alas not all kept, but regrettably parted with and not, so far as I can see from the evidence, by the poet's own wish. I think some sort of explanation is due from Holt and the editor: until one is convincingly forthcoming I would advise you to save, as I have, the $10.95. If you don't already own a *Complete Poems, 1949* look up, by dint of hard labor, a secondhand bookstore where they will very likely have a copy someone recently and mistakenly has replaced by the new edition.

Atlantic, October 1970

Epistolary Eliot

In this beautifully appointed and superbly edited first volume of T. S. Eliot's correspondence (there will be four volumes in all), Eliot's widow, Valerie Eliot, uses as epigraph to the whole enterprise a passage from a lecture her husband delivered in 1933. The lecture has not survived, but Eliot's brother Henry recorded two sentences which addressed, with T.S.E.'s usual originality, the matter of how one should feel about writing letters, or about having one's letters read by others, or about reading letters not written to us:

> The desire to write a letter, to put down what you don't want anybody else to see but the person you are writing to, but which you do not want to be destroyed, but perhaps hope may be preserved for complete strangers to read, is ineradicable. We want to confess ourselves in writing to a few friends, and we do not always want to feel that no one but those friends will ever read what we have written.

So although he might not have been thrilled at the prospect of a complete stranger like myself eavesdropping on a 1915 confession to Pound—"Besides, I am constipated and have a cold on the chest"—Eliot has tactfully allowed us to feel tactful about reading his outgoing mail.

In fact, and although he once wrote his friend Conrad Aiken that "Letters should be indiscretions—otherwise they are simply official bulletins," most of these letters, which extend through 1922 (the year *The Waste Land* was published and Eliot began his editorship of the *Criterion*), are neither indiscreet nor simply "official." The either-or choice laid down to Aiken fails to take into account the number of different ways in which Eliot's prose can be interesting. At least one reviewer of these letters has already found, however, that Eliot's ability to assume different voices depending on whom he is addressing ("He do the police in different voices," as the canceled allusion to Dickens from *The Waste Land* had it) is a measure of his inauthenticity or fragmentedness as a human being. This seems to me nonsense: why should one write one's mother, one's Harvard professor in Indian philosophy, and Ezra Pound all in the same

The Letters of T. S. Eliot, volume 1, *1898–1922*, edited by Valerie Eliot. Harcourt Brace Jovanovich, 1988.

voice? If one demands that a consistent voice permeate a writer's correspondence, one should go to D. H. Lawrence, who tended to harangue everyone he wrote to in the same terms and tone. Eliot is more discreet—even in his indiscretions—and the commendable manners of his epistolary style show in his taking the recipient into account.

For example, a 1914 letter to J. H. Woods, his Harvard philosophy professor, written from Merton College, Oxford, where Eliot is reading Aristotle, is partly an "official bulletin"—since Eliot had promised to keep Woods "au courant" on his studies there—but also something more. He tells Woods he is following three courses of lectures: Harold Joachim's on the *Ethics,* R. G. Collingwood's on the *De Anima,* and J. A. Smith's Logic. He is finding the *Posterior Analytics* "very difficult" and accompanies his study of it "with the commentary of Zabarella, which is remarkably good, and very minute, so that this reading takes most of my time." There follow descriptions of Joachim's good lectures and Collingwood's method with the *De Anima.* Although, from Peter Ackroyd's biography, we knew that Eliot studied Aristotle with Joachim at Oxford, the extent of his immersion in the *maestre de color che sanno* is now more clear. And Eliot's "bulletin" to Woods helps explain the passionate force with which Aristotle is invoked in "The Perfect Critic" (the opening essay in *The Sacred Wood*) where the "living force" of the philosopher is celebrated as well as the "universal intelligence" he applied to everything. Aristotle, says Eliot, wasn't a poet who looked to write critical prose in order to satisfy "impure"—creative—desires:

> In whatever sphere of interest, he looked solely and steadfastly at the object; in his short and broken treatise [the *Poetics*] he provides an eternal example—not of laws, or even of method, for there is no method except to be very intelligent, but of intelligence itself swiftly operating the analysis of sensation to the point of principle and definition.

This famous definition of "method," in other words, came out of some hard antecedent study.

A month after Eliot wrote Woods on how his Aristotelian studies were progressing, he struck a quite different pose to Conrad Aiken in wondering whether to return to America and take up a career of philosophy at Harvard. He is currently suffering, so he informs Aiken, from "indigestion, constipation, and colds constantly"; the university atmosphere is oppressive; the War is suffocating; and how can one like a country that is "satisfied with such disgusting food?" England is surely uncivilized, but then, and even less appetizing, there is Cambridge, Massachusetts, and the college bell, and the "people . . . whom one fights against and who absorb one all the same." The young man continues to put himself on stage for Aiken:

> The great need is to know one's own mind, and I don't know that: whether I want to get married, and have a family, and live in America all my life, and compromise and conceal my opinions and forfeit my independence for the sake of my children's future; or save my money and retire at fifty to a table on the boulevard, regarding the world placidly through the fumes of an apéritif at 5 P.M.—How thin either life seems! And perhaps it is merely dyspepsia speaking.

Dyspepsia perhaps, or perhaps the accents of "Portrait of a Lady," that very artful portrait of a young man who doesn't know his own mind.

In fact, this is one of the last glimpses we are given of the Laforguian or dyspeptic aesthete, conjuring up the world through apéritif fumes. By June of the same year, 1915, Eliot has married Vivienne Haigh-Wood, and a month later is writing his father in quite un-Laforguian terms: "I am *convinced* that she has been the one person for me. She has everything to give that I want, and she gives it. I owe her everything." It is extraordinary to think that this twenty-six-year-old, whose to-be-famous poem, "The Love Song of J. Alfred Prufrock," had just the past month been published in Harriet Monroe's *Poetry*, should without consulting or informing his parents suddenly decide to throw in his lot with Vivien (as she liked to spell it) and England. Eliot appears to have counted on his friends to convince his parents that the life he had chosen was a viable one. Two days after the marriage, Pound—under Eliot's request—sent a long letter to Henry Ware Eliot that was meant to serve as "some sort of apologia for the literary life in general, and for London literary life in particular." It is a fascinating letter, at least as much for what Pound says about himself as about Eliot; although one cannot feel confident that Eliot père was disarmed of his fears and reassured by such claims as "Again if a man is doing the fine thing and the rare thing, London is the only possible place for him to exist." (London was at any rate, as Pound put it in a letter to his own mother, some centuries nearer the "Paradiso Terrestre" than was St. Louis.) A few months after Pound's letter to Henry Ware Eliot, Bertrand Russell wrote Charlotte Eliot in an effort to convince her that, financially and intellectually, it made sense for her son to remain in England: that he could both teach school at High Wycombe *and* pursue the doctoral degree; and that not only was Vivien "thoroughly nice," but her good offices could already be observed insofar as T.S.E. "is no longer attracted by the people who call themselves 'vorticists,' and in that I think her influence is wholly to be applauded." (Eliot's father had remarked, apropos of Pound and Lewis's Vorticist showpiece, *Blast,* that he hadn't known there were enough "lunatics" in the world to support such a magazine.)

Five years after the marriage, with *The Sacred Wood* about to appear, Eliot wrote his mother a letter filled with, among other things, interesting literary gossip, an item of which concerned the arrival in London of the American "vagrant poet and man of letters" Maxwell Bodenheim. Bodenheim hoped to make a living in London by his pen, and Eliot noted sardonically that, as he had informed the new arrival, "getting recognised in English letters is like breaking open a safe—for an American, and that only about three had ever done it." Of course by this time he had broken open the safe, Pound having already instructed him that while he (Pound) threw rocks through the front windows of English Letters, Eliot was to climb in the back way and "make off with the swag." A year after marrying Vivien, Eliot was up to his ears in reviewing: "Philosophy for the *Monist* and the *International Journal of Ethics,* reviews for the *New Statesman,* the *Manchester Guardian* and the *Westminster Gazette. . . .*" From the beginning of 1917 to the end of 1919 he produced roughly seventy-five reviews and essays—most significantly in the *Egoist* and *Athenaeum*—among which are to be found some of his most memorable and lasting prose work: essays on *vers libre,* Henry James, Turgenev, Kipling, Henry Adams, Stendhal, Marlowe, Swinburne, *Hamlet,* Ben Jonson, "Tradition and the Individual Talent." (That the bulk of these reviews and essays still remains uncollected is one of the continuing frustrations of contemporary letters: Faber and Mrs. Eliot, please take note.)

At the same time—as is well known, but not till now so grindingly documented—the writer was not only working full-time at Lloyds Bank, but offering courses of lectures to fill out his income. Eliot comes through at his most appealing when he describes to his cousin Eleanor Hinkley (who always provokes him into lively letters) one of these courses, taught in early 1917:

> My greatest pleasure however is my workingmen's class in English Literature on Monday evenings. I have steered them through Browning (who arouses great enthusiasm), Carlyle, Meredith, Arnold, and am now conducting them through Ruskin. There are not many working *men* at pres-

ent, except one very intelligent grocer who reads Ruskin behind the counter; most of them are (female) elementary schoolteachers, who work very hard with large classes of refractory children all day but come with unabated eagerness to get culture in the evening (stimulated, I hope, by my personal magnetism).

A year later he is in the midst of another series of lectures, "cramming George Eliot for the last two weeks in preparation," and he tells us that for the occasion he has read *Mill on the Floss, Scenes of Clerical Life,* and *Adam Bede* (after work hours at Lloyds and after the latest review had been sent off). By this time—the spring of 1918—one feels that the young man of twenty-nine has come into his full powers as a critic. The sweep and confidence of his literary judgments, as conveyed in the following sentences, again to Eleanor Hinkley, are all the more impressive for also being true:

> I am very glad you like James. . . . He is a wonderful conscientious artist, one of the very few, and more European than most English or Americans. I think he has about the keenest sense of Situation of any novelist, and his always alert intelligence is a perpetual delight. As a critic of America he is certainly unique. I am reading *R[oderick] Hudson* now in preparation for an article for the James number of the *Little Review.* I am writing on the Hawthorne influence on James, which comes out at the end in an astonishing unfinished book *The Sense of the Past* (read the scenario at the end). *Hudson* I find dull and stilted and old fashioned; but it is a very early one. I think you might like Turgenev. I admire him as much as any novelist, but especially in the *Sportsman's Sketches.* His method looks simple and slight, but he is a consummate master with it. . . . I come more and more to demand that novels should be well written, and perceive more clearly the virtue and defects of the Victorians.

He then proceeds to have at Thackeray, Meredith, Samuel Butler, and George Eliot (somehow he missed out on the genius of *Middlemarch*) in invigorating ways. There is some muscle-flexing here, but nothing empty or unfelt in the judgments and comparisons (comparison and analysis, the tools of the critic—as he would put it in *The Sacred Wood*).

His career as a critic coincided, in its beginnings, with the worry that it might be all up with him as a poet; that—as he wrote his brother in September of 1916—"'J.A.P.' [J. Alfred Prufrock] was a swan song." He worried that Vivien would be "bitterly disappointed" if he never equaled it, and confided to Henry that "the present year has been, in some respects, the most awful nightmare of anxiety that the mind of man could conceive"—though, he added, "at least it is not dull." Vivien felt that "Journalism" was bad for her husband, although he loved it: "But I am sure and certain that it will be the *ruin* of his poetry—if it goes on," she wrote to Henry at about the same time. There are a good many of Vivien's letters in this collection, consisting in the main of variations on the theme of her "wretched health" and her over-whelming sense that "life is so feverish and yet so dreary at the same time, and one is always waiting, waiting for something" ("What shall I do now? What shall I do? . . . What shall we do tomorrow? / What shall we ever do?"). The only way, it seems, she could ameliorate her own lot was to worry about her husband's, especially in letters to his mother: "It seems he has not aver-age strength—and added to that he lives as no average man does. The inces-sant, never ending grind, day and evening—and always too much to do, so that he is always behind hand, never up to date—therefore always tormented—and if forced to rest or stop a minute, it only torments him the more to feel that inexorable pile of work piling up against him." Vivien knew how to put words together—just pushing through the sentences, written in June 1917, makes one feel exhausted. Eliot by then had begun work at the bank (hours 9:15 to 5:30, with a break for tea at 4). Surely it was not only the experience of living in wartime London that caused him to describe, in July of that year, his sense of himself as "living in one of Dostoyevsky's novels, you see, not in one of Jane Austen's." As for his health, things weren't so bad—"My teeth are falling to pieces, I have to wear spectacles to read, and from time to time I am contorted with rheumatism—otherwise I am pretty well." He would get worse.

The litany of complaints holds more than the occasional bit of something like comic relief. Note the following italicizations of *key words* in one of Vivien's many letters to Tom's mother on the subject of Tom's clothes:

> Tom did *not* get a new suit, *or* new flannels. I am ashamed to say it. His old underwear is still thick and in *fair* condition, but it needs *incessant darning*. Darning alone takes me hours out of the week. He needs a suit, and I think *must* have one. His pyjamas too are all very old and want constant mending.

This was in March 1917. Eight months later, with winter coming on and Charlotte Eliot having sent money for her son's underclothing, Vivien renders up an account of how that money was spent, in the process of which occurs a sentence-confession it is a delight to misinterpret: "So far the weather has been, and *is,* so unusually warm that neither Tom nor I have made any change in our underclothing since the summer! It is a good thing in a way, but it is *very* damp and enervating at present." Yes, "it" certainly must have been, and for them both. On and on runs the letter, through woollens, vests, under-drawers, socks, and the ever unsatisfactory pyjama situation: "He is still worse provided with pyjamas than anything. . . . He is very rough with his pyjamas, and shirts—tears them unmercifully!" ("I was neither at the hot gates / Nor fought in the warm rain / Nor knee deep in the salt marsh, heaving a cutlass, / Bitten by flies, fought.") But at least he now has a "chest protector," purchased on the advice of Vivien's mother: "The chest protector is quilted satin, and fits around the neck and has a double breasted chest part. It is particularly valu-able for when he goes out in evening dress—which leaves the chest much less protected. . . ." And later: "Tom takes cold *very* much more easily than I do. Most of *my* colds are caught from him. I think he would be better if he had one side of his nose cauterised. . . ." Who was it that doubted we could learn much from Shakespeare's laundry lists? Something like the banality of evil, the everpresent malady of the quotidian, is testified to by these pathetic and oddly gripping outcries of Vivien's, and they provide as much a sense as one could ask for of what the Eliots' life together was like.[1]

The most entertaining and enlivening sections of the correspondence are those in which Eliot is writing to or about Pound, Wyndham Lewis, Richard Aldington, and other modernists. These letters—along with others concern-ing *The Waste Land* and the *Criterion*—I can merely allude to here, since I wish instead to indicate two moments in which Eliot is particularly expressive about his relationship to his parents. The first occurs in a letter to his brother, written in February of 1919, after their father had died. Eliot says that he wished "father could have had more satisfaction out of his children," but doesn't think that his father's life was a very unhappy one—"and after all none of his children was made for the kind of success that he could have appreci-ated" (Henry Ware Eliot was president of the Hydraulic-Press Brick Company in St. Louis). He goes on to speak more personally:

1. There is one teasing, unannotated reference, in a letter of Vivien's [October 3, 1919] written to her friend Mary Hutchinson, to what sounds like Another Man, or at least the possibility of one. After saying how she wants to buy new clothes, but hasn't yet begun, she adds "I dont know what will please Jim most either! Directly that horrible Belgian goes to Bermuda you must begin laying foundation stones for me with Jim." Eliot scholars, get to work!

———————

> I always tried to give as powerful an impression as I could of my position
> here but it was a prominence essentially too esoteric to be of much use in
> that way. Now, I find that I think more of his own youthful possibilities
> that never came to anything: and yet with a great deal of satisfaction; his
> old-fashioned scholarship! his flute-playing, his drawing. Two of the Cats
> that I have seem to me quite remarkable. I feel that both he and mother in
> spite of the strength of their affection were lonely people, and that he
> was the more lonely of the two, that he hardly knew himself what he was
> like. In my experience everyone except the fools seem to me warped and
> stunted.

I think that the loneliness Eliot sensed in his parents' lives was at least as much
projected as discovered; but it is the tone here that compels—for those who
find Eliot's melancholy compelling—and that final surprising sentence which
seems to come out of nowhere and makes the best, glum case for the consequences of not being a fool. (He was about to review *The Education of Henry
Adams*.)

The other moment occurs in a letter written to his mother a few weeks later,
in which—in the words just quoted about his father—Eliot attempts "to give
as powerful an impression" as he could of his literary position. He is explaining why he has turned down an editorial position on the *Athenaeum* and why
he will continue on at the bank and avoid the "intrigues of journalism":

> I only write what I want to—*now*—and everyone knows that anything I do
> write is good. I can influence London opinion and English literature in a
> better way. I am known to be disinterested. . . . There is a small and select
> public which regards me as the best living critic, as well as the best living
> poet, in England. . . . I really think I have far more *influence* on English
> letters than any other American has ever had, unless it be Henry James. I
> know a great many people, but there are many more who would like to
> know me, and I can remain isolated and detached.

Such remarks, he admits, are "conceited." Yet they are also nothing less than a
true measurement of the distance he had come. To be able to write it out to
one's mother, as if to offer (in Yeats's words from "Among School Children")
"A compensation for the pang of his birth, / Or the uncertainty of his setting
forth"—this is the success story told by these letters, played out against marital
failure, and against physical and psychic distress. Out of that distress he came
to formulate his sense of the admirable writer—"perfectly cool and detached,
regarding other people's feelings or his own, like a God who has got beyond

them; or a person who has dived very deep and come up holding some hitherto unseen submarine creature" (September 19, 1917). One recalls, at this point, the familiar sentence from the "Tradition" essay about how "only those who have personality and emotions know what it means to want to escape from those things." To that may now be added a correction he made, not without its quotient of slyness, to John Gould Fletcher who had read "The Perfect Critic" and decided Eliot was insufficiently generous to the claims of "emotion." Responding to Fletcher, Eliot wrote that "Certainly I don't deny the importance of emotion. I often find it present to me when other people find only frigidity. . . ." That was a way of putting it, rather more than satisfactory.

MacLeish Revisited

Archibald MacLeish died last April just as he was about to be honored on his ninetieth birthday by a large gathering at Greenfield Community College (near the MacLeish home in Conway, Massachusetts) to which he had given his papers. His death prompted few attempts on anyone's part at revaluating his achievement as a poet, or even at thinking twice about his career as, pre-eminently, America's elder statesman of poetry. Increasingly since the death of Frost in 1963 he had played the role of America's poet laureate without portfolio. If Richard M. Nixon requested a poem from him on the occasion of the moon landing of 1969, MacLeish, a lifelong Democrat, courteously obliged; after all, the president in his inaugural address a few months previously had already quoted from his poem about the Apollo Eight mission. He was equally ready to celebrate the city of Boston (with "Night Watch in the City of Boston") at the behest of a Bicentennial committee in 1976. There has scarcely been a poet of this century more ready to write poems employing public speech in the services of saluting heroism, political commitment, sacrifice in the service of some high ideal. And MacLeish's recently published *Letters* (Houghton Mifflin) reveals the kind of distinguished person he was in the habit of communicating with: Henry Luce, Franklin D. Roosevelt, Felix Frankfurter, McGeorge Bundy, Adlai Stevenson, Dean Acheson—in addition to various significant poets and novelists headed by Pound and Hemingway.

This willingness to consort with the high and mighty, along with the penchant for noble, large-sounding affirmations of the deathless spirit of man, or poetry, or America, caused many students of modern poetry to treat MacLeish's own work with condescension at best. Here I must account myself one of those students. It was amusing on occasion to see the poet—acting as suave public moderator of a symposium on verse drama at the Harvard Summer School—slightly discomfited, when after he thought to conclude the discussion by artfully suggesting that perhaps *all* the participants would write their next play in verse, Lillian Hellman shot back, "Well, *I* damn well won't!" But it was not only aspiring critics like myself (who loved John Ransom's poems, so how could I love MacLeish's?) who judged his poetry or his rhetoric less than matchless, as we note from the responses of his literary contemporaries. Pound, to whom MacLeish confessed his deep indebtedness and to whom he sent his long poem *Conquistador* after its completion in 1932, thought the poem was (in MacLeish's words) "damn bad" and told him so. MacLeish wrote back, thanking Pound "quite honestly" for the criticisms, saying that he had been asked to write something about the *Cantos* but that "You would probably prefer the praise of someone whose work you respected." Courteous as always, the reply is nonetheless painful. Hemingway, for whose work he had the most profound respect ("The world of this book [he said of *A Farewell to Arms* when it appeared] is a complete world . . . to subject the whole experience of a man's soul to the pure & perfect art of your prose is a great, a very great, achievement. I send you my complete praise & profound respect. You become in one book the great novelist of our time"), paid him in return with the following observation to Malcolm Cowley in 1945: "Does Archie still write anything except Patriotic? I read some awfully lifeless lines to a Dead Soldier by him in the Free World anthology. I thought good old Allen Tate could write the lifeless-est lines to Dead Soldiers ever read but Archie is going good. You know his bro. Kenny was killed in last war flying and I always felt Archie felt that sort of gave him a controlling interest in all deads." Very funny, and more than a touch cruel, it is I'm afraid accurate as a response to MacLeish's poem "The Young Dead Soldiers." Robert Frost, who had a few years previously amused or annoyed a Bread Loaf audience by setting afire some paper while MacLeish was giving a poetry reading, was moved during a conversation with some Harvard students about *J.B.*, to name the following list of related phenomena: "Sociology, and the New Deal, and the New Testament, and Archie, and so on. . . ." I think it fair to say that as more public distinction accrued to MacLeish, the more he became available for satiric and condescending treatment by fellow artists like those just mentioned, or in clever parodies and withering reviews by Edmund Wilson, Randall Jarrell, and others.

As is evident from the letters, early on in his career he was haunted by a sense of having come too late, and though a modern theorist like Harold Bloom would find such fears entirely natural and unavoidable, they seem to have been especially sharp in MacLeish's case, as when he wrote Amy Lowell in 1924 about how it was impossible for him to write Imagist poetry and how his own words "were all ships which have carried ivory & peacocks between England & the Levant for two hundred years." What can replace them, he asks? Not "Eliot's multisyllables" and not the "commercial-jargon impersonalities of Miss Moore." He says he has decided to stop writing, and will learn Italian, read Dante, Laforgue, de Gourmont, and other English poets: "But I am more than haunted with the fear that it is too late. That this rhythm & vocabulary which my intelligence knows for second rate are me, my 'style,' all that I have." A later letter to Amy Lowell mentions his "basic problem of verbiage," and in the same year he wrote John Peale Bishop about the problem of coming after Eliot. Eliot had opened a world to him from which he couldn't "retire"—but what then was he to do?: "Recognize the great man's prior claims and shut up? And what if we can't shut up? Talk about the tragedy of the man who is ahead of his age: it is nothing to the tragedy of the man who comes after the man who is."

This was a wise formulation. MacLeish did not "shut up," of course, but nothing he wrote in the 1930s and the war years which followed showed a resolution of the problem of "verbiage" or of coming after Pound and Eliot. Perhaps there was no possibility for a resolution in the terms he set it, or perhaps he had already resolved it by writing a poem which couldn't be confused with either of those intimidating modernists, nor with Yeats. I have in mind the poem "Eleven," from *Streets of the Moon* (1926) in which the young child

>   . . . would leave
> On tiptoe the three chairs on the verandah
> And crossing tree by tree the empty lawn
> Push back the shed door and upon the sill
> Stand pressing out the sunlight from his eyes
> And enter and with outstretched fingers feel
> The grindstone and behind it the bare wall
> And turn and in the corner on the cool
> Hard earth sit listening. And one by one,
> Out of the dazzled shadow in the room,
> The shapes would gather, the brown plowshare, spades,
> Mattocks, the polished helves of picks, a scythe
> Hung from the rafters, shovels, slender tines
> Glinting across the curve of sickles—shapes
> Older than men were, the wise tools, the iron
> Friendly with earth. . . .

Here he made use of the same "ships" which had carried all that English poetical freight so well for so many years, and there is no way that the poem could be saluted as a new development in American writing (as, say, Edmund Wilson had just saluted Hemingway's *In Our Time*). As with all MacLeish's poems—early or late—there is a principled avoidance of what, in a letter to Allen Tate in 1932, he called "the personality of the poet" in its more dramatic form—the anguished "I" making dramatic capital out of its difficulties. "Indeed," wrote MacLeish, "it seems to me that the personality of the poet is merely the instrument, the voice, and that its qualities will enough color his poetry without a conscious and introspective labor of self-exploration and self-definition." In "Eleven" this coloring is attractively evident, even as the words and rhythms are those familiar to traffickers in English poetical freight. That the poet who wrote "Ars Poetica," with its fancy talk about how a poem should be "palpable and mute / As a globed fruit," should have written "Eleven" at about the same time, goes to show how much more interesting MacLeish's poetical practice could be on occasion than was the presumed "pure" program he laid down for it in "Ars Poetica." It is unfortunately the latter poem rather than "Eleven" by which the anthology reader will encounter MacLeish.

"Eleven" was not an isolated piece of good work. Unless one is enslaved to modernist ideas of what a poem must or must not do, the rhythmic impulse of these opening lines from "Cook County" (published in *Poems 1924–1933*) can be admired:

> The northeast wind was the wind off the lake
> Blowing the oak-leaves pale side out like
> Aspen: blowing the sound of the surf far
> Inland over the fences: blowing for
> Miles over smell of the earth the lake smell in.
>
> The southwest wind was thunder in afternoon.
> You saw the wind first in the trumpet vine
> And the green went white with the sky and the weather-vane
> Whirled on the barn and the doors slammed all together.
> After the rain in the grass we used to gather
> Wind-fallen cold white apples.

As with "Eleven," there is little interesting to note about the poem's form. Its power is a matter of sensations presented, Hemingwayesque—if perhaps ennobled by the long sonorous verse lines—and as with "Eleven" quite untouched by ironical contemplation whether Poundian or Eliotic, of the materials it presents. Surely they are remembered materials (MacLeish grew up in

Glencoe, Illinois) which are celebrated lyrically without a trace of criticism or ambivalence ("Pony Hill" is another possible example of this celebration). These poems seem to me immensely preferable to the anthologized early MacLeish we have been given for years—"Ars Poetica," the over-praised "You, Andrew Marvell" with its reference to Ecbatan (which annoyed Pound, who felt MacLeish was poaching on his sacred places!) but also "The End of the World" ("Quite unexpectedly as Vasserot / the armless ambidextrian . . . etc." or "Immortal Helix" ("Hereunder Jacob Schmid, who man and bones . . .") or the portentous "Immortal Autumn," which a contemporary called the most moving poem written by anyone in MacLeish's generation. MacLeish had no gift for the satiric in his poems (though the letters show an occasional good hit) and unlike the remembered particularity of "Eleven" and "Cook County," "Immortal Autumn" strikes the vatic note which would too often become his key signature:

> I speak this poem now with grave and level voice
> In praise of autumn, of the far horn-winding fall.
>
> I praise the flower-barren fields, the clouds, the tall
> Unanswering branches where the wind makes sullen noise.
>
> I praise the fall: it is the human season.

Those last words—the perfect title for an inspiring book of verse by some humanist or other, perhaps by MacLeish himself.

His longer poems from the 1930s had an uneven reception. *Conquistador* was praised by Tate for its "flawless craftsmanship" and excellent management of terza rima, but Tate also judged it sentimental and as hovering over nothing of substance. Previous to that, *The Hamlet of A. MacLeish* (1928) had been devastated by R. P. Blackmur in *Hound and Horn*, judged by him to be fraudulent and "personal" in the most vain, self-posturing sense. Finally, in the *New Yorker* in 1939 (could such a thing happen today in that well-mannered magazine?), Edmund Wilson, who had given measured praise to MacLeish twelve years previously, wrote his amusing and quite scornful parody, "The Omelet of A. MacLeish," some lines of which will give its flavor:

> Anabase and The Waste Land:

> These and the Cantos of Pound: O how they came pat!
> Nimble at other men's arts how I picked up the trick of it:
> Rode it reposed on it drifted away on it: passing

> Shores that lay dim in clear air: and the cries of affliction
> Suave in somniferous rhythms: there was rain there and moons:
> Leaves falling: and all of a flawless and hollow felicity . . .

In the margin, Wilson supplied glosses à la Coleridge: "MacLeish breaks an egg for his omelet"; "He puts plovers' eggs and truffles into his omelet"; "He slips in a few prizes for philosophers"; "The omelet becomes a national institution and gets into Fanny Farmer." Wilson's poem caught well the portentous self-questioning toward which his subject was inclined:

> And the questions and questions
>   questioning
>   What am I? O
>
> What shall I remember?
>   O my people
>   a pensive dismay
>
> What have I left unsaid?
>   Till the hearer cried:

> "If only MacLeish could remember if only could say it!"

Wilson's conclusion was that MacLeish's career demonstrated "that the poet need not be a madman or even a bounder" and that all in all he was

> A clean and clever lad
>   who is doing
>   his best
>   to get on. . . .

In response, MacLeish wrote to Hemingway a satirical poem about Wilson, speaking "As one on whom / The Triple Stinker publicly hath stunk," but otherwise refrained from comment. Yet though Wilson was wholly sarcastic in hanging the clean-living award around MacLeish's neck, there was an engaging side to MacLeish's civility, as when—a year or so before the Wilson parody—he wrote, apropos an exhibition of his own works at Yale, that "There is a point beyond which mediocrity cannot be inflated to look like the real thing, and I think that point has been well reached at Yale in the Rare Book Room." Here was a fully engaging and humorous modesty, well bred in the best sense.

These traits of character, this liberal and modest decency of response were borne out in a confidence he dropped to Paul Engle when MacLeish was working at the Library of Congress in Washington during the Second World

War, having resigned from something called the OFF (Office of Facts and Figures—"one of the deepest satisfactions of my life," he wrote McGeorge Bundy). Engle had enclosed a poem of his own and made some remark about Frost, and MacLeish attempted, candidly, to say why Frost's poetry had not meant all that much to him: "I don't, as I think you know, share the more enthusiastic view about his poetry. In fact, his poetry has meant little or nothing to me since *North of Boston* and even *North of Boston* didn't really get under my hide." And he went on to speak about the "mysterious thing"—how much "Robert desired fame." In his public statements about Frost and in his exemplary encouragement of him to help in the freeing of Pound from St. Elizabeth's Hospital, MacLeish came to some kind of terms with Frost; yet that poet's example of the speaking voice, the "sound of sense," had indeed not gotten under MacLeish's hide, as had not the witty-cruel way of saying, or resaying, things Frost had made himself a master of. (When in conversation somebody mentioned to Frost MacLeish's famous ending to "Ars Poetica"—"A poem should not mean / But be"—Frost suggested, as a rewrite, that "A poem should be mean.") That was a way of behaving, or writing, not to MacLeish's taste.

So it is odd and moving to encounter something like a Frostian poem in MacLeish's late and probably best book of poems, *The Wild Old Wicked Man* (1968). The Yeatsian title acknowledged the poet whom MacLeish most admired during his late years, and Yeats's presence was pervasive, indeed oppressive, in a collection of short lyrics he published during the 1950s called *Songs for Eve.* In *The Wild Old Wicked Man,* MacLeish curbed his desire to speak largely and grandly about men and women, love, death, mankind; to my tastes at least, the best poem in the book is a wholly modest, subtle, heartfelt one which goes as follows:

> Mark's sheep, I said, but they were only
> stones, boulders in the uncropped grass,
> granite shoulders weathered to the bone
> and old as that first morning where God was.
>
> And yet they looked like sheep—so like
> you half expected them to startle,
> bolt in a leap because some tyke
> had barked, because a bluejay darted—
>
> dart of shadow under blue of jay—
> or someone shouted by the water trough,

slammed a car-door, drove away,
or squirrels quarreled, or a gun went off,

or just because they must: that terrified
impulse to be somewhere else
browsers and ruminators seem to share
as though they knew, they only, the sky falls

and *here* is dangerous (as of course it is).
But Mark's sheep never startled from the grass.
They knew their place, their boulder's business:
to let the nights go over, the days pass,

let years go, summer, autumn, winter,
each by itself, each motionless, alone,
praising the world by being in it,
praising the world by being stone.

"Mark's Sheep"

Here, to one reader's ear and eye, MacLeish's best poetic self was expressed, and it had little to do with modernism, nothing at all with *Conquistador*. There is no reason to tie it to Frost's insistence on the sound of sense (and I suspect the plangent repetition in the final lines would have bothered Frost, as it does me slightly); but surely this is a poem which shares qualities with the man who wrote the complicated, thoughtful, sometimes ironic, sometimes troubled letters MacLeish wrote. If it is, as I assume it to be, "about" Mark Van Doren among other things, it is a wholly appropriate tribute to that uneroded face and intelligence and to the impressive calmness one suspects to have been Van Doren's. But it is beautiful—and surprising too—for its fine poise between public and private, and for the way, within its stanzas and rhymes and nicely managed syntax, that a quality of life is made memorable through a small and witty fable. The personal reference is unmistakable, and "Mark's sheep I said," is in some ways the most telling thing any "I" of MacLeish's ever said.

"Mark's Sheep" is a poem of his old age, and there would be ones to come, like "Crossing" and "Hotel Breakfast," which caught poignant moments of mixed memory and desire in the private life. The public or official life in the 1950s was high-minded: a letter to an editor begins, "What I wanted, as of course you understood, was a clarification of our conversation at the Century" (this about a prospective volume of poems, discussed at The Club); while talk about the Function of Poetry, or of Harvard, is equally lofty, as most strikingly demonstrated in these sentences concluding a letter to Bundy, written in a spirit of optimism just after Nathan Pusey was installed as president of Harvard (with Bundy as dean of the Graduate School):

> I feel in my bones a new age—a new era. Not only the vitality you both have and the complementary intelligence which so patently create a new kind of thinking. . . . It is the fact that this Harvard cares about values. . . . Keats is right in the great Ode—the human equation combines with the order imposed by nature, the order imposed by the imagination. When one can say, understanding what he is saying, that Beauty is Truth, Truth Beauty, one has spoken like a man.

As a graduate student at Harvard in the 1950s, I must confess to having missed out on that new era, as well as all that institutional caring about values, Keats, beauty, and truth. Perhaps it was going on in Eliot House, to which in the following fall MacLeish was inviting J. Robert Oppenheimer to dinner with an "agreeable party," then for talk with "some twenty boys" afterwards, a conversation which would carry on from dinner "in the hope that some of the lads might eventually join us but with no insistence that they do unless so moved. It would all, in other words, be as easy and civilized as we could make it. . . ." Not "palpable and mute / As a globed fruit," those occasions! Somehow one hopes that a few of the equivalent of Mark Van Doren's sheep were there to keep things a bit stony, to not let Beauty become Truth, Truth Beauty, without some recalcitrance.

MacLeish was most admirable when, in his art or his life, he resisted the temptation to unionize Beauty and Truth, or their siblings. In his later years, as earlier, this did not often happen; but when it did, the effect is more startling and enlivening than one could have imagined, given the "official" ring of so many letters and the noble, often monotonous tone of so many poems. So in a late poem called "Family Group" he managed to write about his brother dead in World War One in a way that is freshly affecting:

> That's my younger brother with his Navy wings.
> He's twenty-three or should have been that April:
> winters aged you, flying the Dutch coast.
> I'm beside him with my brand-new Sam Brown belt.
> The town behind us is Dunkirk. We met there
> quite by accident, sheer luck.
> Someone's lengthened shadow—the photographer's?—
> falls across the road, across our feet.

MacLeish Revisited

The other's afterward—
after the Armistice, I mean, the floods,
the week without a word. That foundered
farmyard is in Belgium somewhere.
The faceless figure on its back, the helmet buckled,
wears what look like Navy wings. A lengthened shadow
falls across the muck about its feet.

Me? I'm back in Cambridge in dry clothes,
a bed to sleep in, my small son, my wife.

The fine thing about this poem, and what makes it so different from anything MacLeish would have written in his earlier days, at least about his brother's death, is of course its final two lines where there is presented—with whatever implications of dumb luck one can invoke—the sadness and the undeserved good fortune of life.

A final moment, not surely to be reckoned with by biographers of MacLeish (R. H. Winnick, editor of the letters, is preparing an authorized one) but good for showing the distinguished man and poet in a little-known and for that reason attractive light. Two graduate students in English at Harvard have encountered one another in the stacks of Widener Library, have realized that they were undergraduates together at another eastern university, and begin, rather loudly, to trade stories and memories from the good old days. The problem is that their loud conversation is taking place virtually on the door-step of Professor MacLeish's Widener study. He, perhaps composing a sequel to *J. B.*, or some poem or speech or other—perhaps just plain reading Dante or Yeats or Li Po—has at all events suddenly had enough. The door opens, revealing to the surprised, voluble graduate students Harvard University's Boylston Professor of Rhetoric (angry), who glares at them solidly, then booms out with unconcealed irritation, "Will you two please shut the hell up?" Along with the things for which Archibald MacLeish will be remembered, I would hope this moment of rash, unsympathetic, undemocratic temper may be granted a minor place.

Poetry, Spring 1983

Big Spender

At one point in his *Journals,* Stephen Spender recalls Auden saying to him, when they were undergraduates at Oxford, "You will be a poet because you will always be humiliated." (Spender's 1951 autobiography *World Within World* has Auden saying ". . . because you are so infinitely capable of being humiliated.") A few years later, Virginia Woolf paid him the following tribute: "He talks incessantly and will pan out in years to come a prodigious bore. But he's a nice poetic youth—big nosed, bright eyed, like a giant thrush." It is typical of Spender in his *Journals* that he should refer again to Auden's analysis of his capacity for humiliation, and that he should quote—as if he were proud of it— Woolf's prediction that he would become a prodigious bore. And in case the predictions of his betters were not sufficient to establish the quality of his character and talent, he himself steps in and lays it on the line: "Looking back on the evening it seems to me I did most of the talking. Boasted. Was falsely modest about my own writing—difficult for me not to be falsely modest— because it is rubbed into me by every stroke of my pen that my natural talent, facility, concentration is something to be modest about." In a few more strokes of the humiliating pen, he has rubbed it in further; and indeed these hundreds of pages of journals, added to the two hundred pages of poems he wishes to preserve, should convince any reader that Spender's artistic talent is one truly to be modest about. At the same time, such a recognition deters him not at all from adding two more books to an already bursting bibliography of novels, plays, literary and political criticism, cultural commentary. Stephen Spender is a unique literary and public phenomenon.

It is a phenomenon that—as F. R. Leavis said about the Sitwells—belongs more to the history of publicity than of poetry. Thus there is much more to say about the *Journals* than about the poems, which, if some of them were ever alive in the 1930s, are now dead as doornails. Although Spender has pruned and trimmed the products of almost sixty years, the result is less than inspir-

Collected Poems, 1928–1985, by Stephen Spender. Random House, 1986; and *Journals, 1939–1983,* by Stephen Spender, edited by John Goldsmith. Random House, 1986.

ing. The old thirties chestnuts are there yet once more—"The Express," "The Landscape Near an Aerodrome," "The Pylons," "An Elementary School Classroom in a Slum," the poem about his parents that begins in matchless bathos with "My parents kept me from children who were rough"—above all, the egregious "I think continually of those who were truly great" (now given a new boring title, "The Truly Great"). In "content," their level of flatulence is extremely high:

> The guns spell money's ultimate reason
> In letters of lead on the Spring hillside.
> But the boy lying dead under the olive trees
> Was too young and too silly
> To have been notable to their important eye.
> He was a better target for a kiss.

Tiens! one says to that silly last line from the first section of "Ultima Ratio Regum"; just as well for the silly young lad to have been put out of his misery, rather than hanging around, a target for kisses.

But it is not merely the flatulence count of these early poems that makes them so dispensable; it's also their rhythmic inertness. It was bad enough for Spender to have gone on about how he thought

> . . . continually of those who were truly great.
> Who, from the womb, remembered the soul's history
> Through corridors of light, where the hours are suns,
> Endless and singing.

(One thinks of Philip Larkin's directive, "Get stewed: / Books are a load of crap.") But forget the content of the poem's second stanza and just listen to how it sounds:

> What is precious, is never to forget
> The essential delight of the blood drawn from ageless springs
> Breaking through rocks in worlds before our earth.
> Never to deny its pleasure in the morning simple light
> Nor its grave evening demand for love.
> Never to allow gradually the traffic to smother
> With noise and fog, the flowering of the spirit.

"What is precious, is never . . ."; "Never to allow gradually the traffic to smother"—the ineptness of these rhythms is staggering, until one realizes that

---

Spender doesn't presume to be any great shakes as a prosodist: "Continued sonnet on Berlin Wall. . . . Usual torments of writing poetry . . . my utter incompetence technically and lack of certainty about form I want." He said it, I didn't.

As a poet, his utter absence of humor is crippling, as is his commitment to a high, "spiritual" diction that fills poems with Spirit and blood and love and death. For him, the neck of eloquence somehow never got wrung—he really *did* think continually of those who were truly great: "Instead of being a fake great man, I wanted to be a real great writer. I have resisted my own ambition by sabotaging it for years." In fact, when in poems at the end of this collection he relaxed a bit and wrote about MacNeice or Stravinsky or Auden, drawing on remembered details of his experiences with them, the result is welcome. But such poems are very much the exception. In the *Journals,* by contrast, relaxation is the rule, and if they don't contain much overtly humorous material, they do show engaging instances of Spender regarding himself with less than monumental seriousness, sometimes even emerging as a comic hero.

Inevitably for such a jet-setting lit man, there is a good deal of name-dropping, or at least naming: Oppenheimer and Kennan, Boulez and Bob Craft, Margot and Rudolf and Jackie O. When he drives T. S. Eliot to the Savoy Hotel—as if that in itself weren't enough—it is of course to meet Stravinsky; when—in the *Journals*'s most bizarre episode, he appears to be marooned in Oneonta, New York, after a lecture, the pathos is that he's on for dinner that evening in New York City, with Mrs. Onassis and her daughter, Caroline ("I had not seen Jacqueline for twenty years or so . . ."). The *Journals* exploit bodily embarrassments that the poems avert their eyes from. In Japan, he is squired about by a "boring professor" who invites himself to Spender's hotel room and announces that "We shall now take a multitudinous bath, after which you will feel greatly refreshed." In probably his finest moment, Spender boldly confides to his journal that, "the idea of having a bath with this professor really infuriated me." Nevertheless, it seems, he had it. On the lecture circuit in Las Cruces, New Mexico, he is afflicted with violent diarrhea at the beginning of his talk, hangs on gamely, then afterwards dashes for a lavatory where he encounters an elderly gentleman emerging from one of the stalls, saying, "Didn't I meet you twenty years ago?" This time Spender firmly draws the line: "Excuse me, I'll speak to you afterwards, outside," and dashes into the vacated place.

My favorite journal entry is his tale of the Wagnerian fart:

Big Spender

Some weeks ago in London I walked along Long Acre from Covent Garden where I had seen *Götterdämmerung*—alone as I thought, along the street I farted. It was much louder, after five hours of Wagner, than I had dreamed it could possibly be! Some boys and girls, rather charming, whom I had scarcely noticed, overheard me, or it, and started cheering. In the darkness I was more amused than embarrassed. Then a self-important thought came in my mind. Supposing they knew that this old man walking along Long Acre and farting was Stephen Spender? What would they think?

The answer is, obviously, that the charming boys and girls were thinking continually of those who were truly great—or at least who sounded as though they might be. Surely the cheers were a version of that acclaim Spender imagines for himself when, in a recounted dream, he is made Pope and waits to deliver his first sermon before a million people.

In effect he has been Poetry Pope, teaching or lecturing or reading his poetry at every college and university in America. That, on the edge of eighty, he should want to do this (he is in residence part of this academic year at the University of Connecticut) has seemed on occasion a mystery even to him: "It seems to me quite ridiculous I should spend so much of my life in such desultory circumstances, at my age when I ought to be surrounded by family, troops of friends, and a little honour."

So he wrote in January 1979, describing the view from his tenth-floor room at the Holiday Inn in Nashville, and comparing it with other grim places of recent abode in Charlottesville and Houston. It can't just be economic necessity (though he pulls in hefty amounts for a lecture) but must involve keeping his name up there in lights: "My heart really does do something journalistic—stop a beat, give a jump—if my eye hooks on to the printed word 'Spender' or even—now I am getting a bit astigmatic—any conformation of letters like it. ('Spring,' for example)." Under such conditions, even reading the daily paper must be an exciting event.

The details of various readings in the States give further confirmation to his success as a public figure. At Bates College seven hundred students (out of an enrolled twelve hundred!) turn up for his reading, which has to be moved to the chapel. "At the University of Maine I was banqueted in a way that I found discomforting. Before the banquet I had to stand in a line with dignitaries. This followed on my reading, which was introduced by the President of the University, who recited lines of 'I think continually' at me." Whether it is

Mt. Vernon, Iowa, or Centre College, Kentucky, or Detroit, Michigan, the beat goes on, as does an accompaniment of self-castigation: "Distracted, lazy, pleasure-seeking, frivolous, ever ready to fall in with other people's wishes, desiring to please them, fearful of losing their good will. Years wasted, slipping hour by hour, day by day in a routine of undertaking external to my own inner tasks—reviewing, editing, party-going, travelling, attending conferences, UNESCO, *Encounter,* teaching." The reader can scarcely keep a dry eye.

Despite large doses of candor, Spender does not quite bare his soul on all matters. There are frequently mentions of "B"—"an ornithologist, who also took my writing course at Gainesville"—whom he visits in the man's trailer near the Sewanee River: "With his pale green-grey shining eyes and dark brown hair, he looks more than ever like a portrait of a young Frenchman by Manet." One's curiosity is ever so slightly piqued. On other occasions he can be sharply forthright, reckless of his own future welfare, as when he describes Germaine Greer as having "the look of an overgrown schoolgirl who has won all the prizes and has never quite got round to tidying herself up. Nor does she want to." Or when, in momentary exasperation, he refers to Archibald MacLeish (whom some thought of as the American Spender) as a "humbug."

The *Journals'* final pages record the ambiguous gifts given to the public man as he approaches his ninth decade. The prime minister recommends him for the knighthood; Sir Stephen did not decline. But on the very last page the then knight-to-be confronts death with only one question in mind: "Will my immortal work be written?" Using the adjective without embarrassment, the old poet still hopes to produce something Truly Great. But perhaps his question was already answered, when he shrewdly compared himself to his father, a Liberal politician and author who had written "journalistic books about subjects he hadn't really studied and hoping that feelings, intuitions, sympathies would carry him through." The son notes that "I have done likewise. What makes me different from him is my self-distrust. Still that hasn't been sufficient to stop me." To which the reader wants only to add, you can say that again.

American Scholar, Winter 1988

Robert Lowell (1917–1977)

"His life was a revel in the felicities of language." Thus Frost in 1935, saying the best that could be said for Edwin Arlington Robinson, recently dead. What can be said about Lowell? Robinson died at sixty-six, but the other central modern poets—Hardy, Yeats, Frost, Eliot, Pound, Stevens, Williams—lived to beyond seventy. In the curve of his life Lowell seems closer to his four friends and fellow-poets who died in their fifties—to Jarrell, Berryman, Roethke, and Delmore Schwartz, all of whom, like him, came into their various flowerings in the years after World War II, though none to such eminence and reputation as he. Put simply: after the death of Frost in 1963 and with the publication of Lowell's *For the Union Dead* in the next year, Lowell became our most admired and respected poet; after the deaths of Eliot, Pound, and Auden he was the premier poet of the English-speaking world.

A poet, then, of classic status, also classical. When Helen Vendler reached out to end her account of Lowell's new book *Day By Day* with a comparison, she found Horace the apt figure with whom to yoke him as practitioners of the "imperial" mode. Years ago he himself had spoken admiringly of the "terrible human frankness" he found in Roman poets like Juvenal and Catullus, Virgil and Propertius: "corrosive attacks on the establishment, comments on politics and the decay of morals, all felt terribly strongly." But he was just as open to the kinds of human frankness in his modern predecessors whom, miraculously, he didn't need to reject or even take occasional pot shots at. We have on record, in his *Paris Review* interview, wonderfully generous, intelligent, and incisive comments about Pound's beliefs: "even if they're bad beliefs . . . and some were just terrible of course . . . they made him more human and more to do with life, more to do with the times"; or about Crane: "he somehow got New York City, he was at the center of things in the way no other poet was"; or about Frost (to whom as a young man he had presented a long epic poem for inspection, only to have Frost read aloud to him Collins's "How Sleep the Brave" and say "That's not a great poem, but it's not too long"): "It's the deep, rather tragic poems that I value most . . . but there's an abundance and geniality about those poems [*North of Boston*] that isn't tragic."

There will be many assessments of Lowell's contribution, tracings of his poetic career through his books, and I wish only to provide a few impressions and memories fleshed out with some moments in the poems. I had read his early ones in *Lord Weary's Castle* but first became aware of Lowell himself when, after Frost had read his poetry for an hour at Boston's Jordan Hall (this in 1955) and then asked the audience what he should read next, a tall figure behind me in the balcony rose and in an exceedingly humble (was it regretful?) tone asked if "Mr. Frost" would read "Directive." Recognizing Lowell, Frost complied. I heard him read often in the mid-1950s at various places in Cambridge, mainly at Sanders Theatre, but first at Wellesley where he kept making jokes about Catholicism and I figured he was playing up to the girls. Having recently de-converted he often read aloud and publicly fussed with a poem called "Beyond the Alps" which describes a train journey from Rome to Paris but is really about Lowell's leaving the City of God for more mundane, earthlier haunts:

> There were no tickets for that altitude
> Once held by Hellas when the Goddess stood,
> prince, pope, philosopher and golden bough,
> pure mind and murder at the scything prow—

You didn't always know what lines from this poem meant, and Lowell himself couldn't decide just how he wanted them to go, but they were terrific to declaim, especially in the shower or late of an evening. In 1959 I spent a summer on an island off the coast of Maine, and since the terns and seagulls sounded like the ones that trembled at Warren Winslow's death in the same ocean I memorized "The Quaker Graveyard in Nantucket":

> Sailor, can you hear
> The Pequod's sea wings, beating landward, fall
> Headlong and break on our Atlantic wall
> Off 'Sconset, where the yawing S-boats splash
> The bellbuoy, with ballooning spinnakers,
> As the entangled, screeching mainsheet clears
> The blocks . . .

Particularly appropriate for recitation on solitary car trips, these blocklike pentameters.

But he was changing his style, to the unblocklike colloquial irregularities of *Life Studies,* some of whose poems were published in *Partisan Review* of

Robert Lowell (1917–1977)

Winter 1958. Newly married, I came home for supper one evening with a copy containing five poems, among them "Man and Wife" and "To Speak of Woe That Is in Marriage": "Tamed by Milltown, we lie on Mother's bed . . ."; "your old-fashioned tirade— / loving, rapid, merciless— / breaks like the Atlantic Ocean on my head." My God, what was he saying! And she? "My hopped up husband drops his home disputes, / and hits the streets to cruise for prostitutes, / free-lancing out along the razor's edge." Not very good as a role model for marriage, but it livened up my life, especially by providing words for Eisenhowerworld:

> where even the man
> scavenging filth in the back alley trash cans,
> has two children, a beach wagon, a helpmate,
> and is a "young Republican."

There is really no adequate way to convey the astonished, excited surprise with which I read lines like these. In a novel, maybe, they might have been found— but in a lyric poem? Lowell was doing something nobody else was doing: getting the "times" into his verse; making poetry as interesting as did Pope or Byron.

There were also—and who could have foreseen them—the playful strokes of verbal brilliance that inevitably brought alive something in the world (Nabokov was currently doing the same thing, with *Lolita*). "Skunk Hour," the last and most famous poem from *Life Studies*, was, granted, a portrait of a man in torment ("My mind's not right"); but the poet's mind had just played itself around late summer in a declining Maine small town with unforgettable characters like the following:

> And now our fairy
> decorator brightens his shop for fall;
> his fishnet's filled with orange cork,
> orange, his cobbler's bench and awl;
> there is no money in his work,
> he'd rather marry.

The fairy decorator, to be seen here and there in Cambridge as well as in Maine, became part of my poetic mythology. As did Father Lowell himself, "Home After Three Months Away" from McLean Hospital, recuperating, addressing his daughter, who has stolen his shaving brush, in the following lovely apostrophe:

Dearest I cannot loiter here
in lather like a polar bear.

Life Studies remains for me Lowell's most compelling book, although *For the Union Dead*, with its splendid title poem, is a close second.

Not long after *Life Studies* appeared and I was teaching at Amherst, Lowell came to read his poetry to the students who had just ended their term of "Introduction to Literature" by studying the book. It was a January snowstorm through which he'd driven down from Boston, somehow by way of the Notch (a road through the Holyoke Range connecting South Hadley with Amherst), where he saw—he told the assembled before beginning to read—a sign announcing Dinosaur Land. "I guess all poets live in Dinosaur Land" he said in that wondering, slightly apologetic, seductive tone of voice which could infuse even ordinary statements with magic life. I recall opening lines from the new poems he mainly read:

My old flame, my wife!
Remember our lists of birds?

No longer to lie reading *Tess of the d'Urbervilles*
while the high, mysterious squirrels
rain small green branches on our sleep!

Bed, glasses off, and all's
ramshackle, streaky, weird,

I rub my head and find a turtle shell
stuck on a pole,
each hair electrical
with charges . . .

Sometimes I have supposed seals
must live as long as the Scholar Gypsy.

At a party afterwards he drank tomato juice, was polite but firm when I tried to convince him how good a poet Charles Tomlinson was ("No, the poems seem arid to me"), was not the least interested in being a center of attention. It was the last time I ever heard him read in person, and no poet except Frost ever put on a more satisfying performance.

In the late sixties as he turned out sonnet after sonnet, revising them as fast as he wrote them, it became increasingly hard to maintain perspective, sometimes even to know whether the poem was "good"—indeed to know just what you thought of it anyway. "I always went too far" says one of the sonnets, and in them Lowell went too far so many times that parody was an understandable, even welcome response, as in this ending to "Revised Notes for a Sonnet" by one "Robert Lowly":

> My mind's not right.
> With groined, sinning eyeballs I write sonnets until dawn
> Is published over London, like a row of books by Faber—
> Then shave myself with Uncle's full-dress sabre.

Yet we've barely begun to discover the riches of *Notebook* (1970) and the volumes into which he later divided it. His last book, *Day by Day*, I feel unready to speak about; but even having read it through only once, I find Lowell's death easier to accept, callous as that may sound. "I'm tired / Everyone's tired of my turmoil," he once wrote, and in the concluding poem to this last volume says "I hear the noise of my own voice." I don't think one can read through *Day by Day* without feeling that this was the only way his literary career could have ended: "The book is finished and the air is lighter."

The best single paragraph ever written about Lowell is found in *Armies of the Night*, by his rival-admirer Norman Mailer. The situation is their appearance together at a rally two nights before the march on the Pentagon in 1967, but the context is sub specie aeternitatis, as Mailer imagines what it must be like to carry around the "moral debt of the Puritan" and speculates that "Lowell's brain at its most painful must have been equal to an overdose of Halloween on LSD." But the poetry?

> Lowell's poetry gave one the sense of living in a well, the echoes were deep, and sound was finally lost in moss on stone; down there the light had the light of velvet, and the ripples were imperceptible. But one lay on one's back in this well, looking up at the sky, and stars were determinedly there at night, fixed points of reference: nothing in the poems ever permitted you to turn on your face and try to look down into the depths of the well, it was enough you were in the well—now, look up! The world dazzled with its detail.

This about says it, and perhaps it will be for the dazzle, the detail of the world that Lowell's poetry will be most read and loved. Personal and yet not merely personal, the dazzle is found especially for me in a sonnet, "The Heavenly Rain," a poem with a New York setting from which I quote the last ten lines in gratitude and farewell:

The rain falls down from heaven, and heaven keeps
her noble distance, the dancer, seen not heard.
The rain falls down, the soil swims up to breathe:
the squatter sumac, shafted in cement,
flirts its wet leaves to heaven like the Firebird.
Two girls clasp hands in a clamshell courtyard to watch
the weed of the sumac aging visibly;
the girls age not, are always young as last week,
wish all rains one rain—this, that will not wash
the fallen leaf, turned scarlet, back to green.

Amherst Student, October 1977

Larkin's Presence

"I think in one sense I'm like Evelyn Waugh or John Betjeman, in that there's not much to say about my work. When you've read a poem, that's it, it's all quite clear what it means." Thus Philip Larkin, parrying an interviewer's asking whether he had profited from reading criticism of himself. One takes the point: this is a poet who made every effort, and successfully, not to write poems that—as he said Emily Dickinson's too often did—"expire in a teased-out and breathless obscurity." And even though relative obscurity can occasionally be found in Larkin's poetry, especially in earlier work like "Dry-Point" and "Latest Face" from *The Less Deceived*, his poems typically have "plots," are narratives with beginning, middle, and end, spoken by a voice that invites trust (though not all speakers in his poems are trustworthy), and seeks what Frost said good poems issued in—a "clarification of life." Not necessarily, as Frost went on to say, "a great clarification, such as sects and cults are founded on," but "a momentary stay against confusion."

Larkin's remark about his poems being so clear in what they mean that there's not much to say about them should not however be dismissed—like Waugh's responses to interviewers—as merely a way of eluding questions. Not that he's above discomfiting the questioner, as when, asked what he had learned from his "study" of Auden, Yeats, and Hardy, he snapped back with "Oh, for Christ's sake, one doesn't *study* poets! You *read* them, and think, That's marvellous, how is it done, could I do it?" (The best riposte to one of his parryings was Auden's. After asking Larkin how he liked living in Hull and having Larkin reply that he was no unhappier there than any other place, Auden clucked at him "Naughty, Naughty.") But a glance at criticism of the poems doesn't reveal interpretive disputes about them or strikingly divergent notions of which are the best ones. It seems generally agreed that his poetic output, if small, was distinguished; that whether his range is thought to be relatively narrow or wide as life itself, the poems are like nobody else's. If there are readers of poetry in England and America who don't at all share these sentiments, they have kept quiet about their dissent. But if indeed there's "not much to say" about the poems—as there is, for example, a great deal to say about James Merrill's poems: charting allusions, sizing up the tone of a line, proposing and correcting particular "readings"—there may yet be something of interest to be said about the challenge Larkin's work presents to contemporary ideas about poets and poetry. This would require an attempt to characterize the reader of Larkin who feels that this challenge is a splendid thing to have occurred. And with Larkin more than with most poets the challenge is one the reader takes personally: why does this body of work matter so much to *me*?

More than thirty years ago Randall Jarrell said in a letter to James Agee that writing poetry involved one in struggling "both against the current of the world and the current of the World of Poetry, a small world much more interested in Wallace Stevens than in Chekhov, Homer, and Wordsworth combined." Looking around him, shortly before the publication of Ginsberg's *Howl* and the domestic poems of Lowell's *Life Studies,* Jarrell saw in American poets under forty (he had just turned that corner) what he called "the world of Richard Wilbur and safer paler mirror-images of Richard Wilbur"—the era of "the poet in the grey-flannel suit." Three years later, looking through an anthology of English and American poets under forty, he saw little to contradict his picture of poets and poems that didn't take enough chances: *New Poets of England and America* (ed. Hall, Pack, and Simpson) mainly presented—and seems three decades later still to present—work for which the word accomplished comes all too readily to mind. Yet in that anthology Jarrell found and read with pleasure seven poems by Philip Larkin, including "Church Going," "Poetry of Departures," and "At Grass," from *The Less Deceived.* (The book had not yet been published in America, but serious readers of poetry knew about it in the late 1950s, when it could be ordered from England for ten shillings and sixpence.) Lowell, then well into his *Life Studies* poems in the new style—he included a version of "Skunk Hour" in a letter to Jarrell about the anthology—told him that he had been reading Larkin since the previous spring and liked him better than anyone since Dylan Thomas, indeed liked him better than Thomas. He was not only the most interesting of the "movement" poets, but "unlike our smooth younger poets says something." In reply, Jarrell said he was "delighted" with the remark about Larkin, since he himself was "crazy about him."

I mention this little episode in literary history to point out that for all the critical tendency to patronize Larkin as a wistful ineffectual angel ("He is plain and passive . . . a sympathetic figure as he stands at the window, trying not to cloud it with his breath"), his voice in its early manifestations struck two of the best American poets as a fresh accent, put to the service of saying something, as in the opening of "Poetry of Departures":

> Sometimes you hear, fifth-hand,
> As epitaph:
> *He chucked up everything*
> *And just cleared off,*
> And always the voice will sound
> Certain you approve
> This audacious, purifying,
> Elemental move.

The voice's accent commands not only a lively, slangy idiom in which chuckings up and clearings off are at home, but in addition a cool Latinate superiority to people who get so excited about that idiom that they can't imagine anyone hearing it in a different way. Having so deftly laid down those ironic adjectives—"audacious," "purifying," "elemental"—so as seemingly to kill any pretensions to value the "move" might have, Larkin then changes perspective, appearing to entertain a second thought and what follows from it. For the rest of the poem it's impossible to consider stanzas separately since the voice moves through and over them with quietly dazzling changes of pace:

> And they are right, I think.
> We all hate home
> And having to be there:
> I detest my room,
> Its specially-chosen junk,
> The good books, the good bed,
> And my life, in perfect order:
> So to hear it said
>
> *He walked out on the whole crowd*
> Leaves me flushed and stirred,
> Like *Then she undid her dress*
> Or *Take that you bastard;*
> Surely I can, if he did?
> And that helps me stay
> Sober and industrious.
> But I'd go today,
>
> Yes, swagger the nut-strewn roads,
> Crouch in the fo'c'sle

Stubbly with goodness, if
It weren't so artificial,
Such a deliberate step backwards
To create an object:
Books; chain; a life
Reprehensibly perfect.

In reading the poem aloud or typing it out, one discovers just how perfect an object it is, though not "reprehensibly" so. Although I don't propose to talk about Larkin's rhyming, it should at least be acknowledged as the operation that makes everything come together and cohere (as it does with his early master Yeats and his later master Hardy). In "Poetry of Departures" there are full rhymes usually at the end of a stanza (approve/move; bed/said; stay/today), Audenesque off-rhymes (there/order; think/junk; if/life), and comic-looking or sounding ones that vary depending on your Anglo or American pronunciation (epitaph/off; stirred/bastard—in his recording of the poem Larkin pronounced it bah-stud, which makes for a wholly engaging ring).

For all its talk of undone dresses and bastards, "Poetry of Departures" recalls no modern poet more than Frost, not just because Larkin refuses to trade in "a deliberate step backwards" for the call of the wild (Frost wrote a poem titled "One Step Backward Taken"), but for the way both poets need to plant themselves firmly some place so that they can compellingly imagine some place else. Frost's charming poem about Henry Hudson ("I stay; / But it isn't as if / There wasn't always Hudson's Bay") is titled "An Empty Threat" but the threat of departure, however empty, is enough to fill a poem with detail after imagined detail. The same for Larkin, whose little poem of departure plays with the notion of walking out on things, something he can imagine doing only when he has his feet still in the middle of them. Frost is one of the poets from this century, along with Hardy, Sassoon, Edward Thomas, Betjeman, and Wilfred Owen, whom Larkin said he kept within reach of his working chair (no Auden? no Graves?), but it is important that their affinity not be seen to consist in the way they both expunge romantic possibilities from their consciousness. They may—or at least Larkin did—have expunged them from their lives, but only the better to entertain them in their writing.

John Bayley, who has written about Larkin with his usual perceptiveness, calls this temperamental inclination by the title of a poem from *The Whitsun Weddings*, "The Importance of Elsewhere," and calls Larkin also, with Keats and Yeats in the background, the last Romantic. As with Keats—and probably

Larkin's Presence

Yeats too, as it was for D. H. Lawrence who made up the phrase—Larkin's was a case of "sex in the head," or so he would have us believe from the things he said in print. For him, says Bayley, "The erotic is elsewhere and evaporates on consummation." And with Keats's "Lamia" and Larkin's first novel, *Jill*, in mind, Bayley suggests that "the man who creates and contemplates romance is extinguished by its realization or fulfilment." Larkin uses that last word at the end of "No Road," one of a number of poems in *The Less Deceived* that speak, with an unmistakably personal ring, about a relationship between two people which didn't pan out and after which, the poet imagines, time will obliterate the already disused road between them:

> To watch that world come up like a cold sun,
> Rewarding others, is my liberty.
> Not to prevent it is my will's fulfilment.
> Willing it, my ailment.

The poems he wrote were good for what ailed him. Another way of making the same point about life was to reply, as Larkin did when asked if he were happy, that yes he was but that one couldn't write poems about being happy: "Deprivation is for me what daffodils were for Wordsworth," was his happy formulation. In other words, you can and cannot know me through my poems.

Along with sex, the richest "elsewhere" in Larkin's experience was American jazz, even as he listened to plenty of it. For him and Kingsley Amis as Oxford undergraduates,

> Russell, Charles Ellsworth, "Pee Wee" (b. 1906), clarinet and saxophone player extraordinary, was, *mutatis mutandis*, our Swinburne and our Byron. We bought every record he played on that we could find, and—literally—dreamed about similar items on the American Commodore label.

This was no charming exaggeration; Larkin and Amis may have had better ears than any other recent English writers (or is it just that my own ear is tuned to them?), and I can't believe it had nothing to do with how much jazz, Pee Wee Russell and the rest, they listened to. The whole of English poetry was available there in the Bodleian, yet think of all those American Commodore jazz records that were elsewhere, the ones they hadn't heard. Although at Oxford, as in other places, jazz was and is a minority taste, its being more exciting than poetry surely had to do with this relative inaccessibility. Anyone who once yearned to possess sides or albums the record companies had let go out of print (things are better these days) knows what the excitement of such an elsewhere can feel like.

But it wasn't only the music that interested Larkin. Even before he discovered jazz he had listened to dance music, dance bands, and said that he must have learned "dozens of dance lyrics" about which he said to an interviewer that

> I suppose they were a kind of folk poetry. Some of them were pretty awful, but I often wonder whether my assumption that a poem is something that rhymes and scans didn't come from listening to them—and some of them were quite sophisticated. "The Venus de Milo was noted for her charms / But strictly between us, you're cuter than Venus / And what's more you've got arms"—I can't imagine Mick Jagger singing that; you know, it was witty and technically clever.

The lines about the Venus de Milo, from "Love Is Just Around the Corner," seem to have been favorites since he mentions them more than once, and the influence of dance lyrics may be observed, not merely in the fact that Larkin's poems rhyme and scan, but in how they sound, the way—line by line—they swing. There is no better place to observe such a movement than in the opening poem from *The Less Deceived*, the one that thirty years ago introduced this reader to Larkin. "Lines on a Young Lady's Photograph Album" says more about looking at photographs than any poem I know, and it also investigates what it means to pore over the snapped stages of someone whose past you care about:

> My swivel eye hungers from pose to pose—
> In pigtails, clutching a reluctant cat;
> Or furred yourself, a sweet girl-graduate;
> Or lifting a heavy-headed rose
> Beneath a trellis, or in a trilby hat
>
> (Faintly disturbing, that, in several ways)—
> From every side you strike at my control,
> Not least through these disquieting chaps who loll
> At ease about your earlier days:
> Not quite your class, I'd say, dear, on the whole.

The movement of these stanzas is of course more complicated and "unsingable" than dance tunes can afford to be—consider the pauses within the lines, the way cat/graduate slightly off-rhymes, the parenthetical irony. Yet there are also memorable solo lines that seem to have come out of some Golden Treasury of Popular Song: "From every side you strike at my control" or "Not quite your class, I'd say, dear, on the whole"—surely Fred Astaire sang them in some 1930s movie? And there is a distinctly Cole Porterish feeling in a later stanza, which, after insisting that the photographs have persuaded him "That this is a real girl in a real place," goes on to speculate about whether and how much the truth of those images is dependent on their original being no longer present:

> In every sense empirically true!
> Or is it just *the past?* Those flowers, that gate,
> These misty parks and motors, lacerate
> Simply by being over; you
> Contract my heart by looking out of date.

Witty and technically accomplished certainly, but also poignant the way a gorgeous line can be, this last one delivered, again, with the wistful elegance of an Astaire, maybe a Billie Holiday. (And note the wonderful bonus provided by the double sense of "contract.") When Louis MacNeice died in 1963, Larkin wrote a short appreciation for the *New Statesman* in which he called MacNeice a "town observer" whose poetry was the poetry of everyday life. But beyond that poetry's treatment of shopwindows and lawnmowers and its "uneasy awareness of what the newsboys were shouting," MacNeice, he wrote, "displayed a sophisticated sentimentality about falling leaves and lipsticked cigarette stubs: he could have written the words of 'These Foolish Things.'" A lovely tribute which might well be paid to Larkin himself, especially in his earlier poems.

All the best ones from *The Less Deceived,* including of course the best known of all, "Church Going," are poems of tenderness directed at something that is now elsewhere. Their need is nothing so clearly identifiable as nostalgia; nobody who took Larkin's sardonic, unillusioned view of his own childhood can be accused of that:

> By now I've got the whole place clearly charted.
> Our garden, first: where I did not invent
> Blinding theologies of flowers and fruits,
> And wasn't spoken to by an old hat.

> "I Remember, I Remember"

He doesn't write poems out of the feeling that—as in a line from Jarrell—"In those days everything was better." It is rather the difference between now and then (most affectingly expressed in "MCMXIV" from *The Whitsun Weddings*) that moves him and animates a poem. In speaking about something that is elsewhere—maybe past and gone but not quite—Larkin achieves an extraordinary intimacy of tone, both in relation to that subject and to the implicated reader, who, it is assumed, will care just as much about it as the poet does. (His rhetoric never insists on how really splendid something is, in fact.) Think of this passage about a married woman's maiden name:

> Now it's a phrase applicable to no one,
> Lying just where you left it, scattered through
> Old lists, old programmes, a school prize or two,
> Packets of letters tied with tartan ribbon—
> Then is it scentless, weightless, strengthless, wholly
> Untruthful? Try whispering it slowly.
> No, it means you. Or, since you're past and gone,
>
> It means what we feel now about you then:
> How beautiful you were, and near, and young.

"Maiden Name"

Jarrell once wrote that "the poem is a love affair between the poet and his subject, and readers come in only a long time later, as witnesses at the wedding." Such a poetry has its sudden intimacies of tone ("No, it means you"), and—in case there are people who think Larkin's voice lacked passion—its certifiable intensities of feeling, of love, are witnessed by us.

Unlike the almost forgotten maiden name Larkin writes a poem to revive, a name can live on while the bearer of it is forgotten, and Larkin can right that balance too, as in the final poem from *The Less Deceived* about once-famous racehorses now subsided into something else. "The eye can hardly pick them out," "At Grass" begins, but by the fourth stanza Larkin has achieved a beautiful feeling for his subject, those horses that are wholly unaware of his questioning of them:

> Do memories plague their ears like flies?
> They shake their heads. Dusk brims the shadows.
> Summer by summer all stole away,
> The starting-gates, the crowds and cries—
> All but the unmolesting meadows.
> Almanacked, their names live; they
>
> Have slipped their names, and stand at ease.

The touch is so sure that one almost misses the point that those horses shake their heads not to assure the poet they're impervious to memory but merely to twitch away the flies that are plaguing them. About the surprising "unmolesting," as modifying the meadows, faithful in their way to the otherwise deserted horses, one can only say with Larkin, who, when asked how he'd arrived at an image in his poem "Toads," answered, "Sheer genius."

These poems and others from *The Less Deceived* speak to the reader's own need to be less deceived—the need to be intimate with the past and with loss (of a maiden name, of how one used to look, of a horse's once thoroughbred performance) by seizing them through the poet's words. There is little to be done about the present except to endure it as it erodes us; Frost's lines from "Carpe Diem" say what there is to be said on the subject:

> But bid life seize the present?
> It lives less in the present
> Than in the future always,
> And less in both together
> Than in the past. The present
> Is too much for the senses,
> Too crowding, too confusing—
> Too present to imagine.

And when Larkin decides to live for a bit in the future, the consequences are predictably grim, the end of England foreseen:

> For the first time I feel somehow
> That it isn't going to last,
>
> That before I snuff it, the whole
> Boiling will be bricked in
> Except for the tourist parts—
> First slum of Europe: . . .

> "Going, Going"

But on occasion he succeeds magnificently in imagining the crowding, confusing present by writing a poetry of becoming, of flux, and by exulting in the process rather than lamenting it. "Wedding-Wind" (an early, Lawrentian poem) and "Coming" from *The Less Deceived*, "Here" and "Water" from *The Whitsun Weddings*, are examples of such imaginings. And in the second section of "Livings," from *High Windows*, an unidentified speaker, evidently a lighthouse keeper, raptly contemplates a vividly present scene:

> Seventy feet down
> The sea explodes upwards,
> Relapsing, to slaver

Off landing-stage steps—
Running suds, rejoice!

Rocks writhe back to sight.
Mussels, limpets,
Husband their tenacity
In the freezing slither—
Creatures, I cherish you!

It is a remarkably early-Audenesque telegram in which the importance of elsewhere is subordinated to the here-and-now:

Radio rubs its legs,
Telling me of elsewhere:

Barometers falling,
Ports wind-shuttered,
Fleets pent like hounds,
Fires in humped inns
Kippering sea-pictures—

Keep it all off!

Without the author's name attached, no one would guess this was Larkin; its language revels in the attempt to live up to, even outdo, the invigorating chaos of the world it embodies.

A similar, and similarly rich, satisfaction—though most mutedly expressed—occurs when a scene or place in the present engages him because the life has gone out of it, has gone elsewhere. Yet, as with Wordsworth looking at London from Westminster Bridge before anyone is stirring, the place now offers its essential being, seen as if truly for the first time. In "Friday Night in the Royal Station Hotel,"

Light spreads darkly downwards from the high
Cluster of lights over empty chairs
That face each other, coloured differently.
Through open doors, the dining-room declares
A larger loneliness of knives and glass
And silence laid like carpet. A porter reads
An unsold evening paper. Hours pass,
And all the salesmen have gone back to Leeds,
Leaving full ashtrays in the Conference Room.

In shoeless corridors, the lights burn. How
Isolated, like a fort, it is—

Larkin's Presence

> The headed paper, made for writing home
> (If home existed) letters of exile: *Now*
> *Night comes on. Waves fold behind villages*

I suppose that down through the line comparing the hotel to a fort one might call the poem merely expert, the sort of thing one comes to expect from Larkin-on-emptiness. But where on earth did the italicized message come from, imagined to be written home by the imaginary exile? It moves the poem beyond expertise into the surprising, unsettling creation Larkin at his best is capable of.

"Livings" (part II) and "Friday Night in the Royal Station Hotel" offer us, if you will, glimpses of the Sublime; but sometimes Larkin invites us into a present, at least for a moment, by achieving what a student of mine cleverly called The Tacky Sublime. In "The Large Cool Store" we are shown how most of the "cheap clothes" match the workday habits of the working-class people who buy them. Then there is a surprise:

> But past the heaps of shirts and trousers
> Spread the stands of Modes For Night:
> Machine-embroidered, thin as blouses,
>
> Lemon, sapphire, moss-green, rose
> Bri-Nylon Baby-Dolls and Shorties
> Flounce in clusters . . .

Yet this satiric vision of loveliness leads not to further satiric treatment, but rather to a serious meditation on how hard it is to say something conclusive about women and love.

Some of Larkin's best work is to be found in each of the three books of poetry he published at ten-year intervals (I am excluding his early *The North Ship* as not the real thing), and the finest of the three is the last, *High Windows*. Perhaps, with T. S. Eliot in mind, he scoffed at the notion of a poet's "development" (to Ian Hamilton in an interview he quoted Oscar Wilde's line about only mediocrities developing). But *High Windows*, with only twenty-four poems, is the quintessence of all the books and contains four of his richest and most ample works: "To the Sea"; "The Old Fools"; "The Building"; and "Show Saturday" (with Yeats-like stanzas of nine, twelve, seven, and eight lines respectively). Along with his final poem, "Aubade," "The Old Fools" and "The Building" are the darkest, most death-oriented poems he wrote; the other two are equally life-affirming in their blessings on two rituals—going to the beach, going to the fair. "Show Saturday," with its elaborately rhymed stanzas that

---

enjamb themselves one into the next, concludes in a burst of—for Larkin—
positively positive thinking, saluting with alliterative energy the "dismantled
Show," now concluded but to return next year, same time:

> Let it stay hidden there like strength, below
> Sale-bills and swindling; something people do,
> Not noticing how time's rolling smithy-smoke
> Shadows much greater gestures; something they share
> That breaks ancestrally each year into
> Regenerate union. Let it always be there.

Larkin is not, of course, exactly "there," nor is he one of the bathers in "To the
Sea" who persist in making another kind of annual show:

> If the worst
> Of flawless weather is our falling short,
> It may be that through habit these do best,
> Coming to water clumsily undressed
> Yearly; teaching their children by a sort
> Of clowning; helping the old, too, as they ought.

These are the sort of people an Auberon Waugh recoils from in disgust; Larkin
gives them his considered respect.

As for the dark poems, "The Building" and "The Old Fools" lose none of
their original terror—it is not too strong a word—on rereading. The first is an
improvisation, in the mode of Kafka or Fellini, on this unnamed structure (to
call it a hospital would be to commit the Jamesian sin of weak specification)
which signals that "something has gone wrong":

> It must be error of a serious sort,
> For see how many floors it needs, how tall
> It's grown by now, and how much money goes
> In trying to correct it. See the time,
> Half-past eleven on a working day,
> And these picked out of it; see, as they climb
>
> To their appointed levels, how their eyes
> Go to each other, guessing; on the way
> Someone's wheeled past, in washed-to-rags ward clothes:
> They see him, too. They're quiet. To realise
> This new thing held in common makes them quiet,
> For past these doors are rooms, and rooms past those,
> And more rooms yet . . .

Larkin's Presence

The neutral tone belies the hopeless subject: it is as if Larkin has to keep writing in the hope that, for the space of the poem, he can help us fend off the hopelessness. By contrast, "The Old Fools" is more compact and more tonally aggressive, especially in its first two stanzas, at the expense of age's incapacity to know what's happening to it ("Do they somehow suppose / It's more grown-up when your mouth hangs open and drools, / And you keep on pissing yourself, and can't remember / Who called this morning?"). But by the third stanza, in a moment of sympathetic identification the poet makes up for his would-be callousness, giving the old fools some metaphors with which to see themselves:

> Perhaps being old is having lighted rooms
> Inside your head, and people in them, acting.
> People you know, yet can't quite name; each looms
> Like a deep loss restored, from known doors turning,
> Setting down a lamp, smiling from a stair, extracting
> A known book from the shelves; or sometimes only
> The rooms themselves, chairs and a fire burning,
> The blown bush at the window, or the sun's
> Faint friendliness on the wall some lonely
> Rain-ceased midsummer evening. That is where they live:
> Not here and now, but where all happened once.
>   This is why they give
>
> An air of baffled absence, trying to be there
> Yet being here . . .

It is, I think, Larkin's most handsome stanza (comparable to it are the final ones from "The Whitsun Weddings" and "Dockery and Son"), and it encloses perhaps the most beautifully realized and affecting sequence in all his work. The poem doesn't quite end there, and the horror of enduring this "whole hideous inverted childhood" returns, now with the poet including himself in it: "Well, we shall find out." It is the last answer, if another were needed, to Browning's salute to age in "Rabbi Ben Ezra," and not just one further voice in an argument about growing old but a crushing unanswerable statement of fact. Perhaps too crushing, one might argue—too sweeping, too exclusively grim in its portraiture; yet it has a lot of truth going for it. As Lowell remarked, a poem by Larkin "says something." "The Old Fools" says something final about what was always his ultimate subject.

For if Larkin was driven to write about love consummated elsewhere, the young in one another's arms—"Sexual intercourse began / In nineteen sixty-three / (Which was rather late for me)-"—then age and the death about which "we shall find out" was even more irresistible as a subject to be fetched from elsewhere and entertained in the poem. Larkin "developed" into the poet who wrote "The Old Fools" by taking life—as Frost said poetry should—by the throat, exaggerating both his disgust at old-age horrors and his sympathetic tenderness for those people with lighted rooms inside their heads. It issues in a memorableness that has nothing in common with A. Alvarez's calling him the poet of "suburban hermitage . . . and all mod con." "Death kills a man; the idea of death saves him," said Forster in *Howards End* perhaps too chirpily, at least too much so for Larkin, who wasn't about to talk about salvation in any terms. There is testimony in Andrew Motion's fine memorial poem about him, "This Is Your Subject Speaking," that he refused to talk about salvation as being somehow possible through art. In that poem Larkin, visiting Motion for supper, comes across a book-mark which says "Some say / Life's the thing, but I prefer reading," and snaps back:

> *Jesus Christ what balls.* You spun
> round on your heel to the table
> almost before your anger took hold . . .

Later, cooled down, "Larkin" goes on to say:

> *You see, there's nothing to write*
> *Which is better than life itself, no matter*
> *how life might let you down, or pass you by . . .*

This speaking up for life might have taken a sharper edge as he saw his own powers as a poet disappearing. In 1982 he ended his *Paris Review* interview with the terse declaration: "It's unlikely I shall write any more poems" (not many, *any*) and at another moment in Motion's poem he says to the younger man

> *Don't ask me*
> *Why I stopped, I didn't stop. It stopped.*
> *In the old days I'd go home at six*
> *and write all evening on a board*
>
> *across my knees. But now . . . I go home*
> *and there's nothing there. I'm like a chicken*
> *with no egg to lay.*

Larkin's Presence

His last egg, as it were, was one of his very best. "Aubade," published in December of 1977, was written as death in its elsewhereness seemed closer, staying in the poem's words "just on the edge of Vision":

> I work all day, and get half drunk at night.
> Waking at four to soundless dark, I stare.
> In time the curtain-edges will grow light.
> Till then I see what's really always there:
> Unresting death, a whole day nearer now.
> Making all thought impossible but how
> And where and when I shall myself die.
> Arid interrogation: yet the dread
> Of dying, and of being dead,
> Flashes afresh to hold and horrify.

Here, unlike "The Old Fools," the personal edge is felt at the very beginning and only deepens over the poem's five stanzas. It is nothing more than mere total emptiness that horrifies him—"nothing more terrible, nothing more true"—and in the third stanza, with a touch of the younger, slangier Oxford iconoclast, he sees through the religious consolation:

> That vast moth-eaten musical brocade
> Created to pretend we never die,
> And specious stuff that says *No rational being*
> *Can fear a thing it will not feel*, not seeing
> That this is what we fear—no sight, no sound,
> No touch or taste or smell, nothing to think with,
> Nothing to love or link with,
> The anaesthetic from which none come round.

The voice rises, with pressing excitement, to "correct" the blindness of consolatory wisdom that doesn't know the half of it, of the "Waking to soundless dark" at 4:00 A.M. which he has just undergone and which is his undressed rehearsal for the grave. Since "Death is no different whined at than withstood," the poem ends in a getting up, a coming back without illusion to life, which like death had better not be either whined at or withstood, but rather just met:

> Slowly light strengthens, and the room takes shape.
> It stands plain as a wardrobe, what we know,
> Have always known, know that we can't escape,
> Yet can't accept. One side will have to go.

Meanwhile telephones crouch, getting ready to ring
In locked-up offices, and all the uncaring
Intricate rented world begins to rouse.
The sky is white as clay, with no sun.
Work has to be done.
Postmen like doctors go from house to house.

Those three single-line concluding sentences, in which the "intricate rented world" is faced (and what a stroke that "rented" is), are the point in his work beyond which Larkin was not to go, and perhaps for strong reasons. If a poet has to stop writing there is justice for it happening in coincidence with his subject: to maul slightly Emily Dickinson's line, Larkin's work could stop for death. "Most poets have nothing to write about," James Dickey once confided. Larkin knew what he had to write about and when he had done it.

One's response to his death in December of 1985 was then, for all the sense of loss, not a sense that had he lived he would have gone on to write poems he had not quite yet grown into writing. (It would be nice to have been wrong and to have seen him live and write on so as to prove it.) For essentially his work felt complete—as Jarrell's did after *The Lost World* or Bishop's after *Geography III*, or as Lowell's did perhaps even before he published *Day by Day.* On the face of it nothing could be more absurd than to compare the four slim volumes Larkin gave us (counting *The North Ship* this time) with the eight individually much larger ones of his ancestral favorite, Hardy; yet if Hardy's emergence as a poet is dated from *Wessex Poems* (1898), both he and Larkin (dating from *The North Ship,* 1945) had some thirty years of production. We know that Larkin put himself on record as not wishing Hardy's vast collection a single poem shorter, and as calling his work "many times over" the best body of poetry in the century. One of the pleasures in rereading Hardy is of course the discovery of poems one had previously missed, or only half-read: compared, say, to Eliot, he seems inexhaustible. How many rereaders of Larkin's books have a similar feeling? I think I know his poems as well as those of any postmodern poet; still, to reread is to be struck not by their being fewer than 100 poems all told in *The Less Deceived, The Whitsun Weddings,* and *High Windows,* but by the density and weight of the ones there are.

How much this has to do with their being poems of great formal craft, especially (and frequently) in their often elaborately schemed rhyme and stanzas, is hard to specify. My feeling is that the craft has a great deal, maybe everything, to do with it. When compared to two very different contemporary poets of reputation, John Ashbery and Adrienne Rich, the difference Larkin's adherence to traditional metric, stanzas, and rhyme makes is patent. Ashbery may well possess, as David Bromwich has declared, the "original idiom of our times," but as his prolific output testifies it may not take quite as much care or time to write a poem if one doesn't require rhyme and stanza, and if one is more concerned with nonsense than with sense. (I can't believe that Larkin was not making pointed mischief when he said—explaining why his bad hearing kept him from traveling to America—"Someone would say Ashbery, and I'd say, I'd prefer strawberry, that sort of thing.") And it is hard to imagine Adrienne Rich discovering that her poetry had just dried up, that (in the phrase from Motion's poem about Larkin) she had become a chicken with no egg to lay. There will always be some new or old issue of gender and power on which to exercise her poetic will in various free forms. Ashbery and Rich have written many books of poetry; we may see Larkin's relatively few against the background of the formal tests he set for himself in drawing the figures of poems.

The craft, the elegance, the ceaseless wit—how could anyone say, as W. J. Bate and David Perkins do in their recent anthology of British and American poets, that Larkin writes "the poetry of personal statement and dreary realism"? Although thirty years ago Jarrell hailed him as the antidote to "the world of Richard Wilbur," it is Wilbur, born just a year before Larkin, to whom he can be compared in his command of syntax and suppleness and tone. Larkin might not have liked the comparison, might have felt Wilbur more of a high-toned formalist than he. But for all the American poet's fastidious good manners (those who don't much like him call it primness), Wilbur's poetry from *Ceremony* through *The Mind-Reader* unmistakably reveals a distinct presence, a person whose character and inclinations we get to know very well. If Wilbur, in Brad Leithauser's phrase, is "one of the few living American masters of formal verse," then Larkin was its most recent English master of such verse. And for all its difference from Wilbur's, his poetry shows a person at least as distinct in his outlines, his tastes, the clarity of his idiom. Either of them could have written the next to last poem in Larkin's last book:

> Cut grass lies frail:
> Brief is the breath
> Mown stalks exhale.
> Long, long the death

It dies in the white hours
Of young-leafed June
With chestnut flowers,
With hedges snowlike strewn,

White lilac bowed,
Lost lanes of Queen Anne's lace,
And that high-builded cloud
Moving at summer's pace.

In the fewest possible words, "Cut Grass" says much, surely enough to serve as a poet's epitaph.

Raritan, Spring 1987 ("Philip Larkin"); reprinted in *Philip Larkin: The Man and His Work,* edited by Dale Salwak (Macmillan, 1989). Reprinted here by permission from *Raritan: A Quarterly Review,* Vol. VI, No. 4 (Spring 1987). Copyright © 1987 by *Raritan,* 31 Mine St., New Brunswick, NJ 08903.

Entertaining Amis

Kingsley Amis's poems have always made critics a trifle nervous, partly because he is such a rereadable novelist that it seems hardly fair he should perform so well in verse. Then there is the presence of Larkin over his shoulder, a writer whose poems take on depths of gloomy richness that Amis, wisely I think, doesn't attempt to match. Speaking as an American, it's my impression that news of Amis the poet has barely reached these shores; in college classrooms at least, Larkin is read and admired while Amis gets there, when he does, as the author of *Lucky Jim*. This is fair enough, but makes it harder for the poems to receive their due. He has been referred to as a "non-Commissioned Larkin," also fair enough if we remember that the NCO's have their own club at which Amis's poetic act is one of the best things currently viewable. At any rate, as someone who for years has been sending people copies of "Lovely" ("Look thy last on all things lovely / Every hour, an old shag said"), I should like to suggest why his poetry is a civilized resource, the sort of thing you want to read aloud to another person.

What the *Collected Poems* reveals is Amis's development into one of the best English writers of light verse in this century (the book is dedicated to John Betjeman, master of such activity). Reviewers of his poems in the past have sometimes disagreed over whether they qualified for the "light" label or were of a higher (or heavier) nature. Apropos of this question, his Introduction to the *New Oxford Book of English Light Verse* provides a useful gloss on his own work:

> I described *vers de société* earlier as in some degree a continuation of satire. This move can be seen as already in progress by the time of Swift, who was certainly not writing satire in the normal sense of the term, as his avoidance of the heroic couplet would be enough to suggest. . . . We are dealing with a kind of realistic verse that is close to some of the interests of the novel: men and women among their fellows, seen as members of a group or class in a way that emphasises manners, social forms, amusements, fashion (from millinery to philosophy), topicality, even gossip, all these treated in a bright, perspicuous style.

Collected Poems, by Kingsley Amis. Hutchinson, 1979.

These perspicuous sentences about one kind of light verse are so, partly because they have roots in Amis's own poetry and suggest the way in which, like Swift, he is not writing "satire in the normal sense."

Yet in the earliest poems from the *Collected Poems* (the first six of them were originally published in *Bright November*, Fortune Press, 1947) there is little of the flexibility needed for writing *vers de société*. The portentous style is more contrived than "bright," and contrived in the manner of Auden—in the first poem, "Letter to Elisabeth"—even down to the off-rhymed couplets, a practice which seems to be of dubious value in both Auden and Amis:

> In public rooms we guessed at silence, and
> Discussed the end of what has had no end.
> Where none would pause we found an hour to wait
> And clung together when the streets were wet.
> Now in a parted meanwhile rings the beat
> Of married hearts; my scene has shifted, but
> Still flows your northern river like a pulse,
> Carrying blood to bodies at the poles.

There are also Audenesque "fumbling gestures," and resolutions to "speak straight" and "walk without a strut." John Bayley has said of Larkin's first book of poems, *The North Ship*, that "there is a high degree of competence and of effective Yeatsian usage, but no Larkin at all." A similar judgment might be passed on the presence of Auden in Amis's early poems.

Audenesque was not a plausible style for Amis because Amis's poems, unlike Auden's early ones, do not tease us with an unexpected or inexpressive content, a "secret" behind the words.

> That horse whose rider fears to jump will fall,
> Riflemen miss if orders sound unsure;
> They only are secure who seem secure;
> Who lose their voice, lose all.

"Masters," from which these lines are quoted, produces further examples of this principle, then turns round to describe by contrast some unmasterful "losings":

> The eyes that will not look, the twitching cheek . . .
> Only these make us known, and we are known
> Only as we are weak.

It concludes as sententiously as it began:

Entertaining Amis

By yielding mastery the will is freed,
For it is by surrender that we live,
And we are taken if we wish to give,
   Are needed if we need.

This is apt, a sympathetic statement of the "liberal" point of view (surely E. M. Forster would sympathize with its message); yet it also feels like an exercise, the style carefully excluding any personal idiosyncrasy in favor of sanity and objectivity. When listening to Amis read *A Case of Samples* on the Marvell Press recording, one is surprised to note how little expression gets into his voice, and, as compared with Larkin's recordings, how chaste and impersonal is his delivery. Indeed one wishes for a bit more flare.

The flare of a more personal voice is there, though, in "A Dream of Fair Women," which like Amis's other poems has a principled point to make, but on the way to making it provides us with something other than a dispassionate presentation—as when, in the dream, a bevy of females exercises its varied charms on the narrator:

Speech fails them, amorous, but each one's look,
Endorsed in other ways, begs me to sign
   Her body's autograph-book;
"Me first, Kingsley; I'm cleverest" each declares.

Here the "bright, perspicuous style" emerges, as it does in "A Bookshop Idyll" when, after the narrator (may we call him Amis?) finds that gents and ladies tend to title their volumes of poetry in discernibly different ways, he finds also that "a moral beckons":

Should poets bicycle-pump the human heart
   Or squash it flat?
Man's love is of man's life a thing apart;
   Girls aren't like that.

It was very bright of him to bring in the Byron line here (Senator Sam Ervin also quoted it, during the Watergate hearings, in the presence I believe of John Ehrlichman), to reduce the female sex to "girls," and to squash the last line as flat as he managed to do. Generally the poem's daringness seems more pronounced now than it did twenty-five years ago: "Women are really much nicer than men: / No wonder we like them." Name two other English or American poets who would dare to say such a thing in 1979. One hears the chorus of protest, and certainly it takes a really disinterested female reader, blessed with the humorous sense, to like Amis's work.

By not reading his poems or novels very carefully, one could assume that he is simply a professional squasher of the human heart, that he merely delights in letting the hot air out of pumped-up dreams and visions. It is useful then to consider "Romance," the concluding poem in *A Case of Samples,* to suggest how disturbed and moved he has been by this whole matter of romantic inflation:

> The sound of saxophones, like farmhouse cream,
> And long skirts and fair heads in a soft gleam,
> Both scale and are the forest-fence of dream.
>
> Picture a youngster in the lonely night
> Who finds a stepping-stone from dark to bright,
> An undrawn curtain and an arm of light.
>
> Here was an image nothing could dispel:
> Adulthood's high romantic citadel,
> The Tudor Ballroom of the Grand Hotel.
>
> Those other dreams, those freedoms lost their charm,
> Those twilight lakes reflecting pine or palm,
> Those skies were merely large and wrongly calm.
>
> What then but weakness turns the heart again
> Out in that lonely night beyond the pane
> With images and truths of wind and rain?

This lovely and delicate poem does something interesting with the Yeatsian motto "In dreams begins responsibility," by rewriting it more ruefully and disillusionedly: in dreams begins disappointment or weakness—the heart turned out and away, unable for more than a moment to scale the "forest-fence," to capture or to live in that "high romantic citadel" where you must be as glamorous and undaunted as the others. It is Amis's Fitzgerald poem, as written by a Nick Carraway who had read Empson:

> Was it really he who had spent a whole string of autumn evenings fifteen or sixteen years ago in the front room just off the London-Croydon road, playing his Debussy and Delius records by the open windows, in the hope that the girl who lived at the end of the street, and whom he never dared speak to, would pass by, hear the music, look in and see him? Well, it was a

good thing, and impressive too, that he could still feel a twinge of that uncomplicated and ignorant melancholy.

Take a Girl Like You (1960)

One notes also that it is a "youngster" who is allowed both to experience the dream and to suffer its consequences. Amis has always held on hard to the images and truths of youthful—one could say boyish—perception (his imagining of the youth Peter in *The Riverside Villas Murder* is finely done), which is perhaps why in his poems from the last fifteen or so years, the oldster speaking them is scornful and sad. "A Chromatic Passing-Note," from *A Look Round the Estate* (1967), begins with an oldster talking this way:

"That slimy tune" I said, and got a laugh,
In the middle of old Franck's D minor thing:
The dotted-rhythm clarinet motif.

Amis invariably does something fresh with his musical references, classical or jazz. Here it would be a mistake to remember "filthy Mozart" and presume that a Lucky Jim is up again to his old debunking tricks. The poem goes on to point out, quite didactically, that the tune wasn't "slimy" when the speaker was fifteen, but showed rather "that real love was found / At the far end of the right country lane." Now, having learned different, " 'Slimy' was a snarl of disappointment." What saves the "A Chromatic Passing-Note" from abstractedness and mere lesson-teaching is that there *is* such a clarinet motif in the second movement of the Franck symphony; that one loves it when young and (in my experience) eventually turns on it or away from it as too insistent, too importunate. (Thanks to Amis's poem I've now come to happy terms not only with the clarinet motif but with the whole splendid symphony.)

From here it is but a step, and with hindsight a predictable one, to "The Evans Country." "Adulthood's high romantic citadel" has been too pricey a dream, the human heart too weak to engage it for long. So Amis imagines, with fierce satisfaction, the unromantic architecture against which Evans's courting takes place:

By the new Boots, a tool-chest with flagpoles
Glued on, and flanges, and a dirty great
Baronial doorway, and things like portholes,
Evans met Mrs Rhys on their first date.

Here we have moved completely and successfully into the "manners, social forms, amusements, fashion (from millinery to philosophy)" which distinguish *vers de société*, Amis's brand of light verse. The "bright, perspicuous style" continues to engage us as further items of "romance" are cataloged, "the time they slunk / Back from that lousy week-end in Porthcawl"; then the poem reaches its conclusion in a strongly assured and compelling rhythm:

> The journal of some bunch of architects
> Named this the worst town centre they could find;
> But how disparage what so well reflects
> Permanent tendencies of heart and mind?
>
> All love demands a witness: something "there"
> Which it yet makes part of itself. These two
> Might find Carlton House Terrace, St Mark's Square,
> A bit on the grand side. What about you?

Eh, *hypocrite lecteur?* In *The Waste Land* Eliot is also supposed to have squashed flat the human heart; but if one feels, as I do, that the encounter between the typist and her young man carbuncular ("Flushed and decided he assaults at once") has been bicycle-pumped by language into a great caricature that is beautiful (Eliot's language about Ben Jonson), then one can also be truly moved by this moment in the Amis poem:

> But how disparage what so well reflects
> Permanent tendencies of heart and mind?

The question can be asked only when the poet moves beyond the complacencies of more ordinary "satire" ("poking fun," as the undergraduates say) and acts instead as a true witness to love, even Evans's love, by measuring, thus celebrating it in verse.

By the time we reach the end of the final poem in "The Evans Country" ("Aberdarcy: The Chaucer Road") the poet-as-commentator has disappeared. On his way to a quick one with "Mrs No-holds-barred," Evans reflects on "How much in life he's never going to know: / All it must mean to really love a woman." Yet, the poem suggests, there are compensations, as after the event Evans returns home for a quiet evening:

> "Hallo now, Megan.
> No worse than usual, love. You been all right?
> Well, this looks good. And there's a lot on later;
> Don't think I'll bother with the club tonight."

Entertaining Amis

Nice bit of haddock with poached egg, Dundee cake,
Buckets of tea, then a light ale or two,
And "Gunsmoke", "Danger Man", the Late Night Movie—
Who's doing better, then? What about you?

It is a marvelous stroke to take us, by the flash and movement of the catalog of anticipated delights, inside Evans country to the extent that the final question totally disarms us. And the tendencies of Evans's heart and mind have been permanently etched.

One might say the same about Amis, after reading through the eighteen poems, some of them very short, which follow "The Evans Country" and make up his published output of post-Evans verse. Often they are recited (Amis edited *The Faber Popular Reciter*—"poems that sound well and go well when spoken in a declamatory style") by the radical-reactionary controversialist we've become familiar with from various letters and columns in newspapers and weeklies since the later sixties. Ageing and rigidifying, he salutes himself on his fiftieth birthday in "Ode to Me" for having at least lived through *those* fifty years rather than the fifty to come:

After a whole generation
Of phasing out education,
Throwing the past away,
Letting the language decay,
And expanding the general mind
Till it bursts.

He at least was born with a

chance of happiness,
Before unchangeable crappiness
Spreads over all the land.

The crappiness is succinctly noted in some lines from "Shitty" (but why in the collection does this poem not come after, rather than before, the poem to which it seems an afterthought, "Lovely"?):

Look thy last on all things shitty
While thou'rt at it: soccer stars,
Soccer crowds, bedizened bushheads
Jerking over their guitars,

German tourists, plastic roses,
Face of Mao and face of Ché,

> Women wearing curtains, blankets,
> Beckett at the ICA.

The crappiness has spread to Salisbury, where St. Edmund's Church is to be turned into a modern hotel, a prospect particularly apt to produce images of things shitty:

> Fancies of Japanese, back from Stonehenge,
> Quaffing keg bitter by the pulpit stair,
> Swedes booking coach-tours in the chancel.

> "Festival Notebook"

Those Swedes were originally at their deadly work in Oxford too, but in putting "Their Oxford" into the collection Amis (to be fair no doubt) replaced them with other foreigners, engaged in lousing up the "old hotel / Now newly faced." Thirty years ago the hotel was a slow, safe, boring place; today

> You have to do yourself well as you may
> In the dimmed bar, where fifty Finns arrive

> Just before you, and budding businessmen,
> Though dressed like actors, call at bruisers' pitch
> For Highland malt with stacks of ice.

It's possible that a truly decent liberal democrat might find all this unamusing, even repellent. Since such a reader has also taken many courses in anthropology and sociology at his university he would be similarly unappreciative of the poem's ending, when Amis invokes the lostness, the pastness of "that Oxford that I hardly knew": the Oxford of privilege, of "Champagne breakfasts (or were they mythical?)" or the perhaps equally mythical one of "giant" teachers like Bowra and Lewis ("Men big enough to be worth laughing at"). He disapproved of much at the Oxford he attended, but now, when nobody "except the old" cares how it "used to be," does it make any sense for him to disapprove?

> What seemed to me so various is all one,
> A block of time, which like its likenesses
> Looks better now the next such has begun;
> Looks, and in this case maybe really is.

The fine last line gives a slight but lethal kick in the head to the relativist's wisdom about how nothing really changes, about how "you just *think* things were better back then." Maybe they really were, and it is the poem's art to make one entertain that possibility.

Entertaining Amis

Robert Frost used to say that rather than entertaining ideas he liked to try them out to see whether they entertained him. Amis's poems, especially the recent ones, work this way by invoking contemporary crappiness so magnificently and expertly that—like the poet, and perhaps the man himself—we are positively exhilarated by the awful spectacle. The next-to-last poem in the book, "Farewell Blues," uses Hardy's "Friends Beyond" (the Mellstock churchyard poem) to eulogize dead jazz musicians, much of whose music moulders in the vaults of dead 1930s record companies. What is alive, alas, is music made by "Bongo, sitar, 'cello, flute, electric piano, bass guitar" that sounds like this:

> Trumpets gelded, drums contingent, saxophones that bleat or bawl,
> Keyless, barless, poor-man's Boulez, improvising on fuck-all,
> Far beyond what feeling, reason, even mother wit allow,
> While Muggsy Spanier, Floyd O'Brien, Sterling Bose and Henry Allen lie
> in Decca churchyard now.

In the immortal language of one of Larkin's uncollected poems, the contemporary improvisor is "A nitwit not fit to shift shit." But the final stanza of "Farewell Blues" brings together much of what makes up Amis's version of things: contempt and disgust for the crappy present; nostalgia for a time when things were different, just possibly better; commitment to rhyme and exactly measured lines (fifteen syllables in the first three lines, twenty-four in the fourth); respect helplessly paid to the "dream" which was once entertained and which, because it was so good, helped ruin the present. The stanza is about jazz but about more than just jazz:

> Dead's the note we loved that swelled within us, made us gasp and stare,
> Simple joy and simple sadness thrashing the astounded air;
> What replaced them no one asked for, but it turned up anyhow,
> And Coleman Hawkins, Johnny Hodges, Bessie Smith and Pee Wee
> Russell lie in Okeh churchyard now.

Light verse no longer feels very light, has gone "high" instead into a version of pastoral that is affecting and moving. But I speak for myself here, as one for whom since the day I first read *Lucky Jim* back then, Amis has been the most entertaining, the most exhilarating of contemporary writers. Who's doing better then? What about you?

Essays in Criticism, January 1980; reprinted in *Kingsley Amis: In Life and Letters,* edited by Dale Salwak. Macmillan, 1990.

How to Open a Pigeon

Book jacket comments from English reviews of *Gaudete* suggest that we are in the presence of "the most powerful and original voice in English poetry today," a poet who uses words "with . . . astonishing verbal thrust and precision" and who "gives a cosmic significance to his poems." Hughes is no mere moralist or inhabitant of "arid areas of abstraction"; his world is "dynamic" and "frightening." Now although it is an arid pastime for a reviewer to hold up blurbs for scorn, these (spliced together from different reviewers) seem to me so inadequate, misguided, and untrue that I begin my consideration of *Gaudete* by mentioning them. Does this work reveal dynamic particularity and astonishing verbal precision vindicating the claim that Hughes is the most powerful and original voice in English poetry today?

When Ted Hughes's first volume, *The Hawk in the Rain*, was published twenty-one years ago it was admired for going against the grain of the 1950s. In an age of well-made, ironically expert, rhythmically unadventurous verse (so ran the argument) here was a bold fellow who went deep into nature, hawk on fist, apocalyptic horses on the horizon; someone who *really* heard the wind roar or the wren shriek and who was therefore above petty human concerns (or was it that all human concerns were by definition petty?); a young poet at any rate who at age twenty-seven had produced some impressive lyrics. Actually Hughes was, in this book and in the best poems from *Lupercal*, which followed three years later, less an "original" or noble savage than sentimentalists would have had him be. It is instructive, for example, to place certain poems from these volumes next to one's favorites from the early volumes of Richard Wilbur (his third, *Things of This World*, was published the same year as Hughes's first) and see how both poets weave highly mannered elaborations around their material. Query: who wrote the following first stanza of a poem called "Acrobats"?

> Among ropes and dark heights
> Spot-lights sparkle those silver postures:
> (The trapeze beginning to swing)

Gaudete, by Ted Hughes. Harper and Row, 1977.

How to Open a Pigeon

Casually they lean out
Over eyes opened deeper
Than the floored drop. Then fling
Out into nothing, snap, jerk
Fulcrumed without fail
On axes immaterial as
Only geometry would use.

Of course Wilbur usually rhymes, and his lines are more regular; still it would not be absurdly off the mark to suspect he might begin a poem in this way—though in fact it is from Hughes's second book.

Or consider what seems to me a fine poem from *The Hawk in the Rain* which I quote in full the better to compare it with Hughes's latest effort. Here is "The Thought-Fox":

I imagine this midnight moment's forest:
Something else is alive
Beside the clock's loneliness
And this blank page where my fingers move.

Through the window I see no star:
Something more near
Though deeper within darkness
Is entering the loneliness:

Cold, delicately as the dark snow,
A fox's nose touches twig, leaf;
Two eyes serve a movement, that now
And again now, and now, and now

Sets neat prints into the snow
Between trees, and warily a lame
Shadow lags by stump and in hollow
Of a body that is bold to come

Across clearings, an eye,
A widening deepening greenness,
Brilliantly, concentratedly,
Coming about its own business

Till, with a sudden sharp hot stink of fox
It enters the dark hole of the head.
The window is starless still; the clock ticks,
The page is printed.

This is distinguished for its movement, for the way it expresses an "entering"—something "Coming about its own business" with concentrated economy and delicacy. The repeated "now" in stanza three is the opposite of gratuitous; it acts out the step-by-step progress into creation which the thought-as-fox is imagined as making. And the poem is both tactful and forceful in its emphasis, while remaining sanely aware of how much to claim for an individual mind intent on using but not despoiling "nature." Although the fox isn't merely a fox, it isn't merely a symbol either; rather the poem is a metaphor as Robert Frost defined metaphor: the impulse basic to all poetry to say one thing in terms of another.

Let me now for immediate contrast put next to "The Thought-Fox" a typical passage from *Gaudete*, one describing the changeling minister, Lumb, who (in the words of Hughes's prefatory argument) "organises the women of his parish into a coven, a love-society" for the purpose of producing a new Messiah. At the time which the poem covers, the parish husbands are about to end Lumb's game. Uneasily driving along in his van, he has an accident and then a vision conveyed in the following language:

> One by one he finds them.
> The women of his parish are congregated here,
> Buried alive
> Around the rim of a crater
> Under the drumming downpour.
>
> And now he sees
> In the bottom of the crater
> Something moving.
> Something squirming in a well of liquid mud,
> Almost getting out
> Then sliding back in, with horrible reptile slowness.
>
> And now it lifts a head of mud, a face of mud is watching him.

There is some more sliding and stretching and grasping as Lumb, trying to rescue the "something," finds himself embraced by it:

> The rain striking across the mud face washes it.
> It is a woman's face,
> A face as if sewn together from several faces.
> A baboon beauty face,

> A crudely stitched patchwork of faces,
> But the eyes slide,
> Alive and electrical, like liquid liquorice behind the stretched lids.

As throughout the long poem, this speaking voice is toneless, moving from one word to the next by means of "And now" or "It is," and by repeating key words like "mud" or "face" or by beginning lines with the same word—"A face. . . . A baboon beauty face," etc. It is not clear that there is much to be gained by thinking of the poetry in terms of line units; Hughes breaks them off as he chooses, and the "sense" is never syntactically complex enough so that it makes much difference. Would it matter, for example, whether "Alive and electrical" began the last line or ended the next-to-last?

"His is a dynamic world and a frightening one": one sees why such adjectives should be hauled out, since brought up against a toneless, drugged, repetitive insistence on the unspeakable (what *is* that "something" squirming down there?) only scary but "vital" adjectives will do. The voice imagined to speak "The Thought-Fox" seemed to issue from a living person, interested in variations of tone, sometimes confiding in us ("Through the window I see no star"), at other times more concerned with setting the thing before us ("Brilliantly, concentratedly / Coming about its own business"). By contrast, the voice which speaks throughout *Gaudete* is barely a human voice at all. Call it "cosmic" instead—if you like the word, and some do—for it moves almost entirely by deadpan declaratives strung together with the most basic of connectives: "And," "But," "Then." This cosmic, impersonal voice is also curiously subject to purely verbal effects, almost stuttering in its wide-eyed confrontation with deep things. "Something moving" in one line will suggest "Something squirming" in the next; or the voice will be led from one word to similar sounding ones—"Something . . . squirming . . . sliding . . . slowness . . . striking." Usually it finds alliteration irresistible; so "baboon beauty" and "liquid liquorice" don't so much point to anything out there in the object (which is but a verbal nightmare anyway) but spawn one another and harken after Edith Sitwellian vowel effects—"liquid liquorice . . . stitched lids." Hughes even cultivates these effects by playing around with his protagonist's name: "Lumb's mouth lumps with movement. / Sounds lump in his squeezed throat. / His lungs struggle. . . ."; "His lips loll idiot loose. His mask / Is loosened. . . ."

I believe the style of *Gaudete* represents a corrupt or vicious use of language, sensational and self-regarding in its effects. Its impersonality is of a superficial kind, since there is never revealed in the poem any human personality to transform or escape from into art. There is only the dogged language-user, the impartial observer with no subjective preferences, no morality, moving words around like lumps of matter, or running from one sound to the next like liquid liquorice. To this charge the reply might be made that Hughes is not writing "personal" lyrics, as he sometimes did in his early volumes; that *Gaudete* (billed as a "major work") is a long poem, a folktale-narrative the telling of which must be naive and deeply resonant, untempted by the pleasure and responsibilities of a sophisticated consciousness and a social tone.

Considering what we get in place of a narrator with a human perspective on the dreadful events (I presume they can be called that) narrated, the trade-off seems a dubious one. Here the reader must decide whether this reviewer is merely timid and prudish, or whether there is something less than satisfactory about sitting in a comfortable chair and reading passages like the following:

> Maud, in her bare room below, has wrenched the pigeon's head off.
> Her blood-smeared fingers are fluffed with white down.
> Now her hooking thumbs break the bird open, like a tightly-taped parcel.
> Its wing-panics spin downy feathers over the dusty boards.
> She is muttering something.

(Humming *These Foolish Things* perhaps?) These ministrations are performed by Lumb's housekeeper Maud, here entertaining herself with the bird preparatory to getting painted up for the big orgy at the church basement. Once again the "something" sounds very dark and exciting; and in a sense this passage is expert—what a *good* way to describe how to open a pigeon! Having already unbuttoned his shirt, removed his necktie, and laced up his boots (he's already had to wade through a lot of mud) our thrilled reader is presumably not about to ask whether the activity he and the poet are engaged in is morally and humanly defensible. Isn't life a violent and shocking affair? Isn't the poet allowed to do anything with words?

Maybe not with impunity. Hughes's humorless insistence on how awful things are ("bleak pessimism" would no doubt be the word for it) is probably real enough; he is, in Wyndham Lewis's phrase, an authentic "bad-timer." But *Gaudete* overkills. It's hard to get up a real shiver for that poor pigeon when already (or was it a dream?) "a long-handled hook rips the bull's underbelly from ribs to testicles. / Half a ton of guts / Balloon out and drop on to Lumb";

or a mauled dove's head "Dangles like a fob, / Squandering its ruby unstoppably, into the sterile gravel"; or a hunter's knife stabs a swimming stag in the nape "and a whelm of spray and limbs" erupts; or (best of all) a bull's horns are sawed off with a wire. After a while, one says, I can handle anything. There is also, to assure us we're in the realm of Art, Leonard Baskin's inevitable drawing of slimy things gaudily decorating *Gaudete*'s cover; the kind of book that might show up on a coffee table and doesn't necessarily have to be read. There is also a good deal of hot-sex stuff ("Inside Felicity, a solid stone-hard core of honey-burning sweetness has begun to melt / And she knows this is oozing out all over her body / And wetting her cheeks and trickling on her things") to mix in with the blood and the guts. It is as if Terry Southern had not written *Candy*. And suddenly one simply can't resist the thought that Ted Hughes has gotten on to a good thing; that early along somebody praised him for his dark brooding intensity and he has ended up sounding like the Truman Capote of Yorkshire.

In his British Council pamphlet on the poet, Keith Sagar praises Hughes's bravery: "He has left behind the little humanist critics who are afraid of getting their feet wet. Querulously they call to him to come back to the familiar shore, back to the secure humanistic 'reality' in which they have invested their values." Since I'm less than "secure" about the reality I've invested my values in, I'm not calling out for Hughes to come back to it, though I lament the direction his talent has taken. But as a literary critic, even a little humanist one, I must point out the price language is paying for his indulgence in wild and whirling words. Early in *Gaudete*, within the span of eight pages, the following phrases can be found: "as if to remain still were even more futile"; "As if those puzzles held something from her"; "As if she breathed inside the silk of his nearness"; "As if it had crashed in through the window"; "As if he had just failed to save it"; "as if it were all something behind the nearly unbreakable screen glass of a television"; "As if under the intensification of joy"; "as if clearing an aim"; "As if tearing free"; "As if his / rabbiting spade had spilled open a cache of ancient gold"; "As if hours had passed"; "As if in a doctor's waiting room." Frost once ended a tribute to E. A. Robinson by celebrating the metaphorical nature of all poetry: "All virtue in 'As if.' " Hughes's frantic efforts to invest his tale with the truth of poetry results in "as if" run amok. Since everything is as if it were something else, nothing really turns out to be anything in particular. It's all words, the more (and there is always more) the merrier, and the bloodier. In the process something gets betrayed; "English," as Keats said it must be, has not been kept up. We should not rejoice at the publication of *Gaudete*.

Nation, January 21, 1978. *The Nation* magazine/The Nation Company, Inc., © 1978.

An Interesting Minor Poet?

During Sylvia Plath's short life of just over thirty years, she saw only one book of her poems published: *The Colossus* (1960). She had prepared a second one, even worked out the order of its poems, and that appeared as *Ariel* in 1965 after her death, with a number of poems added which were written in her final months. Two further volumes were published posthumously: *Crossing the Water* (1971), containing mainly earlier poems, and *Winter Trees,* in the same year, containing eighteen late ones plus "Three Women," a lugubrious "poem for three voices" written for the BBC. The result of such piecemeal, though perhaps advisable, publication was to create confusion in our minds about those remarkable seven years (1956–1963) in which 224 poems were written and finished. Now, eighteen years after her death by suicide in February 1963, we are at last given a thoroughly responsible presentation of the poems in chronological order, more than a third of them not previously published in book form. The old volume titles have been dropped, and poems are simply grouped under their appropriate year, dated by month and day whenever possible. The result is to make her appear an altogether larger and more satisfying poet than this reader had taken her to be.

Reading these poems through in chronological order calls into question the received idea of the clever craftswoman producing beautifully shaped objects, almost too beautifully shaped, who suddenly achieved a "breakthrough" into—in the phrase of one of that book's reviewers—the "raw genius" of the later *Ariel* poems. You could even read it as a lesson in liberation, with the early volume coming at the end of those evil 1950s (and she went to Smith too!) and the later one heralding, along with Robert Lowell and Anne Sexton and lesser talents, a confessional freedom from the repressive, whether prosodic or personal:

> What a thrill—
> My thumb instead of an onion.
>
> "Cult"

The Collected Poems, by Sylvia Plath, edited by Ted Hughes. Harper and Row, 1981.

Dying
Is an art, like everything else.
I do it exceptionally well.
I do it so it feels like hell.

"Lady Lazarus"

Never mind that in both poems, as in so many of her other late ones, there was not only a bitter but a mockingly self-lacerating and playful wit, a pure revel in felicities of language ("My thumb instead of an onion"—some fun there after you get through wincing), which the desperateness of her running-out life somehow gave birth to. Too many readers, younger ones especially, approached these later poems with religious awe as if "Sylvia" (or as they would now say, "Plath") were to be treated in a manner befitting Jesus Christ; it was she who had died for our sins—so the distressed young student might feel, especially if female. Of course the backlash wasn't long in coming. One college newspaper in the early 1970s printed twenty-four Sylvia Plath jokes, grisly riddles the mildest of which by far went "Why did SP cross the road?" "To be struck by an oncoming vehicle."

Ted Hughes has done an exemplary job in editing these poems, writing notes to them year by year (one only wishes for more notes, since they are so interesting), and giving us a generous selection of the juvenilia pre–1956 poems. And he strikes the right note in his introduction when he remarks that

> her attitude to her verse was artisanlike: if she couldn't get a table out of the material, she was quite happy to get a chair, or even a toy. The end product for her was not so much a successful poem, as something that had temporarily exhausted her ingenuity.

The right note, for surely she was one of the most ingenious poets in this latter half of our century; and to speak of her in terms of artisan and chair-maker, rather than transmitter of pure inspiration from heaven upstairs or downstairs hell, does justice to her resourcefulness and skill as a maker.

She did not always do justice to herself in this respect; or rather, she sometimes spoke as if formal ingenuity and true feeling might not be compatible. For example, this remark made about "Point Shirley," a poem she completed in January of 1959: "Oddly powerful and moving to me in spite of rigid formal structure." "Point Shirley" was written at the time she had begun to attend (along with Anne Sexton and George Starbuck) Robert Lowell's writing semi-

An Interesting Minor Poet?

nar at Boston University, and the poem's debt to Lowell's work is evident. But consider its opening two stanzas, in which her grandmother's house is evoked:

> From Water-Tower Hill to the brick prison
> The shingle booms, bickering under
> The sea's collapse.
> Showcakes break and welter. This year
> The gritted wave leaps
> The seawall and drops onto a bier
> Of quahog chips,
> Leaving a salty mash of ice to whiten
>
> In my grandmother's sand yard. She is dead,
> Whose laundry snapped and froze here, who
> Kept house against
> What the sluttish, rutted sea could do.
> Squall waves once danced
> Ship timbers in through the cellar window;
> A thresh-tailed, lanced
> Shark glittered in the geranium bed—
>
> Such collusion of mulish elements
> She wore her broom straws to the nub.

This may have been, as her biographer Edward Butscher says it was, a deliberate attempt to capture Lowell's seaside grays; but the strict stanza, the rhymes and half-rhymes, above all the careful syntax and enjambed lines—even running over from one stanza to the next—show an attention to (in Frost's words) "the sound of sense" that is compelling and demanding of any reader's agility. The continuations and suspensions which the speaking voice must make to navigate these lines are surely central to the poem's power. If we may correct Sylvia Plath, it moves us not in spite of but partly because of its "rigid formal structure." And it is quite different from anything Lowell had done in *Lord Weary's Castle*—where the blank verse proceeds in a breathless, hurtling way—or was doing in *Life Studies*, which appeared in 1959.

During the preceding two years, Plath had grown extremely skilled at rendering sentence sounds in poems which this volume allows us to read for the first time. Here is the opening of "The Great Carbuncle" (1957):

> We came over the moor-top
> Through air streaming and green-lit,

Stone farms foundering in it,
Valleys of grass altering
In a light neither of dawn
Nor nightfall, our hands, faces
Lucent as porcelain, the earth's
Claim and weight gone out of them.

And it continues just as expertly. Imagine deciding, as evidently she did, that such a poem was not quite good enough to be included in her first book! When she spoke (in another remark quoted by Hughes) with respect to the admirable "Mushrooms" (which did make *The Colossus*) of "my absolute lack of judgment when I've written something: whether it's trash or genius," she spoke with her characteristic either/or absoluteness. But "The Great Carbuncle," or "Above the Oxbow" (here my Connecticut River sentimentality may be intruding), or "In Midas' Country," or "Child's Park Stones" (a first-rate poem), or "Green Rock, Winthrop Bay" are not trash—perhaps not genius either, but something else, less sensational: assured performances, with a technical control wholly adequate to sustain the observant, grave, responsive presence that makes itself felt audibly over the carefully tracked course of stanza and whole poem. John Frederick Nims said it succinctly when he suggested that young writers should be advised to "forget *Ariel* for a while; study *The Colossus*." With the new volume, this study can more intelligently take place.

If she could only "let things slip a bit," said a reviewer in admiration of her earlier poems, she will do something really special. What happened in fact was that she let them slip with a vengeance into the "stream of repulsions" (the phrase is Hugh Kenner's) that inform the poems from the last months of her life. Ted Hughes left her in October of 1962. During that month she wrote or finished twenty-five poems, including the ones for which she is best known. Beginning with one new to me, "The Detective," we read on through, among others, the bee poems, "The Applicant," "Daddy," "Medusa," "Lesbos," "Fever 103°," "Cut," and "Lady Lazarus." Much adjectival overkill has been employed by reviewers attempting in desperation of vocabulary to outdo the poems themselves, and George Steiner, never at a loss on such occasions, has referred to "Daddy" as the "Guernica of modern poetry." But really it is nothing of the sort, reading now like a very clever, very nasty, very hopeless horror song which holds us partly by its resourceful way of exploiting our reticence and embarrassment at what we are hearing:

An Interesting Minor Poet?

I have always been scared of *you*,
With your Luftwaffe, your gobbledygoo.
And your neat mustache
And your Aryan eye, bright blue.
Panzer-man, panzer-man, O You—

Poor Otto Plath, a diabetic professor of biology at Boston University who had the misfortune to combine the diabetes with gangrene and broncho-pneumonia, so double-crossed his daughter by dying too soon, scarcely deserves such a tribute (I know, it's really a myth). And the stanza, indeed the whole poem, contains much that is repellent about Plath's poetry: the clever "gobbledygoo," a word like the one English teachers used to write on freshman themes; the relentless caricaturing of another, in tough baby-talk, all done in the interests of "art." And the panzer-man repetition. Earlier in "Daddy" we hear that "The tongue stuck in my jaw": "It stuck in a barb wire snare. / Ich, ich, ich, ich," and the poet's tongue sticks also in "Elm" ("These are the isolate slow faults / That kill, that kill, that kill"), in "The Bee Meeting" ("They will not smell my fear, my fear, my fear"), in "The Applicant," and elsewhere. There are many more questions now, fired off by an "Ich" whose tongue really isn't stuck at all, but extraordinarily adept and daring in its leaps and spins; like the one done around the first line of "Lady Lazarus," "Dying is an art":

I do it so it feels like hell.
I do it so it feels real.
I guess you could say I've a call.

It's easy enough to do it in a cell.
It's easy enough to do it and stay put.
It's the theatrical

Comeback in broad day
To the same place, the same face, the same brute
Amused shout:

"A miracle!"
That knocks me out.

A brilliant show, but there may be a problem about how many times one wants to watch it again. That is why encountering it here, as poem #198 in a chronological sequence, is a very good thing for its continued life. She had done, could do so much with words; now she had to do this, *would* do this new turn.

But as "Lady Lazarus" goes on to say, "There is a charge . . . a very large charge / For a word or a touch / Or a bit of blood." The sad joke is that the reader—surrounded by all those other poets in the imaginary museum who can be summoned up in a twinkling for a performance—really doesn't have to pay very much to watch the show. It was Sylvia Plath who paid the charge in full, and one feels in reading the final twelve poems in this collection, written in the month and days of 1963 which preceded her death, that they form a sort of coda, or perhaps a rehearsal for a new part to be played somewhere else.

The mood is set by the bleakly wonderful "Sheep in Fog" ("My bones hold a stillness, the far / Fields melt my heart") and holds largely through until the last poem, "Edge," in which "The woman is perfected. / Her dead / Body wears the smile of accomplishment." But just before the finality of "Edge" comes "The Balloons," a touching surprise after the histrionic agonies of more sensational Plath-poems. For four stanzas, composed with that fluidity of motion she had grown so expert at achieving years before, these "Guileless and clear, / Oval soul-animals" are celebrated for being themselves, for living with the mother and her children since Christmas, for keeping them company. Two last stanzas address the daughter:

> Your small
>
> Brother is making
> His balloon squeak like a cat.
> Seeming to see
> A funny pink world he might eat on the other side of it,
> He bites,
>
> Then sits
> Back, fat jug
> Contemplating a world clear as water.
> A red
> Shred in his little fist.

This was finished a week before she died, and unlike the balloons it remains with us, in its own words

> Delighting
> The heart like wishes or free
> Peacocks blessing
> Old ground with a feather
> Beaten in starry metals.

An Interesting Minor Poet?

For years I have endorsed Irving Howe's limiting judgment of Sylvia Plath as an "interesting minor poet." But I don't think anyone who submits to this collection is likely to be comfortable with that judgment. She was rather, was indeed—as the expression goes—something else.

New Republic, December 30, 1981

John Ashbery

In his introduction to E. A. Robinson's posthumously published *King Jasper,*
Robert Frost (in 1935) made a list of some of the ways recent poetry had tried
to be new, those ways largely ones of subtraction and elimination. Among
the things Frost said poetry had tried to get along without were punctuation,
capital letters, metric frame, dramatic tones of voice, content, phrase, epi-
gram, coherence, logic, consistency, and—he added—it had also been tried
without ability. Fifty years after Frost's remarks we have the interesting phenomenon of John Ashbery, as highly regarded a poet as any in this country
(his prizes and fellowships are many), who has now brought out a large
selection from his work of the past thirty years, stretching from *Some Trees*—
the Yale Younger Poet's volume for 1956—to *A Wave,* published just last
year.

Ashbery's is an interesting case because while a bona fide avantgardist (his
affiliations with modern painting are well known and he is routinely compared with Pollock and de Kooning, to say nothing of Webern or John Cage)
his poetry would appear to elude Frost's charge that "new ways to be new"
proceed by subtraction from and elimination of the traditional qualities of
verse in English. For Ashbery's work is expansive and leisurely in its rhythms,
and hospitable, even promiscuous in its entertaining of many levels both of
diction and of subject matter. So "Bird's-Eye View of the Tool and Die Co.,"
whose title immediately causes a readerly twitch of disbelief, begins by rewriting Proust, then serves up some less than astonishing facts:

> For a long time I used to get up early,
> 20–30 vision, hemorrhoids intact, he checks into the
> Enclosure of time familiarizing dreams
> For better or worse . . .

Then as the poem goes on to accommodate words like "meditated," "improvisation," "chorales," and "stricture," we discover that in fact there is really
no "I" nor "he" whom we can take seriously or trust (the way we "trust" and

Selected Poems, by John Ashbery. Elizabeth Sifton Books/Viking, 1985.

John Ashbery

"take seriously" the speaker in a poem by Keats or Tennyson or Yeats or Sylvia Plath) any more than we can trust those hemorrhoids or take seriously the Tool and Die Co. of the poem's title. Someone is playing a game.

These selected poems (about 140 of them) play various games, individually and collectively, as they aspire to leaving nothing out, to saying more rather than less, to inclusiveness rather than exclusiveness in their procedures. Yet the 340-odd pages contain scarcely a single characterizable dramatic speaker who is located *here* rather than *there* and whose individual accent and tone of voice may be distinguished from other accents and tones of other speakers in the volume. To be sure, Ashbery is sometimes a little jokey and earthy, at other times a little dreamy and elevated. Consider a few bits from the poems: "In the evening / Everything has a schedule, if you can find out what it is" ("Two Scenes"); "Worms be your words, you are not safe from ours" ("Sonnet"); "The first year was like icing / Then the cake started to show through" ("More Pleasant Adventures"); "What are your hobbies, girls? Aw nerts, / One of them might say, this guy's too much for me" ("Mixed Feelings"); "No one really knows / Or cares whether this is the whole of which parts / Were vouchsafed— once—but to be ambling on's / The tradition more than the safekeeping of it" ("Daffy Duck in Hollywood"). Ashbery himself is always ambling on, and though he assures us that "everything has a schedule," canny readers soon learn that they will never find out what that schedule is. In one of his most teasing and returnable-to poems, "Worsening Situation," the anonymous speaker concludes his lament by confiding to us that

> Lately
> I've been looking at old-fashioned plaids, fingering
> Starched white collars, wondering whether there's a way
> To get them really white again. My wife
> Thinks I'm in Oslo—Oslo, France, that is.

This poem is fun to discuss with students in poetry classes who furrow their brows and vainly try to decode it, until somebody gets the point—that it's all exactly as real and as potentially charming as Oslo, France. But is it any more than fun, gained by playing itself off against poems by Ashbery's predecessors that are, somehow, for real?

To my mind the large question is, how real is John Ashbery—how seriously are we to take him? Is he more than a clever, resourceful and indefatigable producer of one elegantly surfaced poem after another? His admirers claim much more for him—at least one of them, Harold Bloom, seeing him as the true descendant in the American Romanticist tradition of Emerson, Whitman, and Wallace Stevens. Bloom has said of Ashbery that there is no poet in English, past or present, "who insists upon so subtly unemphatic a pervasive tone"—as if it were a great virtue to be unemphatic. Yet it might be noted that poets in English have usually tried for *emphatic* tones of one or another sort, have thought that changes of tone carried out through a subtly varying voice were qualities for which to strive. The terrible risk that Asbbery takes is the risk of monotony, a risk compounded in a volume of this length whose peaks and valleys are hardly distinguishable from each other.

The problem of monotony becomes most acute in the book's longer poems—"Clepsydra," "The Skaters" (excerpted here), "Self-Portrait in a Convex Mirror," and "A Wave." As the voice in "Self-Portrait . . ." explains:

> The surface is what's there
> And nothing can exist except what's there.
> There are no recesses in the room, only alcoves,
> And the window doesn't matter much, or that
> Sliver of window or mirror on the right . . .

Still one can get quite lost and grow restless on the surface, even though assured there's nothing beyond or behind it. Such is my experience with Ashbery's work generally, but especially in the longer poems. As for the poems-in-prose, one blinks as the ineluctable sentences from "The System" (*Three Poems*) slide by: "Things had endured this way for some time, so that it began to seem as though some permanent way of life had installed itself, a stability immune to the fluctuations of other eras: the pendulum that throughout eternity has swung successively toward joy and grief had been stilled by a magic hand." And one thinks of Randall Jarrell's response when Robert Lowell showed him the prose composition "91 Revere St." which was to be part of his book of poems, *Life Studies*: "But it's not poetry, Cal."

In saying these things one remembers the old cartoon about the puzzled woman confronted by the abstract painting who asks her son what it's about: "It's not *about* anything, Mother," is the son's chilly response. To complain about Ashbery's lack of reference—or to allow that he refers to everything, and that's the trouble—may be to give comfort to the enemies of poetry, at least to enemies of the New. The question must also be asked whether Ashbery could have produced so much in such a seemingly effortless manner if he worked in

John Ashbery

rhyme and traditional stanza, let alone if he attempted to make discursive sense. (Rhyme is rare in his poems, and when the occasional sestina appears—as in the amusing "Farm Implements and Rutabagas in a Landscape"—it is pleasing, though the sestina provides an ideal form in which to make non-sense.) But Ashbery will not abide such questions, surely not answer them. The only "answer" he provides may be taken from some lines in his "Grand Galop":

> And now it is time to wait again.
> Only waiting, the waiting: what fills up the time between?
> It is another kind of wait, waiting for the wait to be ended.

In the meantime there is another poem to write.

Washington Post Book World, December 22, 1985

The Metered Updike

More than once in reading this densely repaying collection of John Updike's poems (the fortieth book he has published with Knopf), I thought of Wordsworth's Preface to *Lyrical Ballads,* especially its stated aims to keep the reader "in the company of flesh and blood" and to write under one restriction only— that of giving "immediate pleasure to a human being." Readers of contemporary poetry have been instructed, by some of our most influential critics, to admire the breezy abstract chatter of a John Ashbery (no flesh and blood there) or the painful solemnities of an Adrienne Rich (not much pleasure there). By contrast, Mr. Updike's poems, regularly appearing over the past forty years, have attracted comparably little attention or praise. Of course he labors under the burden of his fame as a novelist and critic: is it conceivable that such a phenomenon has also produced a body of distinguished verse? It is conceivable, and such is in fact the case.

In his Preface he acknowledges that the poems are "my oeuvre's beloved waifs," but also that the act of writing them is the "highest kind of verbal exercise—the most satisfying, the most archaic, the most elusive of critical control." In the best, indeed the majority of poems collected here, critical control is evident in their intelligent feeling and in the serious humor with which they present a life. By arranging them in two chronological sections (his light verse takes up the last hundred pages), Updike has helped keep us in the company of his own flesh and blood. "The thready backside of my life's fading tapestry," is how he refers to his poems, each of them dated, many of them (as with Wordsworth) supplied with a note on circumstance and place of composition. "Suburban Madrigal," for example, gives us the poet "Sitting in the first house I (et ux.) owned, 26 East Street, Ipswich, Massachusetts, waxing lyrical as I survey my domain." T. S. Eliot thought it a guarantee of a poem's artistry that it should be impersonal, effecting a cutoff between the man who suffers and the mind that creates. But "Leaving Church Early," one of Updike's always interesting familial poems, begins "What, I wonder, were we hurrying to, / my grandfather, father, mother, myself, / as the last anthem was com-

Collected Poems, by John Updike, Alfred A. Knopf, 1993.

mencing?" and we are invited to observe the continuity between the man's remembered life ("The Child is Father of the Man") and the poem that celebrates and explores it.

Flesh and blood, then, but this is not to say that the results are preciously self-regarding. As anyone knows from reading his fiction, Updike's appetite for the ordinary is extraordinary: "To transcribe middleness with all its grits, bumps and anonymities, in its fullness of satisfaction and mystery" has been his aim as far back as the memoir ("The Dogwood Tree") containing these words. Titles from this collection like "Burning the Trash," "Telephone Poles," "The Bicycle Chain," "Dutch Cleanser," "The Grief of Cafeterias," even, yes, "The Beautiful Bowel Movement," testify to a tenderly and wittily attentive eye. Who else (Randall Jarrell, perhaps) would care to consider "The Melancholy of Storm Windows," whose final stanza rounds off the melancholy:

> We, too, are warped each fall.
> They resemble us, storm windows,
> in being gaunt, in losing putty,
> in height, transparency, fragility—
> weak slabs, poor shields, dull clouds.
> Ambiguous, we have no place
> where we, once screwed, can say, *That's it.*

That the poems are haunted by a sense of transience, nostalgia, and wonder comes as no surprise to those familiar with the Olinger or Maple stories and the Rabbit novels. But the qualities and affinities are, again, pronouncedly Wordsworthian.

Wordsworth deplored poetry about which it couldn't be said that the poet's eye had been "steadily fixed upon his object." Updike's steady eye fixes, unerringly, on everything from sand dollars and seals to plumbing and pillows, as well as on larger constellations of events. The question is whether his poetic ear is as good as his eye; whether the poems display distinct felicities of rhythm and movement. Obviously no one can write good light verse (and Updike's is expert) without a trained ear; but in his other poems he sometimes writes lines that aren't to be scanned, as in the opening ones to "Back Bay": "My adult unemployed son and I / (he composes electronic music) / for his birthday traversed the Back Bay / regions of Boston, looking for suitable clothes / as a present. . . ." This reads like fairly casual prose and lets us know we are to be interested in situation rather than sound, content rather than form—a remark one would never make about contemporary masters of poetic form like Richard Wilbur or Anthony Hecht. (Or about the Auden whom Updike resembles in philological and scientific cleverness.) One sometimes feels that an Updike poem discovers its shape as it gets written, and that the final shape may be less interesting than the material it contains.

At other times, in the old phrase, form and content are one: "Enemies of a House" (houses are all over this book) is a sonnet that begins with "Dry rot intruding where the wood is wet" and moves through other natural and animal threats to the house's physical well-being, on into the sestet:

> ice backup over eaves; wood gutters full
> of leaves each fall and catkins every spring;
> salt air, whose soft persistent breath
> turns iron red, brass brown, and copper dull;
> voracious ivy; frost heaves; splintering;
> carpenter ants; adultery; drink; death.

Three powerful last words to fill out the line initiated by carpenter ants. "Enemies of a House" is one of seventy poems hitherto uncollected, written over the past eight or so years and showing Updike at his deepest and best. Many of them are energized—as were the stories in *Trust Me* and in recent *New Yorkers*—by the prospect of encroaching death, the end of one particular organization of flesh and blood. "Perfection Wasted" begins with a finely casual launch into the subject: "And another regrettable thing about death / is the ceasing of your own brand of magic, / which took a whole life to develop and market." It ends with the unanswerable question, "The whole act. / Who will do it again?" Updike has previously written some of his best poems about the death of grandparents and parents (one of his very best is the early "Dog's Death"). But in these recent poems the subject has cut closer to the bone.

And so has sex, on the evidence of poems like "To a Dead Flame" and "Mouse Sex" that take a retrospective and autobiographical look at the *Couples*-like scene of three decades ago. Updike has previously given us sexually incorrect treatments of female privates which are likely to amuse or repel, depending on the reader. (I found "No More Access to her Underpants" a combination of delicacy and nastiness as bracing as its title. Not everyone will.) But the erotic memories in later poems are more humanly generous and vulnerable in tone: "Mouse Sex" remembers a vivid moment in an adulterous encounter when, after a sudden noise from downstairs ("her husband or the wind") the woman urges her partner to proceed ("Put it in me") and the poet enlarges upon the scene:

> Suppose that moment, frozen, were Heaven or Hell:
> our hearts would thump until the death of stars,
> the trees outside would stir their golden edges,
> the bed would squeak, the frightened inch
> between our skins would hold the headboard's grain.

"To an Old Flame" speaks to the now-dead lover in a voice of wondering disbelief: "What desperate youthful fools we were, afraid / of not getting our share, our prize in the race, / like jostling marathoners starting out / clumsy but pulsatingly full of blood." Lines like these aren't to be judged purely as combinations of sound and sense but must be felt with the weight of a life, a history, behind them.

Another late poem, "Upon Looking into Sylvia Plath's *Letters Home*," begins with the shock of confirmation:

> Yes, this is how it was to have been born
> in 1932—the having parents
> everyone said loved you and you had to love;
> the believing having a wonderful life began
> with being a good student; the certainty
> that words would count;

Despite the differences between Plath, dead at thirty, "leaving blood-soaked poems / for all the anthologies," and himself the "wheezing" survivor and celebrity, recipient of (in "Academy") "an ease of prize and praise," the poet says he feels like her twin. For in them both are the tears of things, on which Wordsworth has the last word, with special aptness to Updike's literary career: "Poetry sheds no tears 'such as angels weep,' but natural and human tears; she can boast of no celestial ichor that distinguishes her vital juices from those of prose: the same human blood circulates through the veins of them both."

Boston Sunday Globe, April 25, 1993

Novelists

Aside from *Seeing Through Everything,* a book I published about English writers between the two world wars, almost all my writing about novelists has been in the form of reviews, omnibus or single, not included here. Three of the following eight items, "Glorious Trollope," "Sound and Fury," and "Total Waugh," come at the novelist indirectly through biographies and move from considering how well the biographer has performed his task to an estimate of the novelist's achievement. "The Serpent Hatches" considers the first volume of a massive edition of D. H. Lawrence's correspondence. "Fordie" is a brief account of a one-volume selection of highlights from Ford Madox Ford's voluminous writings. "Pure Literature," about Anthony Powell's novel *From a View to a Death* (1933), issued from an invitation to write about some favorite little-known book. "Almost Austen" was occasioned by a Virago Press reprinting of some titles from a little-known novelist, one of this century's finest, Elizabeth Taylor. "Vidal's Satiric Voices" was written for a collection of essays by several hands in honor of Gore Vidal.

Glorious Trollope

Is there anything more to say about Trollope beyond confessing one's addiction? And doesn't that merely characterize one as a throwback or curmudgeon, resisting contemporary fevers and frets on the cutting edge of *nouvelle critique* (the way we live now) in favor of a simpler time when a gentleman was a gentleman and things were called by their right names? My departmental colleagues on or near the cutting edge aren't likely to spend many hours reading Trollope (the two faculty colleagues who seriously read him are a philosopher and a mathematician), and although there have been a number of solid books written about him over the past couple of decades, he remains far from the centers of critical debate. There are of course Trollope scholars, one of the foremost of whom is N. John Hall. Ten years ago he gave us a beautifully annotated edition of Trollope's letters in two volumes; now he has published an extremely readable biography. It's not the sort of book that is going to make anyone reconsider his or her opinion about Trollope, but that may just be in the nature of things so far as this eminent Victorian is concerned.

One of Trollope's very best books is his autobiography (innocently titled *An Autobiography*), so a biographer is going to have to decide just how to place himself in relation to it. Mr. Hall's frequent practice, not altogether a satisfactory one I think, is to construct his own narrative by splicing together bits from Trollope's, as in the following treatment of the incipient novelist as a young post office employee sent out to investigate the delivery of letters in rural Ireland. Here is Trollope on the subject:

> I have often surprised some small country postmaster, who had never seen or heard of me before, by coming down upon him at nine in the morning, with a red coat and boots and breeches, and interrogating him as to the disposal of every letter which came into his office. And in the same guise I would ride up to farmhouses, or parsonages, or other lone residences

Trollope: A Biography, by N. John Hall. Clarendon Press, 1991. Three other biographies of Trollope, all of them intelligent and thorough, have appeared recently: R. H. Super's *The Chronicler of Barsetshire* (1988), Richard Mullen's *Anthony Trollope* (1990), and Victoria Glendinning's *Anthony Trollope* (1993). This makes four biographies of Trollope in a five-year span, surely sufficient for some time.

about the country, and ask the people how they got their letters, at what hour, and especially whether they were delivered free or at a certain charge. . . . In all these visits I was, in truth, a beneficent angel to the public, bringing everywhere with me an earlier, cheaper, and much more regular delivery of letters. But not infrequently the angelic nature of my mission was imperfectly understood.

He goes on to explain how his abrupt style of interrogation often caused suspicion and consternation in the parties interrogated. Hall retells it in this manner:

Sometimes he was a peculiar sight, dressed in red coat, boots, and breeches, swooping down at nine in the morning on a country postmaster demanding to know the disposal of every letter that arrived in his office. And often similarly attired, he would surprise farmers, parsons, lone country residents and their wives by suddenly appearing and asking questions about the delivery of their letters. . . . He considered himself "a beneficent angel to the public," even though the public did not always understand how this was so.

And so on in this vein, perfectly acceptable as long as you don't compare it to, as it were, the original. When you do, you see what's been lost: the understated comedy with which Trollope portrays himself as the brash interrogator, "coming down" (Hall soups it up to "swooping down") out of nowhere; or the nice touch, quite lost in Hall, of the beneficent angel whose angelic mission is "imperfectly understood" by his audience. In the main Hall is not a very humorous writer; Trollope is often so, and that makes a difference.

Hall is, however, a scrupulous provider—as was Trollope himself—of the financial details surrounding each of the writer's books; and he does a good job in evoking the misery of Trollope's childhood, in tracing the course of his career in the Post Office, first in Ireland, then in the West of England, and later on in following Trollope on his indefatigable travels. Among other countries Trollope visited the West Indies, the United States (five times!), Australia (twice), and New Zealand, South Africa, and Iceland (he wrote books about four of these places). Nor was there anything perfunctory about these visits: in Australia he didn't just go to New South Wales, but to all the remaining colonies including Tasmania, approaching his travels—as he did everything else—combatively:

His sometimes circuitous routes took him thousands of miles by ship, rail, and coach; he went great distances in buggies, over the bush roads, and trails which in England would have not been considered roads; he also travelled much on horseback, sometimes managing "forty, fifty, and even as much as sixty-four miles a day"; he covered hundreds of miles through forests and mountains "so steep it was often impossible to sit on horseback."

In Tasmania he had himself lowered 150 feet down the mine shaft of a gold mine "with his foot in the noose of a rope," in order to explore the stalactite caves toward which he "made his way for a mile underground . . . crawling, creeping, wading in waist-deep water." At this time he was in his later fifties; a couple of decades earlier, investigating postal conditions in the West Indies, he once rode so many miles on a bad horse and saddle that, in his discomfort, he thought of giving up the project. But, as he later told his brother Tom, that night he ordered two bottles of brandy, poured the contents into a large basin, and sat in it. After brief agony he was in shape to proceed on his mission.[1]

This was also the way he went about his writing, up and at his desk by 5:30 A.M., a half hour spent reading over what he'd written the previous day, then two and a half hours in the attempt, usually successful, to write a page every fifteen minutes: total, ten pages—after which it was time to dress for breakfast and repair to his other job in the postal service. Not to write was not to be alive, and Trollope kept himself alive by keeping himself writing. The piles of reports he produced about how to improve conditions in this or that postal district played directly, so he claimed, into his novel writing: "If a man knows his craft with his pen, he will have learned to write without the necessity of changing his words or the form of his sentences. I had learned so to write my reports that they who read them should know what it was that I meant them to understand." Just as with the pages of a novel where, without undue fussing about word and image, character and event could be so lucidly presented as to be thoroughly understood. Once a man really got going there need be no limit to the different narratives he could keep in motion. Noting that at one point in his career he was writing two full-length novels (*Castle Richmond* and *Framley Parsonage*) at the same time, he assures us that

1. It wasn't all painful, though. In New Zealand he went one dark evening with a friend to bathe in a hot spring, already occupied by three Maori women. With pats on his back, they encouraged Trollope to come bathe, and after a time in the water he remarked to his companion, Gilbert Mair, that "he wished he had something to lean against." Whereupon Mair whispered this "to a fine young woman of splendid proportions . . . who immediately set her capacious back against him, whereat he exclaimed, 'Well, Mair, this is very delightful, don't you know, but I think I did wise in leaving Mrs. Trollope in Auckland.'"

when the art has been acquired, I do not see why two or three should not be well written at the same time. I have never found myself thinking much about the work that I had to do till I was doing it. I have indeed for years almost abandoned the effort to think, trusting myself, with the narrowest thread of a plot, to work the matter out when the pen is in my hand.

"When the art has been acquired": once you know how to do it, you'll be able to do it, and do it without undue "thinking." It brings to mind T. S. Eliot's provocative question about Shakespeare: "Did Shakespeare think anything at all?"—a question Eliot answered by asserting that Shakespeare "was preoccupied with turning human actions into poetry." Each morning Trollope preoccupied himself with turning them into prose, as naturally and effortlessly, so it seems, as did Macaulay in his great history. (Trollope praises Macaulay, in the *Autobiography,* for the assistance his example has given to writers of prose.)

Hall observes that there has been little agreement about the best and worst of Trollope's novels, pointing out by contrast that "No one thinks that *Barnaby Rudge* is Dickens's greatest work, or *Philip* Thackeray's or *Romola* George Eliot's. "This may mean that, compared to theirs, Trollope's work is extraordinarily even in quality, containing relatively no peaks or valleys. But it means also that when English novelists of the period are ranked, Trollope brings up the rear, a solid fourth behind the more distinguished threesome. Both Henry James and Tolstoy agreed on this ranking, James stating that Trollope's talent "was of quality less fine than theirs"—a judgment Tolstoy evidently concurred in, although he said in 1865, after reading *The Bertrams,* that "Trollope kills me with his virtuosity. I console myself that he has his skill and I have mine." Condescension to Trollope may have reached its limit with Leavis's *The Great Tradition* in which he is dismissed as a lesser Thackeray (not that Leavis has much to say for Thackeray either) and, in a particularly demeaning sentence, is contrasted to George Eliot and Henry James who are "great novelists above the ruck of Gaskells and Trollopes and Merediths." It's that ugly word "ruck" and the assumption that Trollope and Meredith are equally undistinguished goods that especially infuriate.

Hall is not out to question anybody's ranking, and perhaps a biographer shouldn't be concerned with such matters. Trollope, though, was much concerned to explain, in the *Autobiography,* why he ranked Dickens third to Thackeray and Eliot (Dickens's characters were too stagey and artificial). In that spirit, it may be appropriate that, rather than joining the fan club of

Glorious Trollope

Trollopians, one should push the case for Trollope as great novelist more strongly than it is usually pushed. I would do this not by a comparison with the original genius of Dickens, but by raising the possibility that, taken in the large and over the course of years, Trollope is a more repaying novelist than either Eliot or Thackeray. This is not to deny that *Middlemarch* is a great book, a peak the height of which Trollope could never reach.[2] But whatever one thinks of *Daniel Deronda* (my thoughts are decidedly mixed), Eliot's earlier novels, *Silas Marner* excepted, are not things one looks forward eagerly to rereading. With Thackeray there is the peak of *Vanity Fair*, again perhaps unattainable by Trollope. But there is also the windiness and affectation of *Pendennis*, the sheer overweight of *The Newcomes*, the datedness of *Henry Esmond* and its historical furniture (Trollope thought it the best English novel ever written, superior even to *Pride and Prejudice* and *Ivanhoe*), not to mention the Thackeray novels I haven't read. What I'm arguing is that *Barchester Towers, The Last Chronicle of Barset, The Way We Live Now, The Prime Minister,* and *The Duke's Children,* along with darker horses like the gloomy *He Knew He Was Right* and the sparkling *Ayala's Angel,* plus numbers of other highly entertaining, expertly managed narratives (*The Claverings, Can You Forgive Her?, The Vicar of Bullhampton*), are enough to call for nothing less than the highest claims for their creator.

In the course of his great essay on Trollope published in 1883, the year after Trollope died, Henry James has provided probably the most astute comparison of him to his novelist contemporaries, both in England and in France. One tends to remember from the essay—because it is so often quoted—James's censuring of Trollope for his "suicidal satisfaction in reminding the reader that the story he was telling was only, after all, a make-believe." But of far more use as a rich indicator of Trollope's art are the following sentences from a very long paragraph:

> The striking thing to the critic was that his robust and patient mind had no particular bias, his imagination no light of its own. He saw things neither pictorially and grotesquely like Dickens; nor with that combined disposition to satire and to literary form which gives such "body," as they say of wine, to the manner of Thackeray; nor with anything of the philosophic, the transcendental cast—the desire to follow them to their remote relations—which we associate with the name of George Eliot. Trollope had

2. In a letter to Trollope, Eliot called his books "pleasant public gardens, where people go for amusement and, whether they think of it or not, get health as well."

his elements of fancy, of satire, of irony; but these qualities were not very highly developed, and he walked mainly by the light of his good sense, his clear, direct vision of the things that lay nearest, and his great natural kindness. There is something remarkably tender and friendly in his feeling about all human perplexities; he takes the good-natured, temperate, conciliatory view—the humorous view, perhaps, for the most part, yet without a touch of pessimistic prejudice.

After judging that his later works do savor of some bitterness, particularly *The Way We Live Now,* James returns to positive appreciation:

> [Trollope] represents in an eminent degree this natural decorum of the English spirit, and represents it all the better that there is not in him a grain of the mawkish or the prudish. He writes, he feels, he judges like a man, talking plainly and frankly about many things, and is by no means destitute of a certain saving grace of coarseness.

The phrase that sums it all up and forms the paragraph's first sentence is rightly famous: "His great, his inestimable merit was a complete appreciation of the usual." I would argue that even while James ranks Trollope below his three English contemporaries, the very strength and justness of his claims make a case for Trollope's greatness that James never made for Dickens, or Thackeray, or George Eliot.

Trollope's "robust and patient mind," wrote James, had no "particular bias." In fact James wasn't the first to perceive this, since an unsigned notice in *The Times* some years previously had pointed out, generalizing from *He Knew He Was Right,* that Trollope's writings "have no aesthetic purpose; they mean nothing more than they say; they are not written *at* the reader; the author thinks of nothing but how his work may be made a correct copy, complete and minute." This is a move toward defining the novelist as realist. In what looks to me the most adventurous and original of recent critical books about Trollope, Walter Kendrick, using the language of post-structuralist discourse, ingeniously describes the difference between Trollope's realism and the mode of other kinds of writers such as poets, the "sensation" novelists (who were his contemporaries), and Post Office employees who make a first draft of a report with the intention of improving it subsequently:

> These writers have in common . . . that they put on paper words that are not exact—whether the form be a plot outline, an early version of a poem, or a first draft of a report. All of them are willing, then, to transform this

writing by means of other writing—filling in the outline, refining meter and metaphor, polishing phrases. Such nonrealistic writers treat words as words; they deal with words in their interrelations, apart from their connections to the things they signify. For the Trollopian realist, writing is valuable only because it is necessary to make the reader's experience of the characters as similar as possible to the novelist's experience of them before he begins to write. But there is no value in intertextuality. Indeed, there is less than no value in it, because the admission of an intertextual relation does harm to the achievement of equivalence that is the goal of the whole novel business. If any participant in that business considers a text as a text, then reality has been compromised. All the opponents of Trollopian realism . . . share the antirealistic habit of admitting that writing has value as writing, rather than as the pure conveyance of what is other than itself.[3]

Accordingly Kendrick understands the authorial intrusions of which Henry James complained as Trollope's attempts to "degrade" the text, the better to enhance the "equivalence" between the novelist's apprehension of reality and reality itself (Trollope knew what that was).

Even when Trollope's prose calls attention to itself for its more than usual density, the novelist assures us that in fact we really don't need his words. In an extraordinary passage from *The Prime Minister* when the villainous Ferdinand Lopez—whose machinations Trollope manages to make continuously interesting—is about to throw himself under a train, the site of his suicide is introduced this way (Lopez is at Euston Station bound presumably for Birmingham on business):

> After a while he went back into the hall and took a first-class return ticket, not for Birmingham, but for the Tenway junction. It is quite unnecessary to describe the Tenway junction, as everybody knows it.

But you must *show*, not *tell*, cries the neophyte Creative Writer, and even though everybody knows what the Tenway is like, Trollope will describe it anyway, no big deal:

> From this spot, some six or seven miles distant from London, lines diverge east, west, and north, north-east, and north-west, round the metropolis in every direction, and with direct communication with every other line in and out of London. It is a marvellous place, quite unintelligible to the uninitiated, and yet daily used by thousands who only know that when they get there, they are to do what some one tells them. The space oc-

---

3. Walter Kendrick, *The Novel-Machine* (Baltimore, 1980).

cupied by the convergent rails seems to be sufficient for a large farm. And these rails always run one into another with sloping points, and cross passages, and mysterious meandering sidings, till it seems to the thoughtful stranger to be impossible that the best trained engine should know its own line. Here and there and around there is ever a wilderness of waggons, some loaded, some empty, some smoking with close-packed oxen, and others furlongs in length black with coals, which look as though they had been stranded there by chance, and were never destined to get again into the right path of traffic. Not a minute passes without a train going here or there, some rushing by without noticing Tenway in the least, crashing through like flashes of substantial lightning, and others stopping, disgorging and taking up passengers by the hundreds.

Wonderfully caught up in the place he's describing which "everybody knows," Trollope finally informs us that "over all this apparent chaos there is presiding a great genius of order," but isn't so immodest as to admit that the genius is himself. The best way succinctly to demonstrate the difference between Trollope and Dickens is to compare this passage about the Tenway junction with Dickens's equally brilliant creation of the railway junction that has replaced Staggs's Gardens in the London of *Dombey and Son*. For all that Trollope's presentation of Tenway stands out from the less memorable character of his usual prose, it still issues in what James called a "complete appreciation of the usual"—after all, everybody knows about Tenway junction. What Dickens does to the junction that's replaced Staggs's Gardens is to write it up into the noticeably unusual through paragraphs of fantastic figuration.[4]

In other words, Dickens is always noticeable in his writing, always the resourceful performer endlessly deploying his bag of tricks. By contrast Trollope brings off his effects without inviting us to be conscious of the way he writes them up. Ford Madox Ford placed him in the company of Chaucer and Jane Austen as, before all things, a "snooper," and Ford uses the testimony of Trollope's nephew, a Mr. Synge, to weave a picture of the novelist as clubman-snooper:

4. "To and from the heart of this great change, all day and night, throbbing currents rushed and returned incessantly like its life's blood. . . . The very houses seemed disposed to pack up and take trips. . . . Night and day the conquering engines rumbled at their distant work, or advancing smoothly to their journey's end, and gliding like tame dragons into the allotted corners grooved out to the inch for their reception, stood bubbling and trembling there, making the walls quake, as if they were dilating with the secret knowledge of great powers yet unsuspected in them, and strong purposes not yet achieved." (*Dombey and Son*, Chapter 15)

Glorious Trollope

> Trollope was extraordinarily unnoticeable. Wherever he was, it seemed to be absolutely natural that there he should be. . . . When he entered a club smoking-room no one interrupted his conversation; when he shot no one noticed his bag. Synge said that, occasionally, when Trollope was the last member in the lounge of the old Club, St. George's Hanover Square, the waiters would put out the lights, not noticing Trollope, although he was under their eyes.[5]

Ford goes on to surmise that therefore he must have heard more "gossip"—the best gossip in the world—than any writer except perhaps Jane Austen. He calls Trollope "the greatest of all specifically English novelists," and, in one of Ford's shrewdest sentences, notes that "He is less of an artist than she but he is male, and that counts." What "counts" is of course male privileges such as being allowed to snoop at the club in Hanover Square.

Style, said Robert Frost once, is the way a person carries himself toward his ideas and his deeds. In speaking of Trollope one wants to add that such carrying is done, essentially, through a narrative voice. It's doubtless unconscionably vague to speak about "voice" and how getting to recognize and love Trollope's over the course of time is such a rewarding activity. But an early reviewer of *Barchester Towers* struck the right vocal emphasis when he said that Trollope sounded "like one's father should sound." And this father was willing to put himself on the line by speaking about basic human values. Trollope said about the Pallisers—Lady Glencora and her husband Plantagenet ("Planty Pal," the Duke of Omnium, the once Prime Minister)—that they were "safety-valves by which to deliver my soul." He delivered it most movingly in *The Prime Minister,* a novel which, mysteriously, was met with disdain—"worse spoken of by the press than any novel I had written," wrote Trollope regretfully in a footnote to the *Autobiography.* This book and its successor, *The Duke's Children,* seem to me to constitute the peaks of Trollope. Coming near the end of his career (1876 and 1880) they refute James's verdict on the inferiority of the later works.

Trollope resigned from the Post Office in 1867 and George Eliot worried about the consequences: "I cannot help being rather sorry. . . . But it seems to me a thing greatly to be dreaded for a man that he should be in any way led to excessive writing." But Trollope lived by writing excessively and in the fifteen years left to him produced some of his very best novels. He was excessive as well about the consumption of cigars, at one point, in a letter to Eliot, gener-

5. Ford Madox Ford, *The March of Literature.*

ously offering to share the 8,000 cigars, which had just arrived from Cuba, with Eliot's common-law husband, G. H. Lewes. His love of hunting also remained unabated, as we learn in a passage from the *Autobiography* which gives us the Trollope voice about as clearly as we ever hear it. He tells us that he's never been able to analyze to his own satisfaction his delights in this amusement and that in fact he knows very little about hunting (remember that he begins the book by calling himself "an insignificant person the details of whose private life would naturally bear little interest to readers"):

> I am too blind to see hounds turning, and cannot therefore tell whether the fox has gone this way or that. Indeed all the notice I take of hounds is not to ride over them. My eyes are so constituted that I can never see the nature of a fence. I either follow some one, or ride at it with the full conviction that I may be going into a horse-pond or a gravel-pit. I have jumped into both one and the other. I am very heavy, and have never ridden expensive horses. I am also now old for such work, being so stiff that I cannot get on to my horse without the aid of a block or a bank.

What's left then? Nothing less than everything:

> But I ride still after the same fashion, with a boy's energy determined to get ahead if it may possibly be done, hating the roads, despising young men who ride them, and with a feeling that life can not, with all her riches, have given me anything better than when I have gone through a long run to the finish, keeping a place, not of glory, but of credit, among my juniors.

Among his juniors, the novelists who came and come after him, his place is not of credit merely, but of glory.

The Serpent Hatches

Early along in this first of what will be an eight-volume collection of D. H. Lawrence's correspondence, the young man on the verge of his twenty-first birthday writes to Louie Burrows about her literary style: "I like above all things your enthusiasm, and your delightful fresh, youthful feeling. Don't be didactic; try and make things reveal their mysteries to you, then tell them over simply and swiftly, without exaggerating as I do." Good advice for the young woman, doubtless, but more interesting when held up against these nearly six hundred letters and postcards in which we see the young Lawrence become a man and a writer: author of three novels and a book of poems; proponent of "a belief in the blood"; defender of the centrality of marriage between man and woman; and mate of a particular woman, Frieda von Richthofen Weekley, who has given his life new spirit and purpose. As man and writer, Lawrence wants to reveal the mysteries of things, but he knows that his own tendencies are toward didacticism, willfulness, and exaggeration—the qualities of "genius"; perhaps even knows that those latter impulses may thwart the former intention. From this tension the letters derive much of their energy.

It should be a reader's privilege and responsibility to speak back to the voice that registers itself on our consciousness so unmistakably throughout these six hundred pages. Yet it is difficult, particularly in the early part of the volume, to hear Lawrence's voice, surrounded and interrupted as it is by the editing of James Boulton, who is also general editor of the series. To put it succinctly, he has annotated Lawrence within an inch of his life. For example, the fifth item in the book, a postcard to a childhood friend from Eastwood, has an introductory sentence that looks like this: "Do you[1] like this, it's not cats.[2]" Footnote one tells us that the "you" is Gertrude ("Grit") Cooper (1885–1942), who suffered from tuberculosis, whose father died in 1918, who then lived with Lawrence's sister, and who was buried in the same grave as Lawrence's parents and brother. Footnote two, the one for "cats," confesses that "The reference is obscure." The postcard's other three short sentences attract three further

The Letters of D. H. Lawrence, Volume 1: *September 1901–May 1913*, edited by James T. Boulton. Cambridge University Press, 1979.

footnotes, and one begins to wonder who in the world, aside from a mad Lawrentian specialist, would have any conceivable interest in all this flurry. At one time the reader is conceived of as someone who would like to know where "Grit" Cooper is buried, or who the nurse was who sat with Lawrence when he was critically ill with pneumonia in 1911 ("Despite a Croydon address for 'Nurse' in DHL's address-book, her identity cannot be traced"). At another time, the reader knows absolutely nothing, needs to be informed of the first names and dates of Shaw and Verlaine, needs to be told that "mewling and puking" is a reference to *As You Like It* (II, vii, 144). Anyone who is neither a Lawrence freak nor a tabula rasa will find his gorge rising.

The trick is to ignore the overkill as best you can, be grateful for the editor's hard labor, and try to make out a story that fits the Lawrence of these years. My own version goes something like this: In the early part of this book we hear the voice of the young, the Eastwood Lawrence, observant and thoughtful, often playful in the manner of Keats's great letters from a hundred years before. Eastwood Lawrence writes like this, nearly always to a woman:

> I am so lazy; having just gathered some gooseberries for a pudding, and picked them out here on our little mat of grass, sitting in the united shade of an elder and a lilac bush, I am disinclined to go indoors to the table. . . . Now the vivid potentillas just move in a little breeze that brings hot breath of hay across the permanent spice of pinks. From the field at the bottom of the garden, I hear the 'chack' and jingle of a horse-rake; the horse is neighing; there, they come into sight between the high larkspur and the currant bushes!; the man sits like a charioteer; his bare arm glistens in the sun as he stretches forward to pull up the tines; they have gone again. It is a true mid-summer day. . . . Only the bees are busy, nuzzling into some wide white flowers;—and I am busy too, of course.

Such diligent indolence is worthy of his Romantic predecessor, as is the following thought, reminiscent of Keats's comparison of life to a "mansion of many apartments": "I believe that a man is converted when first he hears the low, vast murmur of life, of human life troubling his hitherto unconscious self. I believe a man is born first unto himself—for the happy developing of himself, while the world is a nursery, and the pretty things are to be snatched for, and pleasant things tasted; some people seem to exist thus right to the end. But most are born again on entering manhood; then they are born to humanity, to a consciousness of all the laughing, and the never-ceasing murmur of pain and sorrow that comes from the terrible multitudes of brothers." The young man knows the weariness, fever, and fret, can no longer believe in the Christian answer to it, feels himself born into poetry, becomes a man who must speak to men.

The Lawrence of Eastwood days is an appealing figure, seldom hectoring his correspondent, able to say "it is my fault—my temper is so variable." This figure persists, indeed becomes even more expressive and resourceful, after he moves to Croydon in the fall of 1908 and begins his career as a schoolteacher. Croydon Lawrence abounds with superb sketches of London and its environs, like the railway embankment he can see from his back garden in Colworth Road: "In the dark, as if suspended in the air, little trains pass bright and yellow across the uncurtained door. The little trains have only one carriage, something like a tram car, and often there are no passengers; sometimes two, taking the space of one, fancying themselves secure in the privacy of a corner. It is quaint, like looking out on the world from a star, to watch them jog slowly past." Or he visits Richmond Park: "One of the few remaining parts of the old world of romance. The hills rise up and look on the great oaks writhing and twisting—the beeches are tremendous steel shafts—there are broad spaces and great fierce groves, where the pale deer flee, where, I vow, there are dryads and fauns, where you might find a Viking asleep, where there are outlaws and knights in armour and ladies who exist solely to be succored."

Such fantasy and romance, the essential genius of Lawrence's fiction, combine in this portrait of the Dulwich Art Gallery: "a lovely and lovable little place, full of old, fascinating pictures—Colonel Lovelace looking with full, womanly glance; the saddening face of Chas II—pale Chas I—all the old people in one dear nook. There is a fine collection of Dutch pictures. . . . I love the human, sturdy, noble Dutchies. . . . Many quaint interesting Poussins— such a splendid little gallery—so little, so rich." Or he travels to Brighton, "big, stately, magnificent, with a sea like pale green jewels—is lapis lazuli green?— and all wavering, shimmering, intermingling with purple—lovely—inexpressible." Then, in a burst of Keatsian humor: "But Brighton is stately, and I'm not, so I pushed my way through the wind, and here I am at Rottingdean."

Lawrence's generosity toward landscape extends as well to the books he was reading and that he needed to share with his correspondents. Writing from unstately Rottingdean to Louie Burrows, he recommends and praises *Manon*

Lescaut, Tolstoy, and H. G. Wells ("read, *read, Tono Bungay;* it is a great book") in the same paragraph. Similar enthusiasms—expressed during the exciting period in 1909 when Ford Madox Hueffer "discovered" him, publishing his poems in the *English Review* and introducing him to literary London—are directed at Arnold Bennett, Galsworthy, Synge, and George Moore. Everything seems to be opening up ("I am going to dine with Ezra Pound tonight. We shall meet a crowd of other literary folk"), *The White Peacock* is being rewritten, fine short stories and poems are produced—all the while the writer continues to be a conscientious, hardworking teacher at the Davidson Road school.

In retrospect it all seems miraculous and about to explode, particularly the balancing act he effects with his women: with Jessie Chambers to whom he remains betrothed until November 1910; with Louie Burrows to whom he becomes engaged in the following month; with Helen Corke, his friend in Croydon ("a new girl—a girl who '*interests*' me—nothing else") whom, in a letter to another friend, Blanche Jennings, he mentions along with Agnes Holt ("my latest love? Well—she's off again—I don't like her") and Jessie ("the old girl"). Truly a dream of fair women.

But the most important woman of them all was of course his mother. During her fatal illness he writes that "it is true, we have been great lovers," and says that "I have muddled my love affairs most ridiculously and most maddeningly"—referring to the particular breaking off with Jessie Chambers, but with more general application. The death of Mrs. Lawrence at the end of 1910, his bout with pneumonia in the next year, the eventual break with Louie in February 1912, all seem to clear the stage for Frieda to make her entrance, which she does most dramatically in the single sentence of a Lawrence note to her in March 1912: "You are the most wonderful woman in England."

After that a new story begins, and a new Lawrence, whom I confess to finding a less attractive customer. By June of 1912 he is in Munich with Frieda, writing home to an unhappy colleague at the Davidson Road school, "I tell you, find a woman you can fall in love with. *Do* it. . . . You are wasting your life. How miserable your last letter! Nowadays, men haven't got the courage and the strength to love. You must know that you're committing slow suicide." Note the appeal to "men" here, in this strident attempt to set Arthur McLeod right. After all, McLeod is in England, and "I hate England and its hopelessness. I hate Bennett's resignation. Tragedy ought really to be a great kick at misery." So *Anna of the Five Towns* "seems like an acceptance," and is therefore inadequate, as is McLeod, as is England. Since William Heinemann declines to publish *Sons and Lovers*, "Curse the blasted, jelly-boned swines, the slimy, the belly-wriggling invertebrates, the miserable sodding rotters, the flaming sods, the snivelling, dribbling, dithering palsied pulse-less lot that make up England today. . . . Exterminate them, slime." Not very imaginative invective, but prophetic of much to come in the later Lawrence.

Up to this point his letters had shown almost no animus toward England and the English—indeed, quite the contrary. But Eastwood-Croydon Lawrence has now given way to Genius Lawrence, with Frieda behind him (sometimes rather far behind, since the editor surmises that already by the end of 1912 she has seduced Harold Hobson, their traveling companion in the journey south from Germany). Lawrence is now at heroic odds with the rest of the world, and reading one novelist tends to be like reading another. So *Under Western Eyes* (1911) is boring because "I can't forgive Conrad for being so sad and for giving in." Only someone convinced of his own genius would think it his prerogative to forgive or not to forgive Conrad anything.

Now come the famous pronouncements about the blood being wiser than the intellect, about how his life work will be "sticking up for the love between man and woman." Meanwhile, he says, Frieda reads the letters he writes; thus (to Edward Garnett) he must choose his words carefully, but he promises to write Garnett some day when she is out! Frieda not only reads the letters but helps write them; or she will begin a letter to David Garnett and Lawrence will interject gems like "*Shit*," "balls-aching rot," "bitch!" and "arse-licking." This may be an example of the love between man and woman, of healthy unrepressed "blood"; but one winces, wishes the high jinks were funnier, isn't quite convinced that it all travels very well. By contrast, the bold talk about standing naked "for the fire of Almighty God to go through me," and how "terribly religious" one must be to be an artist, may seem yet another kind of rhetorical inflation, a bragging that can't quite conceal the rattling of chains—even though the chains are attached to the most wonderful woman no longer in England.

No matter: *The Rainbow* and *Women in Love* are to come. But in one's natural impulse to salute the development of an artist, to hail his passage from youth to maturity, one might also pause and give a thought to what has been lost: the "delightful fresh, youthful feeling" he wrote of to Louie Burrows; the impulse *not* to know what is best for other people, or for England; the willingness to let things reveal their mysteries—all that negative capability which the later Lawrence, in his willfulness and didacticism, sold short.

Inquiry, October 29, 1979

Fordie

"Good literature is produced by a few queer people in odd corners," T. S. Eliot wrote to Ford Madox Ford in 1924, the occasion of Ford's launching his second and short-lived magazine, *The Transatlantic Review.* One of Eliot's typically throwaway definitions of big subjects (Poetry is "a mug's game," *The Waste Land* nothing more than "rhythmical grumbling"), it was appropriately directed at a very queer person indeed who by that date had brought forth some sixty-four titles—poems, novels, biography, children's fairy tales, polemic, and sociology—held together only by their author's personality and their devotion to literary impressionism. Until very recently, all or almost all of those titles, plus the twenty-four or so others Ford added to them during the last fourteen years of his life, were—except for *The Good Soldier*—out of print. (I more than once had to forgo teaching *Parade's End* because of its unavailability.) Now a glance through *Paperbound Books in Print* reveals not only those novels but two of Ford's memoirs (*Memories and Impressions; Return to Yesterday*); a selection from his criticism; a selected poems; his historical novel *The Fifth Queen;* and a few other titles (*No Enemy; Provence*). Could it be that, almost fifty years after his death, Ford's reputation in this country (though not in England) has stabilized itself?

Not, I think, if it means that aside from *The Good Soldier* and the first volume of the Tietjens tetralogy, *Some Do Not,* his books are much read or taught. Over the past few decades, along with Arthur Mizener's solid biography there have been a number of critical studies, mostly of Ford's novels, by American academics; but the outstanding recent contribution to our understanding of him has been Sondra Stang's. Five years ago she put together a first-rate collection of essays about Ford (*The Presence of Ford Madox Ford,* University of Pennsylvania Press) and has now followed with an ample selection from his own writings. In a foreword to the book, Graham Greene, probably the English novelist who most admires Ford, tells us that for reasons of copyright Mrs. Stang could not reprint parts of *The Good Soldier* or *Parade's End.* But those books need to be read in their entirety, and the idea of a Reader

The Ford Madox Ford Reader, edited by Sondra Stang. Ecco Press, 1986.

should be to point people who know some of Ford's books in the direction of others they don't know so well or at all. In fact Ford is not the kind of novelist—if there is such a kind—who takes well to excerpting, and the first section of the Reader, with bits from seven of his lesser-known fictions (justly lesser-known, I should say), is tough and not especially profitable going. (I was pleased with the section from his romance about Henry Hudson, *The 'Half-Moon,'* but otherwise found myself just turning pages.) The good things come later and include selections from Ford's memoirs and reminiscences; his literary, cultural, and art criticism; his poetry; some miscellany; and a concluding group of sixty unpublished letters.

Ford believed—he and Conrad believed it together—that the English language was ill-suited to good prose because of what he called "the associations that, like burrs, cling undetachable to every English word." Even the simplest English sentence, especially by comparison with a French one, "is forever blurred because it can always have several meanings." Thus his endless praise of Flaubert's *Coeur Simple,* or of Turgenev ("the beautiful genius"), and the relative deploring of Dickens and Thackeray, English producers of what he disparagingly called "the nuvvle." (Yet Ford, at least in his late work *The March of Literature,* rightly praised Trollope as a great realist.) He said repeatedly, probably every morning upon arising, that the "exact use of words" was the most important thing in the world, but whatever standards of exactness he held didn't prevent him from turning out books of all sorts at an astonishing clip, most of which do not cry out for the kind of microscopic attending-to that an "exact use of words" would seem to demand. My own feeling is that this battle cry of exactitude was an homage to France, but that Ford's writing needs to be appreciated in rather different terms. He memorably characterized Hemingway's words as striking the reader "each one, as if they were pebbles fetched fresh from a brook. They live and shine, each in its place." With Ford it's not so much words, rather the voice that utters them which charms us.

He charms us with this voice when, in a section from his pre-Raphaelite memoir, *Ancient Lights* (*Memories and Impressions* in this country), he evokes the voice of one of those poets who used to read aloud at his father's house:

> Mournfully then, up and down the stone staircases, there would flow
> two hollow sounds. For, in those days, it was the habit of all poets and
> poetesses to read aloud upon every possible occasion, and whenever they
> read aloud to employ an imitation of the voice invented by the late Lord

Tennyson and known, in those days, as the *ore rotundo*—"with the round mouth mouthing out their hollow o's and a's."

The effect of this voice heard from outside a door was to a small child particularly awful. It went on and on, suggesting the muffled baying of a large hound dog that is permanently dissatisfied with the world.

As is typically the case with Ford's effects, even at deeply serious moments from *The Good Soldier* or *Parade's End*, there is something funny in what's going on. Ford's stature as a humorist hasn't been paid sufficient attention to because critics are busy being earnest about what a crafty, resourceful novelist he was. But it is a humorous craft.

The humor, the fun (something funny going on) is in no way a comic relief from more serious matters. Probably Ford's best account of how the novelist gets the effect of "life" in his work occurs in his memoir of Conrad (Sondra Stang includes the passage) and is directed against the notion that a novel should report or narrate life directly. No, says Ford, that is not the way to do it:

> Life does not say to you: in 1914 my next-door neighbour, Mr Slack, erected a greenhouse and painted it with Cox's green aluminium paint. Rather, and if you think about the matter [I excerpt from his account] you will remember, in various unordered pictures, how one day Mr Slack appeared in his garden and contemplated the wall of his house. You will then try to remember the year of that occurrence. . . . You will remember Mr Slack—then much thinner because it was before he found out where to buy that cheap Burgundy of which he has since drunk an inordinate quantity, though whisky you think would be much better for him! Mr Slack again came into his garden, this time with a pale-weaselly-faced fellow, who touched his cap from time to time. . . . At this point you will remember that you were then the manager of the fresh-fish branch of Messrs Catlin and Clovis in Fenchurch Street. . . . What a change since then! Millicent had not yet put her hair up.

He leads us on through Millicent's hair before and after putting it up; to Mr. Mills, the vicar, talking to her; to Millicent's troublesome expression; and so to Cox's Aluminium Paint—"the half-empty tin that Mr Slack showed you—he had a most undignified cold"—etc. And, Ford concludes triumphantly, "if that is how the building of your neighbour's greenhouse comes back to you, just imagine how it will be with your love affairs that are so much more complicated." Really this passage is all anyone needs to become a good reader of Ford's novels in which the Impressionist "method" is at work. But it is memorable, surely, because of the man named Slack, his cheap Burgundy, the weaselly-faced fellow who accompanies him, Millicent's troublesome hair, and, of course, Cox's Aluminium Paint. Something funny about the whole business.

Some of the bits from Ford's writings included in this selection are ones with which only the devoted Fordian would be acquainted: his introduction to Hemingway's *A Farewell to Arms;* a letter written about *Finnegans Wake* to the *Saturday Review* near the end of his life; a fine, short "Memories of Oscar Wilde"; the chapter he wrote for Conrad's *Nostromo* when Conrad was ill and couldn't make his weekly installment; a pamphlet of 1912 titled *This Monstrous Regiment of Women* in which his feelings as an "ardent" "enraged" "suffragette" are aired. And then there are the individual sentences one may or may not have come across: "The first duty of philosophy is to help men live their lives; the first duty of learning is to teach the children of men that the objects of learned study are beautiful" (I think that both Henry James and Secretary of Education William Bennett would approve). Chaucer's *The Knight's Tale* is "the supreme monument of the letters of our country"—a judgment probably shared by no one else you could locate. "Yet the great novels of the world . . . have all been mystery stories"—this, by contrast, is something to think about. In response to his publisher who had objected to *The Saddest Story* (too depressing, especially during wartime) as a title for what eventually became *The Good Soldier,* Ford said, "Why not call the book 'The Roaring Joke'?" A less than roaring but wholly endearing joke is a long one from *Return to Yesterday* about the Gypsy, the Ukrainian, and the porkchop, as told to Ford by a humorous Russian nihilist ("Zay was going along a road and zay saw a porg tchop lying on it . . . 'You poor Ukrainian,' said ze Gypsy, 'you are too stchupid to have ze porg tchop. Zay are for fine Gypsy fellows'" etc.). My favorite single sentence is from a pamphlet of 1923: "By carefully going through the Alphabet, and my calling book, I have found that I know at the present moment 1,642 men and women."

On a grimmer note, there are some dignified but sad complaints about the fate of his writings. In 1929, after the Tietjens books had appeared, he wrote to an admirer saying that his books received good reviews but that "The curious thing is that their voices seem to make no impression whatever upon the public and my sales in England are so small that I have nearly come to the conclusion not to publish there at all." In the final year of his life he wrote his publisher Stanley Unwin, "If you could possibly see your way to lending me

Fordie

say £250 it would be of most immense service to me and in the end would be of some benefit to yourself because it would mean that I could return to France and finish my novel in some peace of mind . . . I know that it is very indecent of me to make this request but my necessities at the moment are very urgent and I see nothing else whatever to do." And he asks Unwin to forgive him for "the pain of having to read this letter." Robert Lowell's lines come to mind—

> But master, mammoth mumbler, tell me why
> the bales of your left-over novels buy
> less than a bandage for your gouty foot

—as does Ezra Pound's tribute of many years earlier: "It is well that one man should have a vision of perfection and that he should be sick to death and disconsolate because he cannot attain it." "Ford, you were a kind man and you died in want," Lowell's poem concludes. One imagines how pleased he would have been by his Reader, so intelligently and lovingly put together by Sondra Stang.

Hudson Review 39, no. 1 (Spring 1987). Copyright © 1987 by the Hudson Review, Inc. Reprinted by permission.

Total Waugh

Martin Stannard's now completed biography of Evelyn Waugh deserves saluting as an exemplary portrait of a man who was not only one of the most extravagant literary personalities ever invented but, just possibly, the premier English novelist of our century. Before pressing that second claim, some remarks are in order about why Mr. Stannard, in the new and the previous volume, is such a good biographer. One can say first that the research aspect of his enterprise looks impeccable: the people interviewed; the sources (libraries, newspapers, periodicals, private unpublished letters) widely drawn on and scrupulously acknowledged; the English terrain—Stannard is a lecturer at the University of Leicester—thoroughly and convincingly present. Beyond that he is a biographer who, after a decade of work and 1,000 pages of the finished product, has managed to stay on good terms with his subject. While no starry-eyed fan of the great man, he avoids lecturing him, though he is quite willing to point out disparities between Waugh's version of an event and facts that contradict or qualify that version. Each chapter title is tagged with the relevant year and month span, so that at any moment readers know where they are temporally. Footnotes are conveniently placed at the bottom of the page—no thumbing to the back in an effort to figure out what goes with what. The index is helpful and the pictures—now glossy, unlike those in the first volume—are splendid.

What is more gratifying and seldom true even of substantial literary biographies is the way this one smoothly works into its ongoing narrative relevant criticism of each of Waugh's books. Even when Stannard doesn't conduct a "reading" of the novel to hand, he manages to place it pertinently in its contemporary context. One illustrative example will do, apropos of *The Ordeal of Gilbert Pinfold*, Waugh's 1957 novel of aural hallucinations which came straight from his own horrible experience of hearing voices while on a shipboard cruise:

Evelyn Waugh: The Early Years 1903–1939, by Martin Stannard. W. W. Norton and Co., 1986, and *Evelyn Waugh: The Later Years 1939–1966*, by Martin Stannard. W. W. Norton and Co., 1992.

Total Waugh

The ease with which it translated into a successful radio play testifies to the quality of its structure and dialogue. Waugh's review of *The Comforters* demonstrates his fascination with Spark's self-referential techniques and suggests that he was working along similar lines. The revision most assiduously tackled was that of the ending: converting it into the beginning of the book we have just read. Pinfold is thus both inside and outside his text and the tale repeats itself seamlessly. As with *Helena*, an argument can be made for *Pinfold* as a "postmodernist" novel. B. S. Johnson and Martin Amis (both of whose writings Waugh would have loathed) later used a similar mixture of fiction and autobiography.

Not only are these accurate remarks about Waugh's novel, but it is placed in relation to Muriel Spark and other novelists currently on the scene, and this can only be done by someone who knows the relevant books and writers to compare. To be guided through Waugh's life by both an active-minded explorer and a more than competent literary critic is a double satisfaction.

We're already familiar with much in Stannard's account of the life if we've read Waugh's letters and diaries, his unfinished autobiography, *A Little Learning* (only the first volume was completed), and the biography by his friend Gerald Sykes. Still this biography, especially the first volume, provides a satisfyingly full and evenhanded treatment of Waugh's troubled relations with his father, the bookman Arthur, and with his brother Alec, who became a slickly professional writer. Evelyn, who despite such troubles seems to have had a genuinely happy childhood, was short, an indifferent athlete, delighting early on in the confusion and anarchy from which his early novels sprang. His friendships and sexual inclinations at Lancing and Oxford were largely directed within the male orbit; at Oxford he fell in love with Richard Pares and he became a member of the postwar generation of aesthetes and writers Martin Green has controversially labeled "Children of the Sun." After taking his degree he spent a desperate year teaching at a private school in Wales, evidently (from Stannard's description) a more ordinary establishment than the fantastic Llanabba Castle into which Waugh transformed it in *Decline and Fall* ("In Wales everybody has black spittle and whenever he meets you says 'borra-da' and spits," says an anthropological note from his *Diaries*). Things went from bad to worse: we are to understand from *A Little Learning* that he prepared a suicide note, carefully checked its quotation from Euripides, then walked into the Welsh seawater prepared, so it appears, to destroy himself.

Such heroic aspirations (or were they really mock-heroic?) were foiled by an encounter with a party of jellyfish sufficiently bothersome to take the fun out of the caper. Waugh headed back to shore, felt like an ass, and proceeded to get on with his life.

For a time this meant drinking everything in sight, especially at visits back to Oxford and environs. Fortunately, on one of those Oxford visits he drunkenly exited a room through its window, fell, and severely sprained an ankle.[1]

His friends carted him back to Golders Green, the Waugh homestead, and there he spent three days convalescing, browsing in Arthur's library, and discovering the pre-Raphaelites: Holman Hunt, Millais, and Dante Gabriel Rossetti. After some delaying he received through the agency of Anthony Powell—who was working at Duckworth and soliciting Oxford talent for the firm—an offer for a book on Rossetti to coincide with the centenary of that artist's birth.[2] *Rossetti* appeared in 1928 to good notices; the career was launched. By September 1930, two years and some months later (he was now twenty-six), Waugh had published two novels (*Decline and Fall* and *Vile Bodies*) and completed his most delightful travel book, *Labels*. He had also married and been separated from Evelyn Gardner ("She-Evelyn") who left him for a man named John Heygate, thereafter referred to by Waugh as "the basement boy," and the model for John Beaver in *A Handful of Dust*. He had also been received into the Roman Catholic Church.

His assumptions about literary art had by now taken shape and are described well by Stannard:

1. The *Diaries* are filled with dipsomaniacal adventures: "Next day I drank all the morning from pub to pub and invited to lunch with me at the New Reform John Sutro, Roger Hollis, Claud, and Alfred Duggan. I am not sure if there was anyone else. I ate no lunch but drank solidly and was soon in the middle of a bitter quarrel with the president—a preposterous person called Cotts—who expelled me from the club. Alfred and I then drank double brandies until I could not walk. He carried me into Worcester where I fell out of a window and then relapsed into unconsciousness punctuated with severe but well-directed vomitings. I dined four times at various places and went to a drunk party at Worcester in someone's rooms I did not know." Different window?

2. Stannard quotes from Anthony Powell's memoirs in which Powell remembers being brought back by Evelyn for cold suppers at his parents' house: "On these pleasant North End Road evenings, Arthur Waugh would tell literary anecdotes at the dinner-table. Mrs. Waugh (whose quiet exterior suggested much inner firmness of purpose) scarcely speaking at all, slipping out at the first opportunity. When the company moved from the dining room Arthur Waugh might continue to chat for a minute or two, then also retire, probably to work. Waugh and I would sit and talk. I usually stayed until nearly midnight, when a last bus could be caught to the neighbourhood of Piccadilly." Those really *were* the days.

Total Waugh

> Waugh's attitudes were, and remained, those of the artist-craftsman. Writer, painter, printer, carpenter—the object of all their labours was to produce useful, pleasurable, well-wrought objects. . . . A writer's business was not to confess or proselytise or to render the states of heightened consciousness of sensitive introverts; it was to entertain and to inform.

In his never less than interesting reviews that began to appear increasingly in the 1930s he praised novelists like Ivy Compton-Burnett, Henry Green, and Norman Douglas, who seemed to him to entertain and inform in a craftsmanly way. (Interestingly enough, Hemingway was another favorite—as he was also for the early Anthony Powell.) During the 1930s he would produce three more novels, four books of travel, and a biography of Thomas Campion. The novels and travel books were consistently ignored by serious (too-serious?) periodicals like Eliot's *Criterion* and Leavis's *Scrutiny*. Not even the publication in 1934 of *A Handful of Dust*—a book that, Waugh said, contained all he had to say about "humanism" and which was a larger achievement than his previous novels—made a difference to literary high culture's assumption that this kind of fictional behavior wasn't in need of real criticism.

There is an odd parallel here with Wyndham Lewis's similar fortune during the decade, a time when Lewis produced his best novel, *The Revenge for Love*, mainly ignored by the critics. No two writers ever insisted more loudly on the primacy of the self, even though—in Waugh's case as a Catholic convert—that self was to be seen against a supernatural background. (It's appropriate also that two writers so infatuated by their own voices should have paid no attention at all to one another's genius.) Throughout the 1930s Lewis dramatized himself as The Enemy, even wrote a poem about it ("If So the Man You Are") and more than once confused his dramatized, exaggerated self with reality. There is an analogy with Waugh's increasing uncertainty, as in the 1940s he became a celebrated writer, about just what sort of self he was or indeed whether "he" had a self. On the occasion of his publishing *Work Suspended* in 1942—an unfinished story or novella which Stannard sees as the germ of his later more introspective, ruminative style—Edith Sitwell wrote "It frightens me, too. By that I mean I am frightened by the condition that one has no idea of what one is really like." A telling remark as applied to Waugh, notes Stannard, since

> Waugh's image of "what he was really like" was becoming increasingly diffuse . . . his physical existence—his body, his clothes, the points at which

he touched others' lives—had become correspondingly vague. Nothing attached him to the world. The space which might have been filled by a sense of "self" had become occupied by self-parody. . . . The ventriloquist's doll was working the master.

Again with reference to Lewis, it is apposite that Lewis's comic novel *Snooty Baronet* (1932) contains a tour de force in which the baronet confronts a store-window dummy that, Snooty decides, may just be more real than he is.

As Waugh lost faith in the rightness of England's—indeed the West's—cause in World War II (Stannard faithfully traces his incredibly complicated and disillusioning military career), his own sense of himself as a valid and significant husband, father, member-of-society, became intermittent. There are moments of satisfied self-congratulation, as on his thirty-ninth birthday when he confides to his diary that it has been "a good year":

> I have begotten a fine daughter, published a successful book, drunk 300 bottles of wine and smoked 300 or more Havana cigars. I have got back to soldiering among friends. . . . I get steadily worse as a soldier . . . but more patient and humble—as far as soldiering is concerned. I have about £7900 in hand and no grave debts except to the Government; health excellent except when impaired by wine; a wife I love; agreeable work in surroundings of great beauty. Well that is as much as one can hope for.

But much of the time it wasn't enough: "I have given up drunkenness for life. . . . It is a cutting of one of the few remaining strands that held me to human society," he wrote to his wife Laura a couple of years later. Stannard notes that when Waugh was clear-headed and others were imbibing he found their jokes and conversation disappointingly flat: "When drunk, Waugh could be amusingly offensive; sober, he was caustic and melancholy." Things didn't get better, necessarily, when he was by himself: "I dined alone sitting opposite a looking glass," he wrote to Nancy Mitford, "reflecting sadly that the years instead of transforming me into a personable man of middle age, have made me into a very ugly youth." How much in this observation is "self" and how much is self-parody? It appears that the ventriloquist's doll is indeed working its master. Over the three postwar years 1945–47, Waugh became—declares Stannard emphatically—an old man.

This didn't mean that stories of his behavior decline in their absolutely insupportable and irresistible outrageousness. One of them must suffice, concerning a young American writer-friend of Carl Van Vechten's. Van Vechten

Total Waugh

(best known for his novel *Nigger Heaven*) had suggested that the young man—a Mr. Paul Moor—write to Waugh. Moor wrote, expecting nothing, but was instead graciously invited to Piers Court, Waugh's Gloucestershire home, and met at the train station by a hired limousine. When the front door was opened at Piers Court, a liveried butler greeted Moor and behind the butler appeared Waugh, "dressed for dinner, naturally, in an old-fashioned tuxedo, replete with dancing pumps embellished with dainty little gros-grain bows." Moor nervously awaited his idol's first words, which came as follows after "an elaborate reaction of exaggerated astonishment":

> " 'But I thought you'd be black! I don't understand. I thought all Carl Van Vechten's friends were black! What a disappointment! My wife and I had both counted on dining out for months to come on our story of this great, hulking American coon who came to spend the week-end. Ah well.' Then he brightened, 'Don't dress for dinner if you don't want to.' He paused, then added, somewhat hesitantly, 'Ah—we always do.' "

Escorted to his room, Moor found affixed to the toilet in the adjoining bathroom a hand-lettered card: "The handle should return to the horizontal when the flow of water ceases. Should it fail to do so, agitate it gently until it succeeds. E. W." At dinner—in a scene which replays—though not quite so severely—the discomfiting of Mr. Salter at the dinner table at Boot Magna (in *Scoop*), Moor is about to have his wineglass filled when Waugh halts the butler, saying—as he gestures at a large jug on the sideboard—"I'm sure you'd prefer iced water." Later, looking ahead to breakfast, Waugh suggests to Moor that, as an American, he would probably prefer something like "Popsy Toasties" to a regular English breakfast. At one point Moor, thinking he is alone, sits down and plays a piece on the piano only to discover, after he has played for some minutes, Waugh's face at the window glaring in. Later at dinner Waugh confides in him " 'I don't like music' and pausing for the proper formulation . . . 'I despise it.' " (Or as Waugh put it alternately during his memorable evening with the Stravinskys in New York City, "All music is positively painful to me.") And so on in this manner. Yet as the weekend drew to a close and Moor announced he would depart after Sunday lunch (expecting Waugh to be overjoyed), the host "appeared to be genuinely dismayed: 'Must you go? . . . Stay as long as you like.' " Moor carried away the impression of a "generous but enormously lonely man," and who is to say him nay? How much of it was the self speaking, or the ventriloquist's doll? Or how much of

Waugh's perverse inclination to pull the carpet out from underneath his guest resulted in a comic inventiveness hard to distinguish from madness?

The last hundred pages of the biography, covering the final years culminating in Waugh's death in 1966, make painful if vivid reading. One thinks of Gerontion's lament as Waugh's: the old man in a dry month, his senses failing, may have come up with something like the famous question, "After such knowledge, what forgiveness?" In the 1940s, suffering from piles, he had an unnecessary (Stannard's word) and painful operation to correct the condition.[3] When he was nearly fifty he wrote John Betjeman that his memory was "not at all hazy . . . just sharp, detailed & dead wrong," and similarly imaginative prose memorializes his attempt to grow a beard: "At present it looks peculiarly repulsive—a mass of isolated, coarse hairs of variegated colouring, but it gives an interest as they say, like a pot plant or flower." His reckless combining of alcohol, bromide, and chloral, in the interests of sound sleep, eventually led to the Pinfoldian hallucinations mentioned earlier, as a consequence of which he became convinced that he was possessed by the devil. When Ann Fleming visited him a year or so before he died, she found him in a "dolorous condition" and later wrote, asking him whether he had seen a dentist: "I did not see a toothbrush in your bedroom, do you use one?" Waugh proceeded to have his remaining teeth extracted. The catalog of various relations between him and his six children has to be read to be believed. At about the same time Laura is quoted as saying to her eldest son Auberon ("Bron"), "You see that dreadful old bore . . . he used to be so witty and gay." Stannard puts it simply: "He wanted to die. All pleasure in his domestic life had evaporated."

What about the enduring value of Waugh's novels—how high a claim should be made for them? Stannard doesn't finally settle down to have his say on the question, although his admiration for the work, both pre- and postwar, is everywhere evident. The main critical issue as it has emerged is whether the postwar books, beginning with *Brideshead Revisited*, are a falling-off from the brilliant entertainments that ended with *Put Out More Flags* (1942). (*The Loved One*, 1948, is a partial return to that earlier way of creation.) Edmund

3. Christopher Sykes has a great account of this event: "Before going I asked about his illness and recovery. He told me that the operation had caused him much pain and that the consequent treatment was such as he could not bring himself to describe. I said I supposed that he was now relieved of much chronic pain and must be thankful it was over.

'No,' he said, 'the operation was not necessary, but might conceivably have become so later on.'

'Not necessary? Then why did you have it done?'

'Perfectionism.' "

Total Waugh

Wilson much admired the early comedies but found *Brideshead* often bathetic, and—although he didn't suggest that Waugh revert to his earlier satiric practices—was unhappy with the new attempt at seriousness. More recently Martin Green has written admiringly about Waugh as a major artist but finds that major quality to be present only in the books where "delight" is uppermost, where Waugh doesn't identify with his protagonists but uses them as vehicles for an amoral, comic inventiveness. By contrast, in the *Sword of Honour* war trilogy, in *Brideshead*, even in—so Green would have it—*A Handful of Dust*, Waugh gives us heroes whom we are asked to take seriously, and this he cannot do without making the books relatively dull, lacking in his truest creative spirit. That was also Kingsley Amis's point when, in reviewing the latter two volumes of the trilogy, he lamented that Waugh had repressed his earlier, anarchic energies in favor of less superficial concerns.

There is a lot to be said for such a critical take on Waugh's literary career; indeed I was once committed to it. A rereading of *Sword of Honour* (in the handsome single-volume final version published in England by Chapman & Hall the year before Waugh died) has made for a change of mind and a conviction that the trilogy was a bright deed in the darkening world of Waugh's last fifteen years. Martin Green has strong words about what fuels the novels that lack delight—"a dull obsessive resentable painfulness, as the good characters fail, the bad ones succeed, vitality diminishes, brilliance fades and tarnishes, gaiety dwindles and cracks—all with a mechanical and masochistic predictability." The assumption is, and I don't share it, that Waugh couldn't write convincingly about Guy Crouchback's failure and diminished vitality; that, compared to Basil Seal—the rogue hero of *Black Mischief* and *Put Out More Flags*—Guy is very much a dull dog and a Catholic one to boot. Certainly nobody would deny that *Sword of Honour,* especially in the second volume (originally published as *Officers and Gentlemen*), has its "flats" (as Dryden said of *Paradise Lost*), but they are allowable in an extended work that needn't maintain a high pitch of comic presentation. (There is, it should be emphasized, plenty of comedy in the trilogy overall.) Stannard points out, as have other recent critics of Waugh,[4] that Guy's progress over the long work (Green might call it rather a dwindling and cracking) is toward a depressed realization that his earlier fervent embrace of the war as a sacred mission was desperately, even criminally, mistaken. When, in the incident near the close of

---

4. See Michael Gorra, *The English Novel at Mid-Century* (New York, 1990), pp. 188–194.

the trilogy (section eleven, "Unconditional Surrender") Guy attempts to help some Jewish refugees out of Yugoslavia, the following memorable exchange occurs with a Madame Kanyi, who will later be executed by the Partisans for her role in assisting Guy. Madame Kanyi says:

> "It seems to me there was a will to war, a death wish, everywhere. Even good men thought their private honour would be satisfied with war. They could assert their manhood by killing and being killed. . . . I knew Italians— not very many perhaps—who felt this. Were there none in England?"
> "God forgive me," said Guy. "I was one of them."

This is worth a good deal more than yet another comic turn, however delightful, from a writer who had won his spurs already in that competition.

Sword of Honour has been compared to Ford Madox Ford's *Parade's End*, and Ford's tetralogy is even spoken of as an unacknowledged influence on Waugh, especially in Ford's hero Christopher Tietjens, stubbornly plugging away at his outmoded beliefs, betrayed by his wife, and shabbily treated by some of his comrades. But there's no indication Waugh ever took the slightest notice of Ford's work (though they both started out as pre-Raphaelites) and anyway the differences in tone and treatment between the two war novels are immense. Furthermore, *Parade's End* opens with Ford's finest piece of sustained fiction, *Some Do Not*, but goes downhill from then on. By contrast Waugh's *Sword* builds slowly, too slowly for some, ending with something substantial having been created, no more nor less than the fact of loss—"lost causes, and forsaken beliefs, and unpopular names, and impossible loyalties," to quote Matthew Arnold's words about Oxford.

One of the minor unfortunate consequences of George Orwell's untimely death in 1949 was that he never wrote the essay he planned to on Waugh's fiction (Waugh admired *Animal Farm* and, with some reservations, *1984*). But Orwell did leave a few interesting sentences in a notebook, suggesting the tack of the unwritten essay and beginning "The advantages of not being part of the movement, irrespective of whether the movement is in the right direction or not. But disadvantage in holding false (indefensible) positions." For Orwell it was mainly Waugh's Catholicism that was indefensible ("One cannot really be Catholic & grown-up," Orwell asserted, as if John Henry Newman had never existed). He concluded that "Waugh is abt as good a novelist as one can be (i.e. as novelists go today) while holding untenable opinions." As novelists go today, fifty years later, Waugh looks better than good, his work from *Decline and Fall* through *Sword of Honour* an endlessly rereadable trove of brilliant comedy and unbrilliant, even depressed, realism. The premier English novelist of this century? I can't think of any, including D. H. Lawrence and Virginia Woolf, who is more repaying.

Hudson Review 45, no. 2 (Summer 1993). Copyright © 1993 by the Hudson Review, Inc. Reprinted by permission.

Pure Literature: Anthony Powell's *View*

The recent appearance in England of novelist Anthony Powell's collected journalism reminded me, gratifyingly, that this subtle artist is still very much in the literary scene, even as he prepares to turn eighty-five. Mr. Powell is best known for *A Dance to the Music of Time,* his sequence of twelve novels about the period of English life that has been his own. Less known, even to readers who love *Dance,* are the five shortish novels Powell wrote when he was in his late twenties and early thirties. Of these, the one that most brilliantly illustrates his peculiar, unique flavor as a writer is *From a View to a Death,* which chronicles the rise and fall of a London painter named Arthur Zouch who attempts to marry into a country house family and, after a promising start, comes to an untimely end. Published in England in 1933, it failed to interest American publishers until a somewhat eccentric one brought it out under the title of *Mr. Zouch: Superman.* A disaster as far as sales went, the book was later republished in 1968 by Little, Brown under its original title. But it soon slipped into obscurity and, like Powell's other pre–World War II novels, is now unavailable.

I regularly teach a large course in contemporary satiric fiction and at the end of it pass out a list of recent titles, some of which the more enterprising students may want to look up. But perhaps it is appropriate that none of my own teachers ever mentioned Powell's name, and I first heard about this quite unacademic writer through what seems an unlikely source. That source was Arthur Schlesinger, Jr., whose 1958 piece in the *New Republic,* "Waugh *à la* Proust," showed Schlesinger to be every bit as perceptive about contemporary English comic writers as he had been about the Roosevelt administration or the Age of Jackson. Reviewing the newest installment of *A Dance to the Music of Time,* Schlesinger singled out the earlier *From a View* as a "seminal work" which had affected the tone as well as the technique of English comic writing. And he pointed to Powell's "precise, deadpan descriptions" of scenes, as well as his willingness to grapple, in a comic novel, with "poverty, madness, and death." At that point I headed for the library to procure a copy, read it with delight, and have been rereading it ever since. What follows is by way of suggesting, in some detail, how attractive are those qualities Schlesinger and others have found in the book.

Its title alludes to the song "John Peel," and Powell provides the relevant words as epigraph: "From a find to a check, from a check to a view, From a view to a death in the morning." The song, written in 1820 by John Woodcock Graves, is a strangely beautiful one whose expressive possibilities most fully appear when arranged for a singing group (Virgil Thomson did one arrangement of it). The relentlessness and haunting melancholy with which John Peel's life and death are detailed is memorably effective, and the song—for all its simplicity—capable of touching deep chords. I think there is an analogy between "John Peel" and Powell's book, insofar as the tonality of his writing often suggests depths beneath the novel's surface of trivia and futility. In its opening paragraph, Arthur Zouch—a self-styled "superman," an artist with a beard—who has procured an invitation to Passenger Court by virtue of his attentions to the Passengers' younger daughter, Mary, is being chauffeured to the country house in a quite remarkable automobile:

> They drove uncertainly along the avenue that led to the house, through the bars of light that fell between the tree-trunks and made the shadows of the lime-trees strike obliquely across the gravel. The navy-blue car was built high off the ground and the name on its bonnet recalled a bankrupt, forgotten firm of motor-makers. Inside, the car was done up in a material like grey corduroy, with folding seats in unexpected places, constructed liberally to accommodate some Edwardian Swiss Family Robinson. This was a period piece. An exhibit. The brakes had ceased to work long since.

Readers who expect verbal high jinks, having heard of Powell as some kind of satirist, will be puzzled by the grave and stately narrative pace (like the car itself) in which Zouch's progress is followed. A simpler writer, eager to make the most of opportunities for humorous play, would have seized on those nonfunctioning brakes and made much of the ludicrous fact. Powell merely writes, "The brakes had ceased to work long since," then immediately goes on to observe other things about the car's interior and its occupant. Later in the novel, Mr. Passenger himself prepares to use this car but, for some reason, can't get it started when his chauffeur cranks it up. Eventually the chauffeur inquires of Mr. Passenger

"Have you got the engine turned on, sir?"
"Have—"
They switched the engine on, and after that the car started fairly easily.

The flatness of that sentence conceals, as it also makes more delightful, the comic point that in starting cars it helps to have the engine turned on.

Zouch plans to ingratiate himself with the Passenger family, but is met with strong resistance, especially from the brooding head of the house, morose Vernon Passenger who, deeply dissatisfied with life, generally spends his time quarreling with country neighbors. His wife is serene and perfectly vague about what goes on around her, and Mr. Passenger early in their honeymoon "had made up his mind to brood about her as little as possible." The Passengers' elder daughter, Betty, is divorced from an Italian duke, has a quite fearsome little daughter named Bianca (who will do her share in making Zouch's lot a hard one), and spends much time smoking cigarettes. Other central points of focus are the Fosdick family, presided over by Major Fosdick and including his wife (disliked by the major) and his hapless sons, Jasper and Torquil, two of the novel's most engaging creations. From time to time we also look in on the Brandons: Joanna (with whom Zouch will have a brief affair at Passenger Court), her valetudinarian mother, and an irascible housekeeper, Mrs. Dadds, who sounds like one of Flannery O'Connor's fearful domestics in the way she combines revolting particulars with moral cant: " 'I got an earwig in my ear yesterday,' said Mrs. Dadds. 'I had to put a lighted match inside before I could get it out. It was something terrible. Terrible it was. Couldn't hear a sound. But it doesn't do any good to grumble.' "

Powell admired Wyndham Lewis's early stories (in a now totally unread book, *The Wild Body*, 1927) and took up Lewis's habit of sketching his characters by concentrating on their external attributes, rather than presenting them psychologically, from within. Most of the characters in *From a View* don't have any inner life, or if they do it is of a most rudimentary nature. We know, for example, just about all we are going to know about Jasper Fosdick from the sentences through which he is first introduced. Jasper, who has served in the army,

> was tall and seemed to be all knees and elbows and his ears stuck out like outstretched wings on either side of his head. He wore a small mustache of clipped ginger hair of coarse quality and his mouth was usually a little

open, hinting of adenoids. He had had several jobs since the Armistice. Nine, to be exact. That was in the first three years after the war. By that time it became clear that he was unsuited to the sort of job that was available.

Exactly what "sort of job" would that be? Powell needn't particularize, but lets the perpetually open mouth do its comic work, "hinting at adenoids."

Of course, nothing is easier than to set up your character with a few grotesque features, then proceed to abuse him for possessing the features you have so cruelly given him. By contrast, Powell is scrupulous to keep his distance, as if he were not personally responsible for the way his characters have turned out. And that "way" is, often in *From a View,* not so much humorous or ridiculous as disturbingly expressive of something gone deeply wrong in the human realm. For example, we are presented with the Fosdick family in church, ostensibly observed by Zouch but with the novelist's full assistance:

> Major Fosdick was in a trance. He was leaning far back in his seat staring cadaverously in front of him as if he saw a vision, and the sun, bursting suddenly from behind clouds, streamed in through the memorial window and poured green and mauve reflections over his face, giving his features the semblance of premature decay.

The elegant long sentence, with its touch of the marmoreal, turns the major into a still life to be admired—in the sense of wondered at—indeed to be appalled by. Compared to him, the other Fosdicks—Torquil trying to "draw on or remove a pair of tight lavender gloves," and Mrs. Fosdick ("a wild-eyed woman wearing a hat like a beehive") whispering into Jasper's ear ("It might have been her memoirs or an epic poem")—are relatively under control, their tics benign, or at least of less than epic stature.

But the book's great creation, Major Fosdick, is built on nobler lines, and the scene in which he is discovered and unmasked is unequaled. Upon being introduced to the major, we learn that he frequently takes refuge from his wife and sons by pleasing himself with a period of "mental relaxation." This involves locking the door of his dressing room and dressing up in a black sequined evening dress and a large picture hat of the sort "no doubt . . . seen at Ascot some twenty years before." He then lights his pipe and proceeds to have a quiet read, perhaps in such volume as *Through the Western Highlands with Rod and Gun.* Publicly he refers to these "temporary retirements from the arena of everyday life" as his "Forty Winks."

Over the course of the novel Major Fosdick becomes more careless about his habitual indulgence, at one point executing a dance step, in costume, and disturbing his wife below. Finally, the house being empty, he ventures downstairs in search of a book, neglecting to change out of the dress and hat, and unfortunately meets Mr. Passenger in the front hall. (Passenger has come to badger him about a land dispute, and steps inside the house, thinking the bell is out of order.) Mr. Passenger assumes that the figure in the dress is Mrs. Fosdick, asks if he may have a word with her husband, then realizes that "Mrs. Fosdick could not possibly have grown a heavy grey moustache" in the days since he has last seen her. Both men are conscious that something is very wrong; neither knows what to do about it. The masterly resolution of the impasse, which eventuates in Fosdick burning his hat and dress, followed soon after by his removal to a "nursing home on the south coast," is one of the great comic moments in English fiction. And the comedy is a function of Powell's detached, slow-motion, buttoned-up manner of exposition, a single example of which must suffice. After the two men recognize one another, Major Fosdick removes his picture hat while Mr. Passenger gropes within himself for assistance: "He had had a romantic friendship with a boy at school who had become in later life a Commissioner in Lunacy. It was things like this which made him regret that he had taken so little trouble to keep up with his old acquaintances." Such are the desperate reaches of an imagination clutching at any straw.

Robert Frost once called the kind of humor he admired "dry humor," and said it was humor that didn't seem to appreciate itself. Frost wished that all literature was similarly dry. There are many moments of such humor in *From a View*, my favorite of which occurs at one of the novel's few "events," a hopeless cocktail party given by Torquil Fosdick. At this party, where the guests are offered either a martini or a "fosdick" (the latter a secret mixture), a group of local street musicians called "The Orphans" perform such numbers as "The Bells of St. Mary's," "Blue-bells of Scotland," and "Les Cloches de Corneville," until one of their group makes a pass at a young female guest, causing great consternation. Meanwhile a friend of Jasper's from Cambridge named Young Kittermaster has the briefest of memorable walk-ons: "He had fair, rather sparse hair and thought himself a little like the Prince of Wales. He was called Young Kittermaster because his father, who farmed on a fairly large scale in the neighborhood, was called Old Kittermaster." That last sentence, perhaps the driest in the novel, suggests in little what the book at large displays as its compositional principle. Powell is not out to "make a point" about moribund English country life, or about something significant that happens when an artist from London intrudes upon it and tries to exploit it. These things simply happen, just as Major Fosdick happens to be prowling about downstairs in his dress and hat the day Mr. Passenger takes it upon himself to enter Fosdick's house. Or as Zouch happens to engage in a one-night fling with Joanna Brandon at Passenger Court. In fact there is nothing fling-like about it, and "it" is not described, only its aftermath: "He looked out . . . towards the fields, at this hour unnaturally close to the house. . . . The grey, mysterious English fields. Small pockets of mist hung a short way above the ground and round the roots of the oaks in the park." So Zouch retrieves his dressing gown and slippers, pads silently back to his room, and we are told about him only that "he was not feeling well at all." It is surely the driest consummation in English literature.

Zouch's death is similarly treated. On his second visit to Passenger Court—after an interim spent in London, painting, taking riding lessons, and shaving off his beard—he attempts to appease Mr. Passenger (a "master of the local pack") by riding to hounds. Instead he becomes the victim of a runaway horse, more like John Gilpin than John Peel. In due course the horse slides on a frozen puddle, goes over, and throws Zouch to the ground, on which he lands with his head. The horse arises, but Zouch does not, his mortal remains saluted by the chapter's final sentence: "Where Zouch had fallen there was some blood on the frost of the road." There is no cause for satisfaction, or for lamentation either: these things happen; the artist records them without fuss or fanfare; we may make of them what we will.

As much as any book I know, *From a View* is "pure" literature, devoid of social purpose or conscience, of moral and political ideas or ideals, and of high "romantic" intentions to "soothe the cares and lift the thoughts of man" (Keats). Matthew Arnold insisted that literature was or should be a criticism of life. Powell's novel refuses to enlist under that banner, but rather exists intensely for itself, within the play of its finely turned sentences and paragraphs. As Hamlet remarked, correctly, "The play's the thing." Powell's version of that play is so unassuming and offhand, its humor so dry, its gaze so equable and fastidiously removed, that only a certain kind of reader will be amused. It is coterie literature, and that coterie probably won't be found in college or university classrooms whose teachers, intent on raising their students' consciousnesses, wouldn't know what to do with such a useless book. *From a View to a Death* thus remains out of print, even as it retains the power—through its exquisitely slanted perspective on human nature—to touch the heart.

Bostonia, September–October 1990

Sound and Fury

This is the season of the heavy biography, three of which have recently landed on my desk. First there was Norman Sherry on Graham Greene at 783 pages (which took Greene only up to age thirty-five); then there was John Paul Russo on I. A. Richards at 843 pages; now, easily topping them all, there is Frederick Karl on William Faulkner at 1,131 pages. Mr. Karl is no stranger to the mammoth biography, having already weighed in with 1,008 pages on Joseph Conrad. In fact everything Karl does is giant-sized: you would think that his work on Faulkner during the past decade would have been enough to have kept him wholly occupied; but during that time he also published two large works on modern fiction, one of them (*American Fictions: 1940–1982*) a 636 double-columned survey of the field. Not only has he read all the novels but all the criticism as well, and he takes pains to tell us what every novel says and what he thinks about it. At no point, seemingly, has he entertained a question about the worth of all this activity. Conrad and Faulkner and American Fictions are indisputably there, like Everest, and the only thing to do after you read them is to write about them—and at length.

It is not clear that Faulkner is in need of such treatment, since Joseph Blotner has already provided us with a massive two-volume work in 1974 which, while it didn't shed much critical light on Faulkner's art, appears to be thoroughly reliable about his life. Karl gets Blotner out of the way in a Foreword by saying that he is not attempting to replace his predecessor's "monumental" biography; rather he will integrate Faulkner's life and work in the attempt "to understand and interpret that life psychologically, emotionally, and literarily." "Psychologically, emotionally, and literarily"—already the language gives us pause, since it suggests a writer who is not averse to slinging words around and seeing where they land. "This study is in the deepest sense a biography," Karl intones reverentially, and that note, struck at the outset of the long journey to come, is a keynote. Faulkner's imagination, he tells us accurately at one point in the journey, was "in thrall of something he could not quite control" and operated characteristically "through looping, overlapping,

William Faulkner: American Writer, by Frederick Karl. Weidenfeld and Nicolson, 1989.

147

and repeated telling." As if in sympathetic thrall to Faulkner, Karl tells and retells the same tale about him: in Robert Graves's words, "There is one story and one story only."

Repeatedly we are invited to "understand" Faulkner—certainly Faulkner as a young man—as essentially a poser. High school dropout, he served briefly in the Royal Air Force in Canada, about which experience (he saw no wartime action) he made up many fanciful tales and came back to Oxford, Mississippi, cultivating a limp. At twenty-three he looked to be, in Karl's words, "without bearing" and was referred to by some members of the community as "Count no 'Count":

> His appearance, pathetic and hostile in its implications, was less that of a down-and-out poet than of a bum or jerk. Worn clothing, stuffing coming from seams, mismatched shoes and socks, and a tongue thickened by liquor—he seemed to be sinking into a manhood which would horrify not only his family but Oxford.

Doubtless a chilling sight, but we know things will come out all right and that the Count will become a Great American Writer rather than a jerk or bum. As for the tongue thickened by liquor, we won't be hearing the last of it, since this was a life drenched in booze. When in his later years Faulkner was asked—by the polite, courteous Japanese students at Nagano—about his drinking, he replied that drinking was "a normal instinct, not a hobby . . . a normal and healthy instinct." The discreet Japanese let it drop there.

But the biographer can't let it drop, since he sees Faulkner's drinking as a key element in the young man's attempt to compensate for his short stature by engaging in masculine pursuits like flying, horsemanship, and hunting washed down with lots of scotch and bourbon.[1] Liquor, in Karl's words, "was a legal means by which he could achieve manhood and self-destruct at the same time." Drinking was "part of some grand mystery: at the crossroads of the obsession to create and the compulsion to self-destruct." Well put, and perhaps that's all there is to say about it. But no, we must be continually reminded that Faulkner "was interested mainly in having a good time, drinking"; that "With all, he practiced drinking and driving at the same time"; that (in Horatio Alger-like language to describe a lout) his tongue was "thickened by liquor"; that "he was the town eccentric with a penchant for liquor"; and

---

1. At five feet, Faulkner was not an extreme shortie like Pope or Keats, but he was shorter than his father and his brothers.

that "he drank heavily with the scouts" (Faulkner at one point became a scoutmaster!). These are but five of myriad references to drink: Karl serves up all the items previously encountered in Blotner, about Faulkner passing out against the hot radiator in his New York hotel room and seriously burning himself and about his periodically being taken to this or that clinic for drying-out. It soon becomes possible to follow these accounts and remain completely untouched by them. At one point Karl hazards the guess that "it may some day be possible to connect Faulkner's long, almost undisciplined sentences to the fact that he started drinking early in the morning as he wrote." This utterly reasonable connection was one I myself made some years ago. But the really interesting question raised by Karl's speaking of Faulkner's "almost undisciplined sentences" is whether those sentences are *really* disciplined—"almost" (but not quite, not in fact) undisciplined. Such an inquiry would involve putting harder questions to Faulkner's style than this biographer wants to put.

Karl's solemn earnestness in dealing with his shifty subject, some of whose utterances one might term almost undisciplined, becomes most awkward when he tries to come to terms with Faulkner and race. We all know that kids say the darnedest things, and so did Faulkner on the subject of The Negro. He once wrote his Random House editor that his agent, Harold Ober, "has four stories about niggers." Such language is, to say the least, embarrassing to Karl, who begins to fidget and try to understand why Faulkner would write to Robert Hass ("a Northerner, a Jew") and use such a word. "Was it out-and-out racism"? After all, we know, don't we, that "he consciously meant well for Negroes." Or was it "merely the baggage of childhood" "ingrained into the white Mississippian's vocabulary"? How could a man "so alert to language and to nuances" not know what he was doing? Karl penetrates, so he thinks, to "its deepest levels" and finds that the word "indicates a racism so unconsciously insistent" that it becomes a force in Faulkner's judgments. However we analyze it, Karl concludes, it is "disquieting."

Yet it seems downright mild compared to the evening Faulkner spent at the Institute for Advanced Studies, at Princeton, surrounded by august presences. One of the august, J. Robert Oppenheimer, told Faulkner that he'd recently seen one of his stories dramatized on television. Faulkner's response to Oppenheimer was "Television is for niggers." Consternation for Karl. *How* could Faulkner have said that when, the biographer notes, he himself enjoyed watching certain television sports events and comedy shows? Maybe he was pushed to the wall, not feeling well? It never occurs to Karl that Faulkner had a streak of mischievous cruelty in him, and that the nastiest, most mischievous remark he could make to the high-minded scientist was the unanswerable one he made.[2]

Perhaps Faulkner's most notorious bit of racism was provoked by an English journalist, Russell Howe, whose interview with the novelist elicited these words: "But if it came to fighting I'd fight for Mississippi against the United States, even if it meant going out into the street and shooting Negroes. After all, I'm not going out to shoot Mississippians." The only way Karl can deal with this horror is to create a "context which, while it could not excuse the comment, would make it seem less like the ravings of a white Mississippian." So, looking around for a handy context, he settles for booze: "It is possible that Faulkner had been drinking heavily . . . was out of his mind with anguish and alcohol." A paragraph or so later, Karl has taken the bit between his teeth: "We must conjecture that Faulkner was drunk, provoked, at the end of his tether, and Howe pushed him over the edge." This seems to me the last refuge of a biographer—to pretend, in the face of an "impossible" remark (Great Artists don't say Such Things) that there are, somehow, circumstances which "explain" it, like the possibility that Faulkner had been drinking heavily. But since Faulkner was always drinking heavily (except when drying out) how does that fact distinguish the interview with Howe from other episodes in his life? And why on earth, given that we are now at page 932 of the biography, should a reader care one way or the other?

The wasteful repetitiveness that makes Karl's book such a trial to read is felt in the way each point, after it is made, has then to be remade and made yet again. On page 151 we are told—about a "semiautobiographical" novel titled "Elmer" which Faulkner worked on in the 1920s—that its hero, a painter, liked to fondle his tubes of paint "caressing them [in Karl's words], feeling their weight, letting them dangle from his hands in their heaviness, and feeling the

2. Maybe Faulkner made the remark because he was that irresponsible sort of human being, the artist. Consider the following exchange, from *The Sound and the Fury,* between Jason Compson and an unnamed salesman:

"And what for? so a bunch of damn eastern jews, I'm not talking about men of the jewish religion," I says, "I've known some jews that were fine citizens. You might be one yourself," I says.

"No," he says, "I'm an American."

"No offense," I says. "I give every man his due, regardless of religion or anything else. I have nothing against jews as an individual," I says. "It's just the race."

swell of the tubes as paint exerts pressure to escape." Karl then remarks that the language carries "insistent images of masturbation," a reasonable enough observation. At the bottom of the same page he refers again to "the fondling of the tubes, with their troubling sexuality." Eight or so pages later, we are told that "Elmer" is full of Freudian images: "To begin with, there is his horror at the color red, signifying fear of the vagina; his fondling of paint tubes, so that touch, color, and shape connect his yearning for art with masturbatory sexuality." Nine pages after that we hear that "Elmer's fear of red also suggests a rejection of the female, since red is associated with the vagina," and "Elmer's trauma with red is transferred, in part, to his love of paint tubes—fat, bulging, erectile tubes, phallic in design and in his pleasure at stroking them." Two pages later there is one more reference "to the infatuation with paint tubes, fear of red, and other obsessions." This is ludicrous. It is as if Karl forgot to listen to himself (did he have an editor?), and the solemn retailing of such dreary "facts" about an abortive piece of Faulkner's work is unfortunately consistent with the book's general sprawl—its lack of ironic edge and pointedness.

Unlike some biographers, Karl does not shirk the task of criticizing his subject's art, indeed spends many pages of commentary on each novel and poem and story right down to the most trivial one: " 'Dull Tale' unfortunately fulfills the promise of its title. It has biographical interest and little else. That Faulkner decided not to publish it in his *Collected Stories* was wise." (Wouldn't it have been just as wise, then, for his biographer to ignore it?) But in fact Karl doesn't so much criticize Faulkner's art as enumerate plots, compare characters one to another, and enunciate "themes" in a manner like the following:

> Holding together the work of this period, then, is a deep concern with ultimate questions. How does the individual handle his own needs in the face of an adversarial destiny? How does a person deal with present life when impingement of history and pastness burdens him at every stage? How does one respond to internal needs which defy social constrictions, which break taboos? Further, how does the individual deal with illuminations (from within) when darkness (from without) seems the dominant shade?

I give up! says the reader: *You* marry Mary Jane. Surely this sort of "ultimate" questioning has little or nothing to do with the excitements and pleasures of reading Faulkner. Karl likes to speak of Faulkner's "thinking" on various issues (race, sex, etc.) as if we were to respect him as a philosopher, and at one point even finds that he "reveals a startling linkage to Nietzschean ideas." Or could it be that he had just been drinking heavily?

At any rate, under the stimulus of Karl's biography I have been rereading Faulkner. It seems to me possible that—to use his own lofty language from the Nobel Prize speech—the parts of his work that will not only "endure" but "prevail" may well be the comic parts: like the Jason section in *Sound and the Fury;* or the "Old Man" chapters from *The Wild Palms;* or "Spotted Horses" and other tall tales from *The Hamlet.* Rereading *Sanctuary* I found myself quite disinclined to take André Malraux's line about how it's really a Greek Tragedy superimposed on a detective story, and I often had a devil of a time figuring out what was happening, exactly, in the narrative (Karl refers to the writing in *Sanctuary* as "aslant," but it sometimes feels simply askew). But the two undeniable gems in the book are comic ones: the sojourn of Virgil Snopes and Fonzo—under the impression they are staying in a rooming house—at Miss Reba's Memphis brothel; and the wonderful conversation, conducted with much drinking of beer and gin, between Miss Reba and her friends, Miss Lorraine and Miss Myrtle. (There is the bonus of Uncle Bud, "a small bullet-headed boy of five or six" who accompanies the ladies and keeps sneaking gulps of the currently available beverage, provoking Miss Myrtle to tell him that she is "ashamed to be seen on the street with a drunk boy like you.") Not surprisingly, Karl's reverential tone toward Faulkner doesn't accommodate to viewing him as a comedian.

Perhaps it is *Light in August* that more than any other of his books separates those who regard him this side idolatry from those, like myself, who are more wary. Karl is either unaware or disdainful of Wyndham Lewis's chapter on Faulkner in *Men Without Art* (1934), which contains some salutary reservations about the novelist's more fevered rhetoric. Lewis quotes the following sentence from *Light in August*—"Now it was still, quiet, the fecund earth now coolly suspirant"—and says that "every time it occurs (every half dozen pages that is) it puts me off (I become 'coolly suspirant' myself)." Lewis points out that there is "a lot of *poetry* in Faulkner, not all of it good," which occurs when the atmosphere is running thin:

> His characters demand, in order to endure for more than ten pages, apparently, an opaque atmosphere of whip-poor-wills, cicadas, lilac, "seeping" moonlight . . . and of course the "dimensionless" sky from which moonlight "seeps."

These properties, Lewis declares, are stored in a "whip-poor-will tank" and pumped into the narrative "in generous flushes" whenever the need is felt.

Apart from being an amusing creative fantasy, Lewis's criticism has a grain of hard sense. When, last spring, I had my students read *The Wild Palms* we paused over a sentence in which Wilbourne, the protagonist of the "Wild Palms" sections, speaks of something as "the mausoleum of love, [it was] the stinking catafalque of the dead corpse borne between the olfactoryless walking shapes of the immortal unsentient demanding ancient meat." This isn't supposed to be funny, but try reading it aloud and see how it sounds. Lewis found *Light in August* "full of wearisome repetitions . . . long-winded to the last degree . . . hysterical and salvationist . . . comical where it is not meant to be." Faulkner, he said, had written "a gigantic 480-page Morality" in which the novelist may be seen "delecting himself with, and turning to good library-sale's account, scenes of chopping, gashing, hacking and slitting." More recently Flannery O'Connor (in a fine comment quoted by Karl) called *Light in August* "a real sick-making book but I guess a classic." One would like to encounter more of that "I guess" feeling in Karl's many pages about the novel in which he finds it to be "among [Faulkner's] most profound commentaries on race" and that it "has cut directly across a profound American theme of identity—who am I? what role do I play? how do I find myself?"

It may be that Faulkner, like D. H. Lawrence, is the sort of writer you encounter at one point in your life (maybe in your twenties) and who takes absolute possession of you. Returned to years later, such writers never quite live up to their original, remembered glory—at least so far as that glory entailed intimations of profundity. What remains is not inconsiderable—the marvelous observation, the voices rendered in conversation, and, as already mentioned, the humor. But Faulkner wanted to do something more, wanted—as he once told Malcolm Cowley—"to put everything into one sentence—not only the present but the whole past on which it depends and which keeps overtaking the present, second by second." About that aspiration, Hugh Kenner has written the best paragraph I've come across in all Faulkner criticism:

> A writer with ambitions of this order cannot but grow obsessed with ceaseless Time: the time that takes away syllables as they are uttered, eroding all possibility of that one polyvalent word; that consumes antecedent actions, compelling him to retrieve them by raids on the past; that consigns the vivid actual to myth; that segments and scatters and blurs and consumes all those lives, volitions, passions whose pressure on the

momentary *now* lends it the meaning he sets out to capture—at what cost, in what serial stratagems. For the show of analysis, the show of syntax, are stratagems forced on the Symbolist by Time. Faulkner was neither an analytic nor a syntactic thinker, but a teaser into words, into sentences, paragraphs, chapters—all necessary, all unwelcome—of what was, to start with, a simple unverbalizable pulsating impulse.

That is one way of putting it, in the process of which Kenner manages to sound almost like the Faulkner whose style he is evoking. Another way was Faulkner's own, in a letter written late in his life to his former lover, Joan Williams:

> And now I realise for the first time what an amazing gift I had: uneducated in any formal sense, without even very literate, let alone literary, companions, yet to have made the things I made. I don't know where it came from. I don't know why God or gods or whoever it was, selected me to be the vessel.

Karl's biography does nothing to dispel this—the really important—mystery, and that at least is all to the good.

Almost Austen

Elizabeth Taylor's first novel, *At Mrs. Lippincote's,* was published in 1946; *Blaming,* her last one, appeared thirty years later, posthumously (she died in 1975). In the interim of steady work, she produced thirteen novels and four volumes of stories. She was increasingly referred to with respect, invariably compared to Jane Austen ("the modern man's Jane Austen," said Arthur Mizener), and—certainly in this country—never taken very seriously. Perhaps the misfortune of her name had something to do with it, since the other Elizabeth Taylor (English too, but with all those husbands) took up so much space. The novelist Taylor had but one husband (the director of a sweet factory) and lived with him until her death. She herself was a child of un-extraordinary circumstances, the daughter of a Reading insurance agent. She attended the Abbey School in Reading where she wrote plays and failed maths; then worked as a governess for a time until she settled down with John William Kendall Taylor, living in Buckinghamshire in the Thames Valley and practicing her craft. Elizabeth Jane Howard, a fellow novelist, remembers her "seated in a big chair . . . writing her novels in beautiful longhand, breaking off whenever one of her two children wanted attention."

The previous quotation and information is from Susannah Clapp's excellent introduction to *The Sleeping Beauty,* one of four Taylor novels recently brought out by Dial Press in the "Virago Modern Classics" series. She might have been amused at being chosen a Virago author, since there is little of the "termagant" or the "scold," indeed very little "man-like" or "heroic" (all synonyms from the Oxford Dictionary), in her novelistic presence. Consider some sentences describing the relationship between the recently widowed Isabella (in *The Sleeping Beauty,* 1953) and her friend, Evalie Hobson:

> She and Isabella had only a superficial acquaintance, but this made it all the more precious to both of them. Talk skimmed along, chocolates were chosen from the box, tea drunk, sherry sipped. Scrawled notes passed between them, handbags were rummaged through for recipes and diet sheets. They met middle-age together—a time when women are necessary to one another—and all the petty but grievous insults of greying hair,

crowsfeet, and the loathed encumbrances of unwanted flesh, seemed less sordid when faced and fought (though fought spasmodically and with weak wills) gaily together. . . . They counted up calories, bought new corsets and tried face-creams; cut paragraphs out of magazines for one another and went together to the Turkish baths. They remained the same—two rather larkish schoolgirls. This they realized and it was the piteous part to them of growing old.

This is from what Susannah Clapp calls, in her introduction, Elizabeth Taylor's most romantic novel. Yet as is clear from the above piece of nicely poised, affectionate satire, the social mode, the civilized voice of placement and illustration, are very much to the fore. Compared to such writing, Taylor's female precursors in modern British fiction—Virginia Woolf and Elizabeth Bowen come to mind—seem very much the fancy writers, quite ready to move away from character and society into flights of speculative lyricism. (Reading Bowen's *Death of the Heart* recently, after a bout of Elizabeth Taylor, one sees how restrained, modest, and lucid is the latter's prose. For all that—or perhaps because of it—the final sentence of the excerpt above has both bite and gravity.)

In important traits of character the novelist shared little in common with her women gaily buying corsets and trying out new face creams. She was, Susannah Clapp tells us, "elegant, reserved, antireligious and a Labour voter." The face which gazes out at us from my 1964 Viking issue of *The Soul of Kindness* (dedicated to Elizabeth Cameron [Elizabeth Bowen]) is composed to the point of placidity, pleasant looking if unglamorous, suggestive of few dark corners in the soul. And the constant comparisons between her and Jane Austen have in part the notion behind them that, like her predecessor, Elizabeth Taylor didn't try to do the French Revolution in her fiction, had no novelistic interest in rendering "issues" on which, as a Labour voter, she probably had pronounced opinions. It is hard not to think once again, in this connection, of Eliot's too often-quoted remark about Henry James having a mind so fine that no idea could violate it. In Taylor's case, rather than making for an emptiness of content, a felt lack of ideation, her inviolability points to something distinctive and satisfying about the quality of her narratives.

They are narratives that do not seem governed by the wish to point a moral that will adorn them. In *In a Summer Season* (1961), the heroine, Kate Heron, has remarried a younger, unreliable, bibulous, unemployed but sexy Irishman named Dermot who eventually dies in a car crash, accompanied by the seductive daughter of Kate's old friend, Charles— whereupon Kate marries the old friend and the novel ends. All the members of the family have various attitudes, mainly critical, about Kate's marriage to Dermot; but their attitudes or "ideas," if such they can be called, have nothing to do with what happens to Dermot and to Kate. In *The Soul of Kindness* it looks as if Flora—always the kind soul who encourages those around her to look on the benign side of things—gets her comeuppance when a protegé, Kit, encouraged by her in theatrical dreams of glory, tries instead to kill himself. Flora is severely shaken by this, even (we speculate) to the point of some painful self-redefinition. But in fact, after being assured by her friends that she is not to blame, she is seen at the end of the book "cheerful, and her old self again." There has been no agonizing reappraisal; life just goes on. In *Mrs. Palfrey at the Claremont* (1971), Mrs. Palfrey, hurrying to navigate the swing doors of the residential hotel in which she lives, falls, breaks her hip, and dies in hospital. The novel ends, yet there is no way in which its final event is presented to us as an ironic payment for any of the little vanities Mrs. Palfrey has indulged in throughout the book.

In fact, it is even less fun than usual to try and "tell" the story of a Taylor novel. Dr. Johnson said that if you tried to read Richardson for the story you would hang yourself; rather it was "sentiment" for which one read him. Although Elizabeth Taylor's books are never long (three of the reissued four hover around the 250-page mark), neither are they page-turners, reading situations in which we are driven along to find out what happens next. But it appears that Elizabeth Taylor made a conscious choice *not* to "drive" her narratives, so that whenever one looks for something to happen, some confrontation between two characters that would produce dramatic and revelatory action, she slides away from it, avoiding the pathos or excitement of a big scene. Mrs. Palfrey's real grandson, Desmond, is a selfish Hampstead twit, but she finds a marvelous substitute for him in a somewhat louche young man named Ludo, who hangs around Harrods getting material for his novel. So as to show the other residents at the Claremont that she has a relative who cares for her, she persuades Ludo to pose as the grandson, invited in for the occasional meal and drink. Eventually Mrs. Palfrey lends him money, he disappears, and it looks as though we are in for some pathos, the lonely old woman exploited by the slick, unfeeling operator. But things in life are more complicated and less definitive than that, as Ludo reappears to visit Mrs. Palfrey in the hospital before she dies:

"You aren't going to die," Ludo said quickly.

"It doesn't really matter," Mrs. Palfrey said apologetically. "Perhaps when Elizabeth [her daughter] comes, she'll see to it that I have a room of my own."

"*I'll* see to it," Ludo said.

"Oh, I should love it if you could. Monday seems to be so far away. I should like my own night-gown, too. And my book of poetry. I lie here trying to remember poems to take my mind off things; but they're all gone—nearly all gone."

"Don't talk any more. You'll tire yourself."

He covered her hand with his, and they sat in silence; she, with her eyes closed, and he staring at the clock above the door and wondering how long before he could get away.

Again the writing slides away from what one might here be expecting—a moving deathbed scene between the pair. It is indeed moving, but partly for the way it refuses to advertise the purity of Ludo's feelings. He does take some caring responsibility, does in fact pay back the fifty pounds she lent him. He is a better "grandson" than her real one. Still, for all that, he stares at the clock and wonders how long he'll be forced to hang around. It is such moments in Elizabeth Taylor's writing that satisfy, even as they don't involve us in any great desire to see what happens next. Will she live or die? She doesn't much care, and neither does her creator, nor do we, since her work in this book has been done and done well.

Taylor's particular genius has to do with her ability to render embarrassment, which is eminently a social feeling and inevitably has to do with somebody's sensitivity of perception. Two examples from *In a Summer Season* suggest why it is in such renderings, rather than the development of ideas or themes, that her writing comes most to life. Kate gives a dinner party while her husband's mother, Edwina, is visiting them (not an easy situation at best), and at this dinner are her Aunt Ethel, her children, a young curate named Father Blizzard, and her father-in-law (from the first marriage), Sir Alfred. There has been a dispute over whether the turkey (purchased already plucked and trussed, which the cook feels is dangerous) has gone "off," but Kate decides to chance it anyway. The results are conveyed by the following paragraph:

"I'm sorry to keep jumping up and down," said Dermot. "We are a little short of butlers at present." As he went round the table he observed the state of plates. Edwina had left her turkey and Ignazia [the son's girlfriend] seemed in two minds about doing so. Father Blizzard had finished his and even wore a look of simple contentment, for which Dermot was ready to forgive him his maddening geniality. "No great meat-eater," Sir Alfred muttered, and put his knife and fork together. Ethel had tried to hide most of hers under some brussel sprouts, not realizing that this would only make Kate wonder if there was something wrong with them, too.

Nothing "hilarious" in the comedy here; just extremely, coolly accurate in the various ways it names responses to the embarrassing turkey.

The second instance is more serious and more intricate in its unfolding. One of the main differences between Kate's deceased husband, Alan, and her present one is that Alan shared with her a passion for books and music, while, aside from sex, Dermot is mainly interested in booze. ("Dermot, for his part, was a minute or two earlier at the drinks tray every evening.") At one point Kate notices Dermot inspecting James's *The Spoils of Poynton*, one of Alan's favorite novels. There he discovers (though he can't identify them) lines from Donne, written in as commemorating Kate and Alan's engagement. Where-upon Dermot closes the book. Later, Kate's friend Charles speaks of someone as "Mrs. Gereth" (a character in *Spoils*), and Dermot innocently remarks that "I've never met Mrs. Gereth." Kate blushes but remains silent, and the narra-tor recalls her saying, years previously, "I could never have married a man who didn't dote on Jane Austen or Henry James." Then, late in the novel, Dermot, brooding and irritated already, again picks up the James novel, glances at the inscription, but this time goes further:

> The uncertainties he always felt on beginning to read a book were in-creased. He turned the pages. "*The Spoils of Poynton*. . . . Preface". . . . *that* he skipped. . . . "Chapter One." His expression fell into lines of great boredom as he began to read. "Mrs. Gereth had said she would go with the rest to church." He frowned, closed the book with his finger in it to mark the place and stared up at the ceiling, wondering where, lately, that rather unusual name had cropped up.

Soon he recollects the scene and "his irritation swerved suddenly into anger. Mrs. Gereth then was simply a character in a book and no one had liked to tell him so. They had preferred to gloss over his ignorance." His wife had been "embarrassed" he decides (and rightly) "as if . . . there was some awkwardness in not having read every novel that ever was written and having the names of the characters at one's finger-tips." And he throws the book across the floor.

On occasion Taylor can bring off an Ivy Compton-Burnett–like exchange, as when an aunt says to her niece that "Perhaps we ought not to discuss people behind their backs," whereupon the niece sensibly replies that "We can't very well discuss them in front of them." But usually the effort is less pointed, more lifelike in the way conversation goes than such a "brilliant" exchange as the one above presents. Occasionally she indulges in the bad habit of skewering a hapless character on the strength of a sentiment he or she has professed, as when, after Sir Alfred claims something for himself, to himself, Taylor comments "This was untrue as well as uninteresting." But at her best she resists twisting her narratives into shapes which too gratifyingly exhibit the witty, moral superiority of the narrator. The result is that more than most recent novelists, even female English ones, she gives us a sense of the real, of life going on (as it were) without the help of a presiding, shaping, manipulative spirit. This is of course an illusion; that it can be entertained at all is a measure of her specialness as a writer.

An end note to each of these four volumes promises that others are to follow. One would like to speak up for *Angel* (1957), about an Ouida-like trashy novelist and unlike anything else she wrote; or *The Wedding Group* (1968), with its superb triangle of husband-wife-mother (-in-law); or her final book, *Blaming,* a little weary and depressed in some of its reflections, but nonetheless moving for that. Meanwhile let us be grateful for what has been re-brought to our attention. She is, as Robert Liddell once said, an exquisite writer; but she is a deep and a wise one as well.

New Republic, March 26, 1984

Vidal's Satiric Voices

Over the years since Gore Vidal published his first novel, *Williwaw*—the un-voiced narrative of a toneless narrator—his work both in fiction and criticism has become increasingly bristling in its tone and subtle in the effects it orches-trates. Literary theorists who like to subvert the notion of a speaking voice in the literary text, by proving there's no such thing, would have difficulty deal-ing in such a manner with a typical passage in, say, "Pink Triangle and Yellow Star," Vidal's 1981 piece in the *Nation* on homosexuals and some of their critics. The essay's most memorable section considers the assumptions and statements made about gays by Midge Decter in her *Commentary* article, "The Boys on the Beach"—except that Vidal does not commonly speak of "gays." He finds that so-called politically correct term "a ridiculous word to use as a common identification for Frederick the Great, Franklin Pangborn and Elea-nor Roosevelt." Vidal prefers to call it "same-sex sex" and to characterize its practitioners with traditionally abusive and contemptuous words like "fag-gots," "queers," and "fairies." Or, more clinically, he employs his own favorite coinage—"homosexualist."

Decter is one of a group of New York Jewish writers who, Vidal claims, engage in "fag-baiting" (in an earlier essay, "Sex Is Politics," he referred to "a Catskill hotel called the Hilton Kramer"). She is introduced in "Pink Tri-angle . . ." with a parenthetical allusion: "Mrs. Norman Podhoretz, also known as Midge Decter (like Martha Ivers, *whisper* her name)." Whether one is generally sympathetic or not to Decter's politics, the allusion to Martha Ivers is diverting since *The Strange Love of Martha Ivers* is a 1946 Barbara Stanwyck movie about a woman on the make. Advance publicity for the film made use of the terse command "Whisper her name," and those of us (like Vidal) whose adolescence or young adulthood took place during the 1940s will catch the fond remembrance even as it warns us to beware of Decter.

Having previewed the excitements to come, Vidal paraphrases some of her observations on the behavior of "pansies" (his term, of course, not hers) at a Fire Island resort called the Pines. Decter observed that, over the years, "the boys on the beach" had become more militant and also (Vidal interpolates) less well groomed: "What indeed has happened to the homosexual community I used to know—they who only a few short years ago ["as opposed to those manly 370-day years," Vidal again interpolates] were characterized by nothing so much as a sweet, vain, pouting, girlish attention to the youth and beauty of their bodies?" Instead of answering her irrelevant question, Vidal pounces on one of Decter's footnotes in order to create what is probably the single most outrageously funny sentence he has ever written:

> "There were also homosexual women at the Pines [Decter writes] but they were or seemed to be, far fewer in number. Nor, except for a marked tendency to hang out in the company of large and ferocious dogs, were they instantly recognizable as the men were." Well, if I were a dyke and a pair of Podhoretzes came waddling toward me on the beach, copies of Leviticus and Freud in hand, I'd get in touch with the nearest Alsatian dealer pronto.

The style accommodates, in a fairly short sentence, "dyke" and "Leviticus" and "Alsatian dealer," even as the alliterative "pair of Podhoretzes" are made to waddle along the Fire Island beach. The sentence begins with a relaxed but ominous "Well," and ends, in a masterstroke, with "pronto," a word nobody ever uses in conversation or in writing, and which has therefore a distinct, archaic charm.

In the words of a now-dead expression, the whole passage is Too Much; like the earlier reference to Martha Ivers, it goes too far. Vidal's scathing contempt for Decter's tone and ideology, nevertheless, feels freer, funnier, and more exhilarating coming forth in a beach-fantasy like the above. Having let himself go this far, a more prudent combatant would have desisted; instead Vidal is spurred to further inventive invective, as if to prove he can top the one he'd just thought up (as indeed he can). So he chooses another of Decter's musings, this one concerning a supposedly relative lack of body hair on homosexuals as compared to their heterosexual counterparts: "We were never able to determine just why there should be so definite a connection between what is nowadays called their sexual preference ["previously known to right-thinking Jews as an abomination against Jehovah," intrudes Vidal] and their smooth feminine skin. Was it a matter of hormones?" Vidal suggests that, because of her "essential modesty and lack of experience," Decter has been privileged to see few gentile males without their clothes on:

> If she had, she would have discovered that gentile men tend to be less hairy
> than Jews except, of course, when they are not. Because the Jews killed our
> Lord, they are forever marked with hair on their shoulders—something
> that no gentile man has on *his* shoulders except for John Travolta and a
> handful of other Italian-Americans from the Englewood, New Jersey, area.

The great strokes here are not only that trick first sentence, with its proffered
formulation comparing relatively hairless gentiles to hairy Jews (which then
takes it all back with the minimally stated but absolute reservation—"except,
of course, when they are not"), but also, later, the marvelous entrance of John
Travolta onto the scene, bringing along with him a spurious demographic
swipe at the Englewood, New Jersey, area.

Hugh Kenner once said about Eliot's "young man carbuncular" in the third
book of *The Waste Land*, "If he existed, and if he read these words, how must
he have marvelled at the alchemical power of language over his inflamed
skin!" One imagines, just for a moment, that when Midge Decter read (if she
ever did) Vidal's retort to her, she might have marveled or even laughed aloud
at what her observations of certain gay lifestyles had been turned into. The
mocking tone of Vidal's extravagantly gleeful correctives is such as to move
any argument he has with someone like Decter to another level—an aesthetic
level, I'd call it (though Decter herself may have found other words for it). At
any rate, for all Vidal's witty ability to deflate someone's oversized ego or to
squelch the wrong-headed opinions of an antagonist, his approach invariably
has something "positive" about it. In this connection, one wonders if John
Simon was able to derive any instruction from the following sketch of himself
in Vidal's essay "Literary Gangsters":

> A Yugoslav with a proud if somewhat incoherent Serbian style (or is it
> Croatian?—in any case, English is his third language), Mr. Simon has for
> twenty years slashed his way through literature, theater, cinema. Clanking
> chains and snapping whips, giggling and hissing, he has ricocheted from
> one journal to another, and though no place holds him for long, the flow
> of venom has proved inexhaustible. There is nothing he cannot find to
> hate. Yet in his way, Mr. Simon is pure; a compulsive rogue criminal, more
> sadistic Gilles de Rais than neighborhood thug.

(A footnote adds: "Mr. Simon has since instructed us that English is his fifth
language.") Vidal knew that with John Simon he had on his hands no mere
neighborhood thug—that Simon's vituperative critical operation deserved

nothing commonplace in the way of abuse. Thus are brought in the meta-phorical chains and the whips, the giggling and hissing suitable to an uncommon "literary gangster."

In 1959, when Norman Mailer had his say about some contemporary American novelists ("Evaluations—Quick and Expansive Comments on the Talent in the Room," in *Advertisements for Myself*), he wrote two interesting paragraphs about Vidal praising his "good formal mind" and the "brave and cultivated wit" of his essays. Mailer opined that Vidal's "considerable body of work" showed as yet no novel that was "more successful than not." But he asserted that Vidal had "the first requirement of an interesting writer—one cannot predict his direction." Although, as often, the essay (and book) was couched in terms of typical Mailerish self-promotion, this was also a prescient statement about Vidal. To measure the distance between *Willwaw* and *Lincoln,* or between *The City and the Pillar* and *Duluth,* is to realize that "development"—the critic's usual term for artistic maturation or change—is scarcely the word to describe such scope and diversity in a novelist's work. I don't propose to explore the subject beyond noting that (in Mailer's phrase) Vidal's "cultivated wit" played almost no part in the early novels, whether their scene was contemporary or historical. But by the late sixties, with the publication of *Myra Breckinridge,* and such essays as "The Holy Family" and "Doc Reuben," he was fully launched on a satiric style that came to full expression in *Myron, Duluth,* and in essays like "Pink Triangle . . ." (noted above).

Or, say, rather, satiric *styles.* To simplify matters perhaps unduly, the "Pink Triangle" style is very much a voiced one, and the voice is marked by its commanding insolence toward the fools and knaves it opposes. I don't know if Mailer's prose work in the 1960s was of any specific use to Vidal in loosening up his own style and broadening the range of his targets, but *Advertisements for Myself, The Presidential Papers,* and *Cannibals and Christians* must at least have had the force of example. In fact, when Vidal made his infamous coupling of Mailer with Charles Manson (in "Women's Liberation meets Miller-Mailer-Manson-Man"), which led to the famous confrontation between the two on *The Dick Cavett Show,* Vidal himself was being rather Mailerish in his aggressive, free-swinging ripostes. And though Mailer has typically been louder and, sometimes, cruder in striking blows against politicians or writers he doesn't admire, he and Vidal do share a savvy wit and a genius for constructing bizarre creative fantasies.

Vidal's Satiric Voices

In the 1970s, as Mailer occupied himself scarcely at all with evaluating the talent of his younger American contemporaries, Vidal grew bolder and (from one angle at least) more conservative in his pronouncements on what sort of fictional thing would or would not do. His special scorn was reserved for practitioners of what he called "fiction's R and D [Research and Development]." These novelists were themselves teachers, and if they were not exactly "scholar-squirrels" or "the hacks of academe" (Vidal's affectionate names for members of the profession), they wrote "teachers' novels." Often in Vidal's opinion, they didn't write well: John Barth's *Giles Goat-Boy* "is a very bad prose-work"; Donald Barthelme's *The Dead Father* "is written in a kind of numbing baby talk" which "of course" Barthelme means to be ironic and that he also knows is "not very interesting to read"; Pynchon's *Crying of Lot 49* is notable for its cute names, bad grammar, and homophobia, while *Gravity's Rainbow* is "the perfect teachers' novel." That these novelists and their professional explicators deserve one another is the clear implication of Vidal's treatment. It may well have been that as his own fiction grew more unexperimental—as he began to write longish historical works that unfolded through a relatively conventional narrative texture, and through sentences not designed (like Barth's or Barthelme's) to "self-destruction"—his contempt for "teachers' novels" sharpened and intensified.

Yet between 1968 and 1983 he published four comic novels whose sentences, if they don't exactly self-destruct, cannot be read with a straight face. Compared to the vigorous insolence and mischief of the "Pink Triangle" satire on Decter, the style of these novels is fastidiously bogus. All of them are written in purposely "dumb" voices, and their construction must have furnished their author with considerable pleasure. These books are filled with movie lore, and in *Myron*, Myra Breckinridge finds herself inside the filming of a 1948 film, *Siren of Babylon*, starring Maria Montez. When, with "spitfire intensity," Maria utters the following question—"You who have debauched thousands and listened to evil councillors, now will you listen to the voice of the One True God?"—to Louis Calhern's King Nebuchadnezzar, Myra can barely contain herself for the thrill of it all:

> Every time Maria says this line I shiver and want to pee and am covered with gooseflesh. Her air to Puerto Rican majesty combined with a Santo Domingan accent result in a performance which is, voice-wise, superior to that of Loretta Young as Berengaria in *The Crusaders* (1935) when Loretta said so movingly to her husband Richard the Lion-Hearted,

"Richard, you gotta save Christianity," and equal to that of Lana Turner's portrayal of a priestess of Ba'al who is stoned to death in *The Prodigal* (1955); a performance which was, very simply, the high point of 1940's movie acting in a 1950's film.

"Voice-wise" this passage is delightful in its "authoritative" pronouncements about Puerto Rican majesty and Santo Domingan accents, and in the precise distinctions and comparisons made among three immortal (camp-wise) films and actresses. (Who else but Myra—or Vidal—could state that Lana Turner's work in *The Prodigal* was "very simply" the high point of 1940's movie acting in a 1950's film—an extremely refined discrimination that could just possibly be true.)

As noted, one occasionally reaches for the term *camp* to label this sort of thing—but Vidal's effects often elude the term and sometimes even have an almost poignant ring to them. In *Myron* there is a mention of an all-but-forgotten 1940s leading man, Lon McCallister, who, though we are told he lives on in Malibu, "is of course no longer the boy who broke your heart in *Stage Door Canteen,* playing Romeo to Katharine Cornell's gracious Juliet nor can he ever again go home, except on the Late Show, to Indiana." It is as if some central part of the writer's own heart has gone into salvaging poor Lon. The most useful and shortest definition of camp I've encountered says that it takes opposite attitudes ("Of course it's dreadful, but it's *wonderfully* dread-ful") toward whatever subcultural artifact (say, Maria Montez's acting) is up for inspection. But Myra isn't camping it up, she simply adores Maria Montez, while Vidal thinks Maria is so awful that she's wonderful. Camp is boring when the "positive" element in it—the "wonderfully" component—lacks con-viction or sufficient inventiveness. Flushed with enthusiasm, the voice of Myra Breckinridge can produce ultimate questions like the following, provoked by (in reference to great film moments) "those strips of celluloid which still endure":

> Could the actual Christ have possessed a fraction of the radiance and mystery of H. B. Warner in the first *King of Kings* or revealed, even on the cross, so much as a shadow of the moonstruck Nemi-agony of Jeffrey Hunter in the second *King of Kings,* that astonishing creation of Nicholas Ray?

Surely a rhetorical question, but both *Myra Breckinridge* and *Myron* (espe-cially the latter) have enough of such reflections to ensure their endurance as minor classics. Indeed, the movie-camp trivia seems to me funnier and more rereadable than the sex-change business in both novels.

A related but somewhat different bogus style is found in *Kalki* and especially *Duluth,* and it has affinities with Terry Southern's procedures in *The Magic Christian* and *Candy.* Southern, his books out of print and his name unknown to younger readers (none of my students, canvassed recently, had even heard of him) was, along with Lenny Bruce, the most remarkable darkish comedian of the sixties. In Mailer's words, he represented, as does Vidal, "the aristocratic impulse turned upon itself," and he produced in *The Magic Christian* what Mailer rightly called "a classic of Camp." Vidal's *Duluth* has similar classic ambitions, though it fails to achieve them because it's rather too long a book (Southern's novel, by contrast, is wickedly short). But sentences like the following, pretending to describe the "barrios" of Duluth, packed with illegal aliens ("over-heated wetbacks") and women "folding their tortillas with practiced fingers," sound exactly the right note of inspired bogusness, as a white alien policewoman invades the aliens' turf:

> Obsidian black inscrutable eyes in age-old Mayan or Aztec faces immediately recognize Lieutenant Darlene Ecks, Homicide, whose recipiency of the Civic Achievement Medal has not gone unremarked in the Spanish press. As Darlene, a dazed smile on her moist lips, pauses at a colorful outdoor market where chiles and peppers and black beans are bought and sold by women in the colorful black dresses of their original homeland, Pablo and two accomplices materialize just back of the chickpea stall.

Such riveting thriller-writing (note the artful repetition of "colorful" and the ominous rising action behind the chickpea stall) is the staple of narrative news in *Duluth*. If *Gravity's Rainbow* is a perfect "teacher's novel" since it gives teacher plenty to do (every paragraph with its own built-in knot to unravel), Vidal's *Duluth* is full of cheesy thirdhand imaginings ("a dazed smile on her moist lips") which don't tempt anyone to interpretive academic strategies.

But neither did the progenitor and masterpiece of all modern comedies, Evelyn Waugh's *Decline and Fall.* In that classic, the Welsh schoolmaster, Dr. Fagan, remarks to Paul Pennyfeather, the novel's hapless hero, that "We schoolmasters must temper discretion with deceit." True enough about schoolmasters, it is also true about satirists like Waugh and a latter-day practitioner such as Gore Vidal. It was in Waugh's second novel, *Vile Bodies,* where the word *bogus* made its appearance in relation to a Bright Young Thing named Archie Schwert ("the most *bogus* man," says Agatha Runcible, spiritedly). But Waugh was already an expert in constructing bogus sentences that discreetly and deceitfully pretended to be observing life—to register the look and feel of a world "out there"—when in fact they were merely opportunities for striking off humorous (sometimes cruelly humorous) juxtapositions. At the end of Lottie Crump's party in *Vile Bodies,* "Judge Skimp was sleeping, his fine white hair in an ash-tray," and the sentence which notes that "fact" pretends to responsibility toward the way things are, even as it scores nicely off the judge. Like Waugh, Vidal decided that it was not for him to explore the mysteries of the human heart; decided that he didn't want to know all, and thus have to forgive all. Instead he became, in his comic novels and prose, a considerable satirist the essence of which activity (as Wyndham Lewis pointed out most clearly) is to be unfair.

To conclude this brief sampling of Vidal's satiric voices, it may be helpful to remember Eliot's remarks about the nature of Ben Jonson's comedy—that it is "only incidentally satire, because it is only incidentally a criticism upon the actual world." Eliot found the source of Jonson's art not to lie "in any precise emotional attitude or precise intellectual criticism of the actual world," and claimed that it was "creative" rather than "critical" in its character. Yet it is probably no coincidence that Jonson was also a fine critic, and surely no coincidence that the journalist-reporter Vidal, who provided us with so many engaging and incisive criticisms of America in the 1960s and beyond, should also figure as a first-rate creative satirist.

Gore Vidal: Writer Against the Grain, edited by Jay Parini. Columbia University Press, 1990. Copyright © Columbia University Press, New York. Reprinted by permission of the publisher.

Critics

There follow some recorded admirations of seven critics about as distinct from each other as one could wish. Most of them share the common quality of having little or no current status in today's academy. For students of literature, George Saintsbury, H. L. Mencken, and F. R. Leavis are figures from a bygone past; George Santayana is little more than a name to aspiring philosophers; and most musicologists regard B. H. Haggin as at best a critical amateur. William Empson has survived the changes in critical styles, but not necessarily for the best of reasons. (Deconstruction takes him to its heart because he can be used to show the instability of signifiers, the unsettledness of all reference.) The only one of the seven still alive is Helen Vendler, a professor at Harvard University and probably the most influential poetry reviewer in America.

The occasions for these pieces were various: the appearance of a full-length book on Saintsbury and a biography of Santayana; the publication of Mencken's diaries; a posthumous collection of Empson's essays and reviews; and Vendler's first collection of her shorter pieces on poets and poetry. The short tributes to Leavis and Haggin were written soon after the death of each.

Bookman

In a telling phrase, Vladimir Nabokov once referred to John Galsworthy as a "stone-dead" English novelist. No English men of letters are more stone dead, so it would seem, than those who flourished a hundred years ago: most prominently and prolifically Andrew Lang, Edmund Gosse, and George Saintsbury. Yet the last of these has been the recipient of two tributes from modern men of letters with whom one doesn't like to disagree. T. S. Eliot dedicated *Homage to John Dryden* to him (Saintsbury himself wrote a still lively book on Dryden), praised his mighty edition of the Caroline poets, and remarked in passing that his *History of Criticism* was "always delightful, generally useful, and most often right." And in two short appreciations of Saintsbury, Edmund Wilson went further, calling him the sole full-length English professional critic of the late-nineteenth and early-twentieth centuries who was of first-rate stature (Wilson mentions Leslie Stephen as possibly another). Moreover Wilson directed attention where it should be directed—to Saintsbury as a writer who had created his own style and "personal rhythm," "a modern conversational prose that carries off asides, jokes and gossip." Wilson found charming and irresistible the way that style conveyed judgments about writers and their work: it was like eating peanuts, he confessed.

Wilson's remarks are now half a century old, and his expressed hope that some of Saintsbury's books would be made available in reprints has not come to pass. At present—with the exception of a few expensive items for libraries—Saintsbury is not to be found. It follows that he is unheard of by students and by many of their professors, certainly the younger ones whose assumption is, anyway, that criticism should be *hard,* reading it like eating not peanuts but the shells. What Wilson found impressive and engaging was Saintsbury's ability to read and criticize for their own sake innumerable English and French writers, especially such minor ones as George Crabbe or George Borrow or Thomas Peacock or William Cowper. Most academics today wouldn't be caught dead practicing such a nontheoretical leisure-class activity (though

"King of Critics": George Saintsbury, 1845–1933, by Dorothy Richardson Jones. University of Michigan Press, 1992.

they might indulge themselves in a film or two) since such reading would stem from no more than a desire to appreciate "disinterestedly." And as we all know, disinterested reading has gone the way of the telegraph and slide rule.

Dorothy Richardson Jones, a professor emerita from Queens College, is of a generation that, in its undergraduate and graduate study of literature, was sent often to Saintsbury's histories and surveys and to his articles in the *Cambridge History of English Literature* on periods, prosody, and poets. She wrote her doctoral dissertation on the man way back in 1938; now she has given us a full, sympathetic, and not uncritical survey, in the old-fashioned sense, of Saintsbury's career in its large outlines and of the formidable array of books he produced over the course of a life of eighty-eight years. She confesses to having read all of his signed and a good portion of his unsigned writings (more than a hundred volumes, Saintsbury estimated), "something no one will do in the 1990's," she quite rightly remarks. This enormous production presents a real problem to a biographer (W. E. Henley called the articles on French writers that Saintsbury produced for the ninth edition of the *Britannica* in themselves "the labor of an ordinary lifetime").

How much time should be spent describing and summarizing the contents of books most of which Professor Jones's (few) readers won't have read? And what is to be made of a man's life spent virtually in reading and writing? Professor Jones sees this overwhelming literary activity as Saintsbury's way of practicing a "life-long habit of evasion and escape from reality into literary fantasy and dreams." Although he married and fathered two children, neither his wife (who became an invalid) nor his sons seem to have touched him in the way books did.

At Oxford Saintsbury's academic hopes were dimmed when he received a second in "Greats" and failed to win a fellowship. There followed a decade of headmastering at less than top-rank schools, after which, in 1877, he settled in London and began the long parade of articles, reviews, and books. His early writing includes, among so much else, a history of French literature, the *Britannica* articles on French writers, and prefaces and bibliographical notes to the forty-volume English edition of Balzac's *Comédie humaine*. Professor Jones says that, compared to Saintsbury's commentaries on French literature, Matthew Arnold's essays on the subject seem restricted, lacking range and depth (Saintsbury later wrote a book on Arnold). He helped make French literature accessible to students—even though he had little sympathy with any writer subsequent to Baudelaire, indeed with literature written after 1880—

and he did much editing and translating of French works. Professor Jones describes his life as a "hardworking journalist"—Saintsbury's words about himself as subeditor of the *Saturday Review:* "It staggers the imagination to picture those crowded days and nights—the editorial work with long days and a long walk home, the steady flow of book packets for review after long nights of reading while the more lasting work for essays, prefaces, and surveys was also going on."

In 1895 Saintsbury accepted the chair in English at the University of Edinburgh, taking over from Milton's biographer David Masson. In his first academic year he delivered 150 lectures and continued, for twenty years, to lecture (without notes), grade papers and examinations, and administer with "an absolute and prompt conscientiousness" (in his biographer's words) his other academic chores. During his tenure at Edinburgh, Saintsbury produced his longest, most notable books, including the three-volume *History of Criticism and Literary Taste in Europe,* the equally thick three-volume *History of English Prosody* (and its accompanying *Historical Manual of English Prosody*), and his *History of English Prose Rhythm.* These enormous labors were accomplished without the aid of sabbaticals, Guggenheim grants, or other emoluments.

In the histories, as in his previous books, Saintsbury's critical "method" was scarcely that. Professor Jones defines it as "impressionistic, appreciative criticism, full of personal enthusiasm . . . regulated by the use of historical knowledge for constant comparisons." In his rewriting of Arnold's famous dictum, Saintsbury defined criticism as "the endeavour to find, to know, to love, to recommend, not only the best, but all the good, that has been known and thought and written in the world." And he spoke of his critical practice as "an endless process of correcting impressions—or at least checking and auditing them till we are sure that they are genuine, coordinated, and . . . consistent." One sees what T. S. Eliot would have admired in this sort of practice (comparison and analysis are the tools of the critic, said Eliot) as well as why current fashion should find it irrelevant or worse.

In a life so free of cataclysmic events and personal horrors as Saintsbury's, the human details, when they come, stand out vividly. He was as overachieving a walker as he was a reader and scholar: twenty-five to thirty miles on an average day (can this really be?) until in his forties he broke a bone in his foot. As for reading—"*Pickwick,* Peacock, *Wuthering Heights, The Antiquary,* Southey's *The Doctor,* Jane Austen, Thackeray, and so forth, all these he *reread* once a year; the *Earthly Paradise* he read twenty times with unfading delight;

Gulliver a hundred times; three hundred volumes of Gautier; all of the *Anti-Jacobin*; *The Anatomy of Melancholy* read twice through (it was 'not easy')." And there is the legend about his habit of reading a French novel before breakfast. He never stayed in bed after 8:00 A.M. and retired as late as 2:00 A.M., but he once remarked to Sir Herbert Grierson that he never worked after dinner. Grierson replied, "I often read a good deal then," to which Saintsbury retorted, with who knows what degree of mischief, "I do not regard reading as work."

There was also his wine cellar to keep up. Saintsbury's *Notes on a Cellar Book* not only classifies the wines but contains a commendable defense of gin. (Kingsley Amis's *On Drink* is an excellent descendant of Saintsbury's cellar book.) Speaking of these "defenses" against doubt and depression, Professor Jones says they were compounded of "the drive for omniscience, hard work, aesthetic enjoyment of beauty, wine, foods, the vicarious life of fiction, the retreat into past literature, and religious and political dogmatism" (he was Anglican and High Tory). It would take a sterner analyst than I to decide that Saintsbury really missed out on the more important aspects of life.

Edmund Wilson thought that *The Peace of the Augustans*—the superb guide to eighteenth-century writers that Saintsbury produced after he retired from Edinburgh—was the best introduction to his work. That seems reasonable, and a curious reader might go on to dip into the histories of prosody, criticism, and prose rhythm, looking at what Saintsbury has to say about particular writers (try the pages on Burke in *Prose Rhythm*, on Blake's *Poetical Sketches* in *Prosody*, on the Wartons in *Criticism*). But my own favorite passage in what I've read of him (a great deal less than Dorothy Richardson Jones) occurs in some brief remarks about teaching ("On the Teaching of English," in *George Saintsbury: The Memorial Volume*) to which Professor Jones doesn't refer. There he argues that lectures should be extempore, not written out, and should consist of "the continuous reading and commenting of texts" rather than airier disquisitions on more abstract matters. He sums up as follows:

> The absolutely ideal literary lecture or schoolhour would be the utterance of what the lecturer or master himself experiences when he reads some good verse or prose for the first time—a little "diluted," so to say, so as to bring it within the range of less trained organisms. The pleasure which he feels at the perfection of expression, the critical doubt at its imperfection; the slight effort of memory needed to recall allusions or facts; the more serious intellectual exertion to explain difficulties and enlighten obscuri-

ties; the further reminiscence of passages in other writers which this recalls; the recognition of idiosyncrasy and felicity in rhythm and metre and
style—all this should be, as it were, extruded from the teacher's own
progress of thought and feeling, and thrown in spoken phantasmagoria
on a screen for the audience's consideration.

Saintsbury admits that nobody but a literary archangel could do this perfectly,
but insists that, still, it can be done: "And if anybody cannot do it at all, he has
no business to be a teacher of English." I should like to think that, with such a
challenge laid down, Saintsbury hasn't dated at all and that we very much need
him today.

American Scholar, Autumn 1993

Santayana's Legacy

I presume I was not the only undergraduate who, having misplaced the religious faith of his youth, turned to philosophy as a hopeful substitute. It was not so much to "philosophy," as to the possibility that some figure from the recent past (Aristotle, Spinoza, and Kant were too far away) might be discovered who could provide sagelike guidance on matters of intimate and ultimate concern: on first principles; the problem of substance; the essence of things. By the time I graduated from college and had submitted to the inclinations of my philosophy teachers, I had found not one but three sages who in their different ways spoke to what I thought I needed. There was William James, with his psychology, his fresh ways of thinking about truth and meaning, about "thinking"; there was John Dewey, to whom I looked for instruction in social consciousness (that never panned out); and, most elusive and most intimidating to me, there was George Santayana, guide to the Life of Reason and the Realms of Being. Santayana's prose was as richly authoritative as any I had read since the King James Bible or the Book of Common Prayer, and was as aesthetic, as literary as anyone could wish for. Many of his books were out of print, but—in addition to libraries—the bookstores in Boston and Northampton, Massachusetts, were well stocked with second-hand copies of those handsome maroon Scribner's editions. For as little as $1.50 you might come home with a copy of *Winds of Doctrine* or *Soliloquies in England* or *Interpretations of Poetry and Religion* or *Scepticism and Animal Faith* (the titles themselves beckoned invitingly). As the years passed these books continued to look good on my shelf, and from time to time I even took one of them down to read, pretending momentarily to be still a student of philosophy.

Today's students, at least the ones I've observed, have simply not heard of Santayana, a consequence of their teachers' not making him known. (Evidently he does not have the requisite rigor, is too "exquisite" to pass as philosophy, while English teachers have other, mostly Continental fish to fry from the great world of theory.) John McCormick in his fine new biography claims that the neglect of Santayana "accompanies a growing consensus" that he was

George Santayana, by John McCormick. Alfred A. Knopf, 1987.

a great man—but I have seen no indication of such a consensus. The publication, concurrent with Mr. McCormick's biography, of Santayana's three-volume memoir, *Persons and Places,* in a single 760-page "critical edition," is a welcome event that inaugurates the MIT Press's promised edition of the complete works. But this scholarly monument to its subject may end up in libraries only, unvisited except for the occasional researcher.[1] And, like the fate T. S. Eliot said had been Ben Jonson's ("to be damned by the praise that quenches all desire to read the book; to be afflicted by the imputation of the virtues which excite the least pleasure; and to be read only by historians and antiquaries—this is the most perfect conspiracy of approval"), Santayana's acceptance as a magisterial writer of "beautiful" prose may be as deadly.

If Santayana continues to be unread it will not be for John McCormick's lack of trying to reverse the situation. His introduction sets an admirable tone for the book to follow when he says that, although he is interested in correcting recent and wrongful neglect of Santayana and in placing him historically, his "first and enduring motives were delight in his character and in his eloquence, agreement with his naturalistic philosophy, and joy at the prospect of a man of his stature who refused to puff himself and forbade others to pound the Santayana drum." It is evident that McCormick derives intense pleasure from reading his man:

> Some philosophers can bring a smile, William James and Ludwig Wittgenstein among them. Some, like Nietzsche, terrify, although not for the reasons he thought he was terrifying. Only Santayana can make me laugh aloud. Insofar as a biographer can determine, he was a happy man and his happiness was contagious. . . . He was not elusive but fastidious, one whose distinctions were subtle but wonderfully available, and not only to specialists.

I don't recall ever having laughed aloud while reading Santayana, but in the course of reading the biography I picked up *Egotism in German Philosophy,* an

1. *Persons and Places: Fragments of Autobiography,* by George Santayana, edited by William G. Holzberger and Herman J. Saatkamp, Jr., with an introduction by Richard C. Lyon, MIT Press, 1987. Santayana's autobiography used to be available in three small Scribner's volumes. The new edition, with a valuable introduction by Richard Lyon, is approved by the MLA's committee on scholarly editions, which means it is edited within an inch of its life. Two hundred of its 761 pages are taken up with notes and textual commentary, discussions of adopted readings, lists of emendations and substantive variants. The index seems to me absurd: the word "Life" is followed by page references to categories such as "academic," "and art," "his attitude toward," and on through some forty-five more, including "sunny side of" and "happiest moments of."

elegant, sardonic analysis of the subject published during the First World War while Santayana was in England. Here is the opening paragraph of the third chapter, "Transcendentalism":

> Fichte called Locke the worst of philosophers, but it was ungrateful of him, seeing that his own philosophy was founded on one of Locke's errors. It was Locke who first thought of looking into his own breast to find there the genuine properties of gold and of an apple; and it is clear that nothing but lack of consecutiveness and courage kept him from finding the whole universe in the same generous receptacle. This method of looking for reality in one's own breast, when practised with due consecutiveness and courage by the Germans became the transcendental method; but it must be admitted that the German breast was no longer that anatomical region which Locke had intended to probe, but a purely metaphysical point of departure, a migratory ego that could be here, there, and everywhere at once, being present at any point from which thought or volition might be taken to radiate. It was no longer so easy to entrap as the soul of Locke, which he asserted travelled with him in his coach from London to Oxford.

My knowledge of Fichte doesn't extend beyond a categorizing label or two, but I have read enough Locke to savor that deadpan final sentence about his soul, and I can delight in Santayana's evocation and expansion of the German breast into a surveyor of the cosmos. This delight is centrally a matter of suppleness of rhythm, aptness of image, and a wry, flexible tone of discourse. Such a masterly exposition *must* be saying something true about Fichte—or so my nonspecialist perception told me; and I had similarly approving and non-specialist responses to the pages on Kant and Hegel, Schopenhauer and Nietzsche from the same book.

Santayana's hospitality to readers who think of themselves as mainly—in that old-fashioned term—"literary" is indicated by the fact that Mr. McCormick teaches comparative literature at Rutgers and has written extensively about fiction. It may be true that, not being a philosopher himself, he doesn't give us a sufficient account of what the *Times* book reviewer called the "professional controversies" in which Santayana engaged—though the six-hundred-odd pages of this thick book, many of them devoted to Santayana's writings, will be found sufficient by most readers. The reviewer's other complaint—that McCormick is too adulatory of Santayana and that he fails to "make the philosophy clear"—seems to me quite off the mark. Most certainly he writes as a long-term admirer of the books; but as for making the philosophy "clear," that is surely not the point. We don't read Santayana and then, puzzled, go to some commentary to find out what he was really saying, what his "philosophy" or "thought" consisted of—any more than we read Proust or Shakespeare, then look up some critic to clear away our difficulties with them. In fact, McCormick's painstaking accounts of the five volumes of Santayana's early *The Life of Reason* and of the four which make up the later *Realms of Being* (along with its introductory marvel, *Scepticism and Animal Faith*) were for me the least engrossing parts of the book. Paraphrasing someone whose language is as delicately itself as Santayana's figures to be a less than rewarding occupation (McCormick himself in his introduction admits that "to paraphrase Santayana is to butcher him"). As with Proust or Shakespeare, the reader would be better advised to pick up the original and go to work. But McCormick makes us want to read or reread the books, which is what counts.

Santayana's memoir has already familiarized us with his childhood, divided between Avila with his Spanish father, and Boston where he lived with his mother and half-siblings. His days at Boston Latin School and as a Harvard undergraduate provide some of the memoir's best writing, especially for me in the account of his economic and domestic arrangements as a freshman living on the ground floor of Hollis Hall in Harvard Yard:

> the rent was forty-four dollars a year. . . . It was so cheap because the cellar below might increase the cold or the dampness. I don't think I was ever cold there in a way to disturb me or affect my health. I kept the hard-coal fire banked and burning all night, except from Saturday to Monday, when I slept at my mother's in Roxbury. . . . As to my lodging, I had to make up my sofa-bed at night before getting into it . . . I also had to fetch my coal and water from the cellar, or the water in summer from the College pump that stood directly in front of my door.

With his "less than a dollar a day" spending money, he managed nonetheless to "dress decently, to belong to minor societies like the Institute, the Pudding, and the O.K. . . . to buy all the necessary books, and even, in my Junior year, to stay at rich people's houses, and to travel." (He goes on to confess, unashamedly, that a friend provided him with a set of old evening clothes so that those rich people's houses could be visited.) By the time he graduated summa cum laude, he had joined eleven different organizations, had studied with Josiah Royce and William James, and had written some seventy-five poems. After studying in Germany and traveling to Paris and Avila, he handed in his doctoral dissertation—three years after graduation—on Lotze, then settled in for twenty-three years of teaching in Harvard's department of philosophy. In that stretch, as with his later sojourn in England during and after World War I, or his last twenty-odd years in Rome, little occurred to disturb the even tenor of his ways. He produced his books at an astonishing rate, with no decline in freshness and never a touch of spirit-weariness.

Apropos of those teaching years at Harvard, McCormick is extremely interesting on the relations between Santayana and William James. He usefully corrects the notion that all James saw in his pupil's philosophy was—in James's too colorful phrase from a letter to his colleague George Herbert Palmer—the "perfection of rottenness." Santayana had admiringly reviewed James's *Psychology* the year after it came out in 1890, and ten years later James, in the letter to Palmer, began his discussion of *Interpretations of Poetry and Religion* by saying that "The great event in my life recently has been the reading of Santayana's book." James meant the phrase "perfection of rottenness" to apply to Santayana's philosophy, but others, like President Charles Eliot, thought the rot went deeper. (Eliot referred—in a letter to Hugo Münsterberg, another colleague in philosophy—to Santayana's way of life as "abnormal," which McCormick takes to be code for homosexual.)

Santayana once insisted to James that apart from temperament, they were closer than James believed. McCormick points to their both being cosmopolitan (each wrote French well—Santayana wrote and spoke it "to perfection"), to their shared reservations about the teaching of philosophy at Harvard (it was moralistic and lacked the Platonic and Catholic tradition), and to their common rebelliousness toward logic and the exalting of "technical" methodology. Both were committed, however differently, to literary ways of writing philosophy (McCormick argues that Santayana was influenced by James); both were humorous but also passionate in their way of taking the things they cared about. When *The Life of Reason* was published in 1905, James called it (in a letter to Dickinson Miller) "Emerson's first rival and successor" and a "great" book, though he found "something profoundly alienating" in Santayana's tone. In a letter to James in response, Santayana took a lively jab at Emerson who, he said, might "pipe his wood-notes and chirp at the universe most blandly," but whose "tender" and "profound" genius was certainly not Santayana's. The latter felt that no one including James had caught what was deepest in his book—the *tears* ("*Sunt lachrimae rerum, et mentem mortalia tangunt*") that he shed not for the lost past but for the lost ideal, the "vision of perfection" which was so elusive. He ends the fascinating letter by saying to

James, "I seldom write to any one so frankly as I have here. But I know you are human, and tolerant to anything, however alien, that smells of blood." Surely that was the right note to strike.

Like Socrates he was fond of the youth, very fond, especially when they were good-looking. When in the 1940s Ezra Pound forced himself on Santayana's attention in hopes of luring him into writing a book (along with himself and T. S. Eliot) that would reform American education, a visit from Pound was surely improved by the fact that Santayana found him to be "taller, younger, better-looking than I had expected." His earlier letter to Guy Murchie, a Harvard undergraduate friend who had conceived the odd idea that he (Murchie) wanted to get married, is an embarrassing classic of single-sex special pleading: "And besides I think marriage for you extremely risky. . . . It is hard for a young man like you to distinguish the charm of a particular woman from that of women in general. . . . If you could weather this storm, the very experience would strengthen you and enlighten you for the future. . . ." No humor there, nor is it there in Santayana's poetry, which is rhythmically conventional and perfectly boring ("Cape Cod" is an exception). The biographer is forthright in calling it a pastiche of dictions that falls short of "genuine" art. Santayana never came to terms with the poetry of this century: except for his sudden and surprising warming, late in life, to Lowell's *Lord Weary's Castle*, his approval of *Georgian Poetry 1911–12* was the last of such he bestowed.

There is no room to go into here what the biography goes into very interestingly—Santayana's conservatism and his anti-Semitism. He wrote Sidney Hook in 1934 that he loved order "in the sense of organized, harmonious, consecrated living"; for that reason, he said, rather too candidly, "I sympathize with the Soviets and the Fascists and the Catholics, but not at all with the Liberals." He went on to add that he would sympathize with the Nazis too if their system were founded on reality rather than on "will . . . therefore a sort of romanticism gone mad, rather than a serious organization of material forces." As for the anti-Semitism, it can be understood in part as yet another example of a widespread attitude among English literary people: McCormick lists Carlyle, Trollope, Meredith, Virginia Woolf ("How I hated marrying a Jew," wrote Woolf to her beloved Ethyl Smyth, "how I hated their oriental jewellery, and their noses and their wattles"). He could have added D. H. Lawrence, and this is to stop short of the Eliot–Pound–Wyndham Lewis team. But however one tries to explain it historically or biographically— Santayana grew up in the Spanish Catholic Church with its anti-Semitic catechism, and in Boston where Jews were disliked as much as the Irish and the Italians—the prejudice is, in McCormick's works, "scarcely comprehensible" emanating from the author of *The Life of Reason*. We are used to "understanding" Pound as a zealot, half-baked on various issues; Santayana should have been taken in by no such immoderate, vulgar prejudice.

It is with relief that we hear him speaking about America rather, and what was wrong with it. The following sentence from a letter of 1927 is more eloquent even than anything in his essay "The Genteel Tradition in America": "It is veneer, rouge, aestheticism, arts museums, new theatres, etc. that make America impotent. The good things are football, kindness and jazz bands." He was soft on athletics and athletes: back in his early days as a Harvard instructor he had to apologize to President Eliot for dereliction of duty when he proctored exams for the Harvard crew at New Haven. As for jazz bands, one wonders what he had in mind—early King Oliver perhaps? At any rate the sentiment is commendable.

Santayana moved somewhat in the Bloomsbury orbit during post–World War I years, enough at least to get invited to Lady Ottoline Morrell's, where he noted what he called Bertrand Russell's "romance" with the lady, and enough to decide that he loathed Lytton Strachey (nobody who loathed Strachey can be judged too severely). Upon reading Clive Bell's *What Is Art?* with its catchword notion of the essence of art as "significant form," he henceforth referred to him as "the tinkling Bell." As early as 1921 Desmond McCarthy, Bloomsbury's omnipurpose reviewer, called Santayana "the greatest of all living critics." But the fullest case for his importance as a literary critic came from very much of a non-Bloomsbury affiliate, none other than Q. D. Leavis, whose *Scrutiny* appreciation of him in 1935 (when she also reviewed his novel, *The Last Puritan*) made a good case for his valuable service. *Scrutiny* found few critics outside their own fold who could be recommended to students of literature, and Santayana was not only named one of them but invited to write for the magazine. He did, publishing his "Tragic Philosophy" in 1936, which then became the occasion for a lively corrective of him by F. R. Leavis (Santayana didn't quite understand how it wasn't "Shakespeare" who spoke, "Out, out, brief candle!" but Macbeth, a dramatic character in Shakespeare's play).

Q. D. Leavis's praise of Santayana was echoed in this magazine thirty years ago by Marvin Mudrick, who called his work "the most comprehensive, the most penetrating, and the most consistently satisfying text of literary criticism originated by any philosophic mind since Coleridge" ("The Life of Reason,"

Santayana's Legacy

The Hudson Review, Vol. X, No. 2, Summer 1957). The places to go to check this for its truth are to the essay on Whitman and Browning ("The Poetry of Barbarism," in *Interpretations of Poetry and Religion*) and the essay on Shelley (in *Winds of Doctrine*). There is the essay on Dickens in *Soliloquies in England* and—though less importantly so, I think—essays on Shakespeare to be found in various places. There is also *Three Philosophical Poets*, from which the chapter on Lucretius is preeminent. But really, if "literary critic" means some-body who writes a lot, and saliently, about literature, then I don't think Santayana has a place—along with Pound and Eliot—in the group of what Mudrick called "the three outstanding literary critics of our language in our century." (I'm not sure Pound belongs there either.) Better to think of "literary critic" as someone who writes penetratingly, with fully expressive resources, about other writers, whether or not they have composed poems, novels, dra-mas. Such criticism in Santayana's case would consist prominently of the aforementioned *Egotism in German Philosophy*; of the masterly *Character and Opinion in the United States*, with its brilliant chapter on William James; or of the moving tribute to Spinoza in the address delivered at The Hague in 1932 ("Ultimate Religion," in *Obiter Scripta*). Moving along the line from criticism to, in Richard Rorty's phrase, "philosophy as a kind of writing," there are the belletristic pleasures of *Soliloquies in England*, and the challenging dialectics of *Scepticism and Animal Faith*, dialectics which—as John Dewey said rightly in his admiring review of the book—are comparable to F. H. Bradley's. And this is to ignore much, and to say nothing of systematic attempts to say it all in the *Life of Reason* and *Realms* books. Santayana himself remarked, in *Scepticism and Animal Faith*, that "The whole of British and German philosophy is only literature." Exactly the same thing may be said about his own writings, espe-cially if we give due prominence to the ambiguities of "only" and "literature."

It is astonishing to hear from Mr. McCormick that *The Last Puritan* quickly sold 148,000 copies in America and was on the best-seller lists for several weeks. It is a book that, try as I may, I can't seem to make my way through. But Santayana doesn't need or ask to be read whole; one can be a sampler, in the best sense of that activity, and come away from even a brief visit fortified with some new way of putting things, or an old way one had forgotten about. Nobody can read him now without thinking of Wallace Stevens's "To an Old Philosopher in Rome," which the biographer quotes entire at the very end of his book (the effect is even finer than when Stevens's poem is read by itself):

So that we feel, in this illumined large,
The veritable small, so that each of us
Beholds himself in you, and hears his voice
In yours, master and commiserable man,
Intent on your particles of nether-do . . .

The poem's final stanza beautifully captures the self-generated, wholly finished nature of the "old philosopher's" work of a lifetime:

Total grandeur of a total edifice,
Chosen by an inquisitor of structures
For himself. He stops upon this threshold
As if the design of all his words takes form
And frame from thinking and is realized.

Hudson Review 39, no. 3 (Autumn 1987). Copyright © 1987 by the Hudson Review, Inc. Reprinted by permission.

Henry Mencken's Prejudices

I have come late to Mencken. His name was infrequently, if ever, sounded in English classrooms of the 1950s, for by that time he had pretty much disappeared as a force in literary criticism. The cerebral thrombosis he suffered in 1948 left him without the ability to read or write, though he lingered on for almost eight years, cared for by his brother, August. But well before 1948 his influence had waned, and not merely because of his opposition to Roosevelt and World War II. In 1928, T. S. Eliot began a discussion of Irving Babbitt's humanism by noting that "It is proverbially easier to destroy than to construct," and adducing Mencken as a critic whose "brilliant attack" was mounted against "aspects of contemporary society which we know and dislike." Thus Mencken's popularity had to do with the familiarity both of his targets and of the terms in which he criticized them. "But there are more serious critics than Mr. Mencken," declared Mr. Eliot in his most churchwardenly manner. By the 1950s, of course, English professors had caught up to Eliot, sort of, and his pronouncements had all the prestige Mencken's lacked.

So Mencken was classified and condescended to as a journalist (as if the many pieces written to deadline by Eliot were something else!) and a dogmatic one at that, whose judgments had not worn well. In his study of modern literary critics, *The Armed Vision* (1948), Stanley Edgar Hyman devoted a paragraph to Mencken in the midst of an unfriendly chapter about Yvor Winters. He saw Mencken as someone, like Winters and like Ezra Pound (but on a lower, "journalistic" level) whose specialty was dogmatic evaluation. Hyman proceeded to devalue Mencken by producing some of his more unconvincing judgments—especially his admiration for the poetry of Lizette Reese—as indications of a lack of literary credentials. In fact, Mencken's early *A Book of Prefaces* contains essays on Conrad and Dreiser that deserve to be called pioneering and are still well worth reading; but out of excessive respect for critics, or out of mere laziness, I never until recently got round to seeing for myself. Thus the publication of this diary, recorded between 1930 and 1948, has provided a much-too-long-delayed entry into the world of a remarkable writer.

The Diary of H. L. Mencken, edited by Charles A. Fecher. Alfred A. Knopf, 1989.

Mencken's six volumes of short essays are titled *Prejudices,* an apt identification of the principal aspect of his critical mind. In a diary entry of 1939, he speaks to the matter without using the word itself:

> It has . . . been assumed on frequent occasions that I have some deeplying reformatory purpose in me. This is completely nonsensical. It always distresses me to hear of a man changing his opinions, so I never seek conversions. My belief is that every really rational man preserves his major opinions unchanged from his youth onward. When he vacillates it is simply a sign that he is stupid. My one purpose in writing I have explained over and over again: it is simply to provide a kind of katharsis for my own thoughts. They worry me until they are set forth in words. This may be a kind of insanity, but at all events it is free of moral purpose.

One could term this statement a prejudice in favor of prejudice. The year after Mencken published his first volume of *Prejudices,* Robert Frost declared, in a vein Mencken might have admired, that "I'd no more set out in pursuit of the truth than I would in pursuit of a living unless mounted on my prejudices." Mencken's "really rational man" is in fact a creature of prejudices, acquired early on and stubbornly adhered to over the years. Such ideas of persistence and adherence crop up in moments when a writer attempts to take stock of where he stands on "ultimate" matters, as when John Updike (in his memoir "The Dogwood Tree: A Boyhood") considers his childhood beliefs in the infinite radiance of art: "How innocent! But his assumption here, like his assumptions on religion and politics, is one for which I have found no certain substitute." Updike puts it delicately, but what he puts forth is—like Mencken's and Frost's declarations—a radically conservative assertion which marks a corresponding temperament.

One sees other marks of such a temperament in the above diary entry. There is Mencken's disclaimer of any moral purpose in what he writes, as well as the insistence—surely an overinsistence—that any "vacillation" where major opinions are concerned is "simply" a sign of stupidity and that his purpose in writing is "simply" cathartic. This is the mode of utterance of a man (and Mencken is always very much a "man") who has followed, so it seems to him, Dr. Johnson's directive to Boswell: "Clear your *mind* of cant." Johnson said that it was all right to *talk* cant (signing a letter "your humble servant" when you were not the recipient's humble servant) but not to think that way. Mencken tried not to talk that way either, so when a neighbor's dog became a nuisance he wrote the neighbor an un-cantish letter:

Henry Mencken's Prejudices

Dear Charlie:

Your dog barked yesterday from about 5.30 p.m. to 7 or thereabout. I called up your house but got no answer; apparently there was no one home. As a result of this uproar I had to abandon some important work on which I was engaged. Such interruptions to my work cost me money, and disturbances of my rest, at my age, are dangerous to my health. I have been aroused from sleep as early as 6.45 a.m. and as late as 12.30 midnight.

I must ask you once more to stop this nuisance. So long as your sister was living I remembered her plea that she felt insecure in the house without the dog. But that reason is now gone. I am therefore trusting you either to teach your dog to stop disturbing the neighborhood or to get a dog less noisy.

"Charlie" (who is later characterized, in the diary entry, as a "complete moron") didn't answer the letter. But the barking subsided.

Readers who have heard about Mencken's diary only through the newspaper publicity surrounding its publication are likely to associate his "prejudices" wholly with his attitudes toward Jews and (in the current phrase) people of color. There's no doubt that Mencken had a fair amount of what Pound called (in reference to his own anti-Semitism) "the cheap suburban prejudice," and that his attitudes toward Negroes were condescending to say the least. (During the years Mencken kept his diary I was growing up in upstate New York and hearing much the same sort of thing from people less interesting than Mencken.) One could argue that a good writer and an important critic who tried to clear his mind of cant should have been harder on his assumptions about race. But in fact some of the people who make noise about Mencken's bigotry are harder to put up with than the bigot himself.[1] Another way to look at the matter is to say that when, in his diary, Mencken remarks

---

1. In this connection, a letter to the *Washington Post* (Jan. 12, 1990) by Doris Grumbach counted twenty-four anti-Semitic references in the published diary, while opining that there must have been many more in the unpublished parts. Grumbach concluded that anyone not offended by these references possessed "an antisemitic sensibility." In reply, two letters defended Mencken, not just by invoking the old line that some of his best friends—like Alfred Knopf and George Jean Nathan— were Jews, but that he had spoken out, in the 1930s, in favor of opening the borders of this country and others so as to admit German Jews. One of the letter writers, himself a Jew, said that Grumbach was free to denounce Mencken the public writer for his private anti-Semitism, but that she had no business condemning *him*, the letter-writer, for possessing "an antisemitic sensibility"—thus doing her own name-calling in public. He concluded by quoting Mencken: "All persons who devote themselves to forcing virtue on their fellow men deserve nothing better than a kick in the pants." I found this a satisfying response to Doris Grumbach's virtue.

that so-and-so is a "clever Jew" or that "it is impossible to talk anything resembling discretion or judgment into a colored woman," he has—in addition to embracing stereotypes—lost his sense of humor. Much of the good writing in this diary, as it sets forth the strong opinions of a man who doesn't change his mind, is instinct with humor. Like the Twain whom he so much admired and the Frost whose humor he underestimated ("sour resignationism" was what he saw in that "standard New England poet"), Mencken is one of the authentic humorists in American letters. The humor is very dry indeed and recalls Frost's observation that dry humor is the kind "that doesn't seem to appreciate itself." Mencken is good at playing this game, especially given the temptation that a diary (composed partly with posterity in mind) presents to an over-appreciating of one's own bon mots.

Some examples: there is the flat recitation of a remark about William Randolph Hearst, passed on to Mencken from someone else: "Hearst married a prostitute, and then gradually dragged her down to his own level." After lunch with F. Scott Fitzgerald, Mencken notes that Fitzgerald went to Paris with the notion of accumulating "new experience" for his novels. "Unfortunately," writes Mencken, "Fitzgerald is a heavy drinker, and most of his experience has been got in bars." An evening with T. S. Eliot left him less than thrilled: "An amiable fellow, but with little to say. He told me that his father was a brick manufacturer in Missouri. . . . I drank a quart of home-brew beer, and Eliot got down two Scotches. A dull evening." (One would have liked to have listened in on that dullness.) On a trip with Joseph Hergesheimer through the Pennsylvania-Dutch territory around Lancaster, Mencken confides that they "passed through towns of such astonishing names as Blue Ball, Bird-in-Hand, and Intercourse. How Intercourse got its name no one knows. The place attracts a great many automobile tourists [it certainly did yours truly] who stop off to send out postcards." And one is hardly surprised, though still pleased, to hear Mencken identify someone as probably a Christian Scientist, since "He had the calm, complacent air peculiar to the brethren, and the pale, somewhat pasty complexion."

On occasion he decides to give an episode full-dress treatment, as in a portrait of his recently dead friend Max Brödel, an anatomical artist at the Johns Hopkins School of Medicine and a fellow member of the Saturday Night Club, a group of amateur music-lovers who met for weekly performances and conviviality (Mencken played the piano, it seems quite expertly). Mencken and a professor of biology named Raymond Pearl are discussing, one night "at the beer-table," the matter of sexual intercourse, which Brödel suggests is overrated since it only lasts about a minute. Mencken and Pearl are dumfounded by this and they question Brödel further:

> The more we cross-examined him the plainer it became that he actually believed what he had said. When Pearl argued that any man who entertained a lady for so little as two minutes was guilty of a gross offense, not only against her person but against the peace and dignity of the human race, it was Max's turn to be astonished. He had simply never heard that copulation could be prolonged at will—at all events, far beyond the limits he had set. . . . On the heels of this grotesque discussion Pearl announced the founding of an organization to be called the Society for More and Better Fucking in the Home.

This could have been ruined by heavy-handed yucking and jeering; Mencken finds just the right mix of tones and diction—from "the peace and dignity of the human race" to "More and Better Fucking"—to bring it off.

He is adept also at handling "vulgar" matters in such a way that they turn into humorous art. At the annual Gridiron Club dinner in 1946 (always a bore, Mencken complained, though he always attended), he is seated at an elevated guest-table, with President Truman two places away on one side and the Duke of Windsor three places away on the other. After getting through a long stretch of the evening, during which Mencken has talked mainly to the British and Philippine ambassadors who flank him, there is at ten o'clock "a sort of seventh-inning stretch" in which "the guests all rush for the pissoirs":

> When I got to the nearest I found dignitaries lined up before each stall, with the Duke at the end of one line. Patterson, who was with me, was enchanted by this spectacle, and whooped it up as a proof of the Duke's democratic spirit. But what else could he do? The brethren ahead of him had full bladders and could not give him place. I was disinclined to get into line myself, so I started to find another pissoir. At the door I met Felix Frankfurter, who suggested that we try the cubicles opposite the stalls. It cost five cents to get into one, but the money was well spent. When I left mine I held the door open and let some other guest in on my nickel.

One hopes that Frankfurter did likewise. Earlier in the evening, Mencken reports, Frankfurter was "very attentive" and urged Mencken and the British ambassador to become friends. After Frankfurter left, the ambassador informed Mencken that he had been warned that Mencken was "anti-English" (certainly a reasonable judgment, given some of his statements) to which "I replied that this was a gross calumny, circulated by Japs." Enough said.

Mencken claimed that his only purpose in writing was to provide a catharsis for his thoughts. If one prefers to avoid cathartic talk, one might say, on the evidence of these diary entries, that he loved to put life into sentences, to state things clearly—and was committed to the idea that they could be stated clearly; never was anyone less of an anguished theorist within the prison-house of language. When in 1939 Al Capone, suffering from paresis, is admitted to the syphilitic clinic at Johns Hopkins, Mencken spends a couple of pages describing Capone's treatment, the circumstances of his admission to the clinic, Capone's temperature (as high as 106 degrees), his way of bearing discomforts ("very philosophically"), and his popularity with the hospital staff: "he is not only a good patient, he is also likely to leave large tips." In this entry we see a writer animated by nothing more than the spirit of pure curiosity: Mencken wanted to know what was happening, to himself as well as to others. As his sixtieth birthday approached in 1940, he kept close track of his physical condition (he had already suffered blood vessel spasms in the cortex) which he assumes involves sclerosis in the coronary artery: "This is an incurable condition, and I can only look forward to its gradual worsening. Thus my life-long feeling that I would probably not live much beyond sixty appears to have been well grounded." There is a disinterestedness in this way of writing about his mortal condition that makes the statement, bleak as it is, something not only he but we can take a modicum of comfort in.

Mencken's writing about women seems to me correspondingly invigorating (his early *In Defence of Women,* 1918, should be looked up). In a discussion of how all of us play parts, thus making "honest autobiography" a contradiction in terms, he speaks about the marital relation:

> Thus a man's wife, however realistic her view of him, always flatters him in the end, for the worst she sees in him is appreciably better by the time she sees it, than what is actually there. What she sees . . . is not the authentic man at all, but a compound made up in part of the authentic man and in part of his projection of a gaudy ideal. The man who is most respected by his wife is the one who makes this projection most vivid—that is, the one who is the most daring and ingratiating liar. He can never, of course, deceive her utterly, but if he is skillful he may at least deceive her enough to make her happy.

This seems to me both disenchanted and humorous to boot, so it is especially touching when the disenchanted man (his wife, Sara, having died five years previously after a marriage of only five years) looks back on their time together in a long entry of which I quote only a small part:

> Marriage is largely talk, and I still recall clearly the long palavers that we used to have. Both of us liked to work after dinner in the evening, but both of us always stopped at 10 p.m. If there were no visitors, which was usually the case, we sat in the drawing-room that she was so proud of, and had a few drinks before turning in. On Sunday nights, with the servants out, she often made supper in the kitchen, and we ate it there. We had plenty to talk of. I talked out my projects with her, and she talked out hers with me. I don't think we ever bored each other. I know that, for my part, the last days of that gabbling were as stimulating as the first. I never heard her say a downright foolish thing.

This is really to say a lot about what a good marriage feels like.

Having a few drinks before turning in, or indeed having them whenever Mencken was not working, is a pleasantly recurring theme in the diary. Early along there occurs a fine anecdote about going with Alfred Knopf to visit Bethlehem, Pennsylvania, in 1931, for a Bach festival, and trying in vain the first day to procure beer. Years later, during the war, the state of beer at New York's Luchow's restaurant is deplored ("I drank a Seidel each of the six beers on draught, and found them all bad") and, after the war, so is the lack of adequate beerhouses and drinkable draft beer in Baltimore: "*Sic transit.* The decent pleasures of life have diminished enormously in my time." All things considered, it was best to stay home where he had a cellar full of excellent wines and liquors and where he could get the best lunch to be gotten in Baltimore: "I go out relatively seldom, and have guests even seldomer. Two evenings out of three August and I have a few quiet drinks together in our living-room, and they are always first-rate drinks." If you don't warm to an observation like that last one, then Mencken is probably not your kind of writer.

As the prejudiced observer grew older, the *sic transit* note is recurrently struck, from the decline of the railroads and the Baltimore *Sunpapers* (with which he was—ever more uncomfortably—associated), to the death of friends and to what he saw as his own decline:

> My health deteriorates steadily, and anything resembling sustained work is now impossible. After my struggle with my mail in the morning I begin to feel exhausted and by noon I am beset by discomforts in the region of my heart. . . . I take a nap every afternoon before dinner, but it restores me very little, and I always awaken feeling wretched, as I do every morning on arising.

This, from 1943, is one of a number of such complaints. The death of Roosevelt, whom he despised, brought with it no satisfaction, only a melancholy deprivation, since the Baltimore saloons and restaurants closed down Saturday night out of respect for the president, whose body passed through the city at midnight: "As a result, the Saturday Night Club missed its usual post-music-beer-party for the first time in forty years." Instead he and his brother went home, "had a couple of high-balls" and went to bed. One recalls the opening of Wordsworth's "Mutability" sonnet:

> From low to high doth dissolution climb,
> And sink from high to low, along a scale
> Of awful notes, whose concord shall not fail;
> A musical but melancholy chime.

I found the melancholy chime in this diary extraordinarily affecting, since most of the time it is struck in a tone similar to the dryly humorous recitation of absurdities found in the pissoirs at the Gridiron Club. A final entry, for May 5, 1946, may provide the proper mood with which to conclude:

> After two weeks of rain, cold and high winds, today (a Sunday) opened gloomily, but by 10 a.m. the sun was shining and in the afternoon the temperature was up to 70 degrees. August and I spent the morning in the backyard. We planted morning-glory seeds, prepared the ground for the petunias that should come in from Cook the florist this week, banked the ferns with peat moss, trimmed the vines, and did a lot of other chores. I became so warm at work that I took off my coat, but in a few minutes a chilly west wind came up, and I had to put it on again. The yard never looked more lovely. The trees, the vines along the fences, and the ivy on the ground all show the bright greens of Spring, and the coleus that I have been setting out (bought in Lexington market) are flourishing. But in a little while this first blush will fade, all the greens will grow darker, and the yard will settle down for the struggle with the heat of a Baltimore summer.

A year before his stroke, he laments his diminished energy: "After three hours at my desk I must stop for rest." What a standard of performance he held himself to! Such persistence, and such a persistent love of life, for all the complaints and the contempt, may provide some nourishment for our own seasonal struggle.

F. R. Leavis (1895–1978)

The facts of Leavis's life—in the sense of colorful, humanizing events to delight the onlooker—are relatively few. Son of Harry Leavis, proprietor of a Cambridge music store ("Leavis means pianos"), he did service as a stretcher-bearer in World War I where he was mustard-gassed, his digestion permanently affected. He studied with I. A. Richards at Cambridge in the 1920s, then taught in the university as a probationary lecturer but was not offered a permanent position until 1936 (Ronald Hayman says, in his biography, that at one point there was a move on to send him to a job in Tasmania, a move which Leavis resisted). *Scrutiny* was founded in 1932 and survived until 1953, much of its copy written by Leavis and his wife, Queenie; while the books published under his name were largely composed of materials that had appeared in the magazine. Except for the D. H. Lawrence book, there was a relative falling-off, in the 1950s, of his critical productions; then at the end of the decade the notorious attack on Sir Charles Snow and the notion of "Two Cultures." Retirement from Cambridge in 1965; part-time teaching at the University of York; a spate of books of which the last appeared in 1976. Leavis liked to wear open-necked shirts, was a runner back before everybody ran, gave legendary classes in which specimens of literature were "dated," presided with his wife at comparably legendary tea-parties where visiting Americans—if vouched for— were well entertained.

I have nothing to add to the public account and little to refining the estimate of his critical achievement, but want instead to describe Leavis's impact on a young aspiring academic and, twenty-five years after the original impact, how he remains in my imagination. I never read him as an undergraduate, indeed had barely heard of his name, although I was deeply under the spell of literary criticism; for example, I had learned (from Stanley Hyman's *The Armed Vision*) that Richards, Empson, Blackmur, and Burke deserved the highest marks as critics, while Wilson, Winters, and Eliot ranked much lower, were flawed and erratic in their practice. Not until I went to graduate school at Harvard did I pick up and read Leavis's work, whereupon I discovered a new hero, a critic who stood at the very head of all the classes. There was a joke going about back then that one could succeed as an English grad student at Harvard if one took pains to be sufficiently dull, and it is true that most, though not all, of my classes were harmless and soporific, relaying information I could have picked up just as well out of standard reference books. Dull or third-rate writers were to be tolerated and appreciated "in their own terms" as the phrase went; for were we not students of literary history preparing ourselves for those moments in our Ph.D. orals when we would be asked about eighteenth-century users of the Spenserian stanza, or challenged to specify the stages of man in "Tintern Abbey," or even to name four picaresque novels and chat about their heroes?

What relation did Leavis have to that sort of thing? His sentences from "Literary Studies" in *Education and the University* made it clear to me why Harvard English was wrong:

> Literary history, as a matter of "facts about" and accepted critical (or quasi-critical) description and commentary, is a worthless acquisition; worthless for the student who cannot as a critic—that is as an intelligent and discerning reader—make a personal approach to the essential data of the literary historian, the works of literature (an approach is personal or it is nothing; you cannot take over the appreciation of a poem, and unappreciated, the poem isn't "there"). The only acquisition of literary history having any education value is that made in the exercise of critical intelligence to the ends of the literary critic. Does this need arguing?

For a rather different reason, it was not about to be argued at Harvard where, except for the example of Reuben Brower (who had studied with Leavis in the 1930s), a very different notion of "English" was current. So we hopeful critics united behind the flag of truth, and I cynically wrote "A" exams discussing Tennyson's view of this and contrasting it with Browning's attitude toward that, saving my real passion for arguments and papers about poems and novels, trying to discriminate between A and B or show that X was better than Y. (Although Harvard English didn't encourage "personal approaches" it was usually tolerant of them so long as you kept your facts straight and handed in a bibliography.)

Anchor paperbacks had just brought out *The Great Tradition* (for ninety-five cents) but Leavis was mostly unavailable in America, and I proudly opened an account at Blackwell's, ordering *New Bearings in English Poetry, Revaluation, Education and the University,* and *The Common Pursuit.* But the great experience was looking up the files of *Scrutiny* in Widener, sitting at a cubicle (the sun was shining outside, other people thought *they* were happy!) and learning the right ways to feel about all sorts of writers: Auden and Joyce and Arnold Bennett; Empson or Santayana or Richards; most of all, D. H. Lawrence. The summer I studied for my orals I remember signing out *Scrutiny* and reading issues during lunch; remember taking over verbatim Leavis's distinctions (in *Revaluation*) among Donne and Jonson and Carew, and his brilliant dispositions of minor eighteenth-century poets. Even if I hadn't read all the poems, I knew my Leavis cold. When the Lawrence book appeared I devoured it with an excitement unmatched since, and once again tried to take over the analyses of *The Rainbow* and *Women in Love*—exactly, of course, the sort of "taking over" that Leavis said one could not, in fact, do.

I don't wish to labor the point, or exult in some piously moral triumph over an earlier self. But though I was all for the unacademic virtues and thought Leavis my standard-bearer, I had precious little of those virtues—"a pioneering spirit; the courage of enormous incompleteness . . . the judgment and intuition to select drastically yet delicately, and make a little go a long way" ("A Sketch for an 'English' School"). I was enormously incomplete all right, but complacent about it too, since I had picked up lines from Leavis about Auden's limitations or Trollope's minorness or Pound's poetic lack of distinction (except for "Hugh Selwyn Mauberley") before I'd even read them, or after superficial acquaintance merely.

What finally turned things around—aside from the human condition of growing up into something more than a graduate student—was my encountering a new writer, Wyndham Lewis, whom Lawrence hadn't liked and for whom Leavis had no respect. Yet Lewis came to figure for me, despite the embarrassments of his political views, as an incomparably richer comic writer than either of them. Whatever *Women in Love* was after three or four readings, it was no longer fun; and hadn't Lawrence himself said that if it isn't any fun, don't do it? And if Leavis could be wrong about Lewis (the "brutal and boring Wyndham Lewis," he called him in the Rede lecture) maybe there were other writers he was less than right about. By the time I finally got to Cambridge, England, for a brief visit in 1964, I was writing a book about Lewis and felt too nervous to attempt an invitation to tea at the Leavises. What would I have said when he asked me my subject of concern? At that time Cambridge was filled with anti-Leavis jokes, helped along by Kingsley Amis's recent appearance on the scene. I felt guilty about that too, but contented myself with observing the great man's entry into a lecture by his old *Scrutiny* colleague, L. C. Knights.

No doubt I have followed the common pattern of the deconverted convert, too eager to find the teacher less flexible, open, or humorous than the newly liberated pupil fancies himself to be. But Leavis for all his fine moments of sardonic, dismissive irony (a sarcastic letter about A. L. Rowse speaks of "These flashes of the brilliance of All Souls—further lights on a famed civilization") was essentially a solemn passionately dedicated critic and teacher. One of his epigraphs to *The Common Pursuit*, an indispensable collection of *Scrutiny* essays, quotes a Henry James letter whose following sentence refers to more than James:

> I can't go into it all much—but the rough sense of it is that I believe only in absolutely independent, individual and lonely virtue, and in the serenely unsociable (or if need be at a pinch sulky and sullen) practice of the same: the observation of a lifetime having convinced me that no fruit ripens but under that temporarily graceless rigour.

More so than James, Leavis lived this role to the extent that serious literary people complained about his graceless behavior as a prose writer. It would be a mistake to dismiss such complaints (one of them, I remember, from Anthony Powell) too quickly, as part of that awful modern England of "the Welfare State, the Football Pools, and the literary culture of the *New Statesman* and the Third Programme" (with cinema, bingo, and the telly thrown in) Leavis so often and so predictably inveighed against. He *had* to be the practitioner of "individual and lonely virtue," more than a pinch sulky and sullen: in the words of a friend's brilliant rewriting of Hobbes's man in the State of Nature, Leavis was "solitary, poor, nasty, British and short." Yet every *trouvaille* of that sort brought with it uneasiness about sociable clubbing which produced such good jokes at the expense of absolutely independent virtue.

The many books Leavis published in his seventies, over the last ten years of his life, will not be much loved or long consulted. The endless repetitive rant against technological-Benthamite civilization, the Robbins report on Education, Lord Annan and Lord Snow; the increasing use of a bludgeoning literary jargon (its key terms "constatation," "nisus," and "*ahnung*," each of which causes my mind to go completely blank)—these are boring, even a shade brutal, and he will not be remembered for them. Yet just two years ago (in *The Living Principle*) he published an essay of some 100 pages, for me his last significant piece of literary criticism, in which he comes to terms with Eliot's *Four Quartets*, trying for one last time to express his admiration for and his

F. R. Leavis (1895–1978)

rejection of the mind, the attitude toward life and poetry—really toward the English language—expressed in that poem. Leavis wants to show why we must finally say *no* to the view of life found there, though as he had said years before in a letter to the *Spectator*, "I have always imagined myself to derive from Mr. Eliot as much as from anybody." He was right, and if in Leavis's hands the early Eliotic strategies of *The Sacred Wood* and the 1921 essays hardened into formulas, they never tried to have things more than unambiguously, nor did they mind (as Eliot came to mind) giving offense.

A few decades ago Leavisian notions of the necessity to read, discriminate, and evaluate were instrumental in saving people from becoming dutiful reporters on the development of the Elizabethan novel or some other crashingly boring phenomenon. Today when literary studies look anthropological, structuralist, linguistical, in a very bad way, and hardly critical, or literary at all, Leavis's example, his books, are more essential than ever.

New Republic, June 3, 1978

Criticism on the Record:
B. H. Haggin (1900–1987)

The death last month of B. H. Haggin, who was a music critic for *The New Republic* for many years, removed from the scene not only a great critic of music and musical performance, but also a distinguished embodiment—a throwback, one might say—of Matthew Arnold's notion of the function of criticism: "To see the object as in itself it really is." To my knowledge Bernard Haggin never referred to Arnold, but he liked to quote Bernard Shaw, whose brief career of writing about musical performances he found exemplary. Shaw gave us his version of the critic's task when he said that some people had pointed out evidences of personal feeling in his reviews "as if they were accusing me of a misdemeanor, not knowing that a criticism written without personal feeling is not worth reading. It is the capacity for making good or bad art a personal matter that makes a man a critic." But this making of art into a "personal matter" is exactly in the spirit of Arnold's praise of disinterestedness: the project of "inflexible honesty," of criticism "resolutely following the law of its own nature." In Arnold's famous though not always admired formulation, the business of criticism is "simply to know the best that is known and thought in the world." Haggin's business was to write about, to further, even to proselytize for, the best that was composed, performed, and danced in the world, and he brought to that business a single-mindedness that makes even Arnold or Shaw look diffuse, though more various, by comparison.

He conducted his critical operations for more than sixty years, beginning with early reviews in the *Brooklyn Eagle,* and coming to maturity in the eighteen years, beginning in 1939, during which he wrote about music and records for the *Nation.* He wrote the Records column for TNR from 1957 to 1966, and served further terms with the *Hudson* and *Yale* reviews. In one of his early books, *Music on Records* (1938), he defended his practice of offering personal judgments that, he admitted, set higher valuations on music by Chopin and Tchaikovsky than did "general opinion," but also set lower valuations on some of Bach and Brahms than did that same opinion. After all, he said, "if I take away with one hand it is to give with the other: if I take away some of Bach's Partitas or Brahms's Intermezzi, it is to give Chopin's Polonaises. . . . If I take away Brahms's Symphony No. 1 it is to give Tchaikovsky's Pathétique—to say nothing of Brahms's No. 4." And he added, convincingly, that the total of what he gave was more than most readers would be able to acquire for a long time—"before the end of which they will have reached the point where they will have tastes of their own, and will know whether they want to accept my judgment or reject it." In that book, and in the ones to follow—the revised *Music on Records*, *The New Listener's Companion* in its various editions, *Music and Ballet*, and his collections of reviews—he spelled out his reasons for preferring one composer, one piece of music, one recorded performance to another. Distinguishing among the best, the good, and the not-so-good work of various artists, he gave and took away; but what he gave in my case was indeed more than I was able to acquire for a long time.

The *New York Times* obituary said, rather disapprovingly, that he "worshiped certain artists, notably Arturo Toscanini, at the expense of all others." Certainly Haggin helped me pay attention to (in an often-used phrase of his) the "plastic continuity" of Toscanini's performances of Beethoven, Schubert, and Dvořák, of Haydn, Berlioz, and Verdi. But, as a pianist, I found most useful his writing about Artur Schnabel's playing of Mozart and Beethoven concertos and sonatas, and of Schubert's posthumous sonatas: about the "meditative" character of Schnabel's approach, which operated both with powerful intellect and with powerful emotion; the greatness of the playing, even as it sometimes contained technical flaws and distortions of phrase. But Haggin didn't "worship" Schnabel at the expense of all other pianists, nor did he worship Toscanini at the expense of all other conductors. He championed, though on occasion searchingly criticized, Lipatti and Cliburn and Gould, Ashkenazy and Pollini. By pointing to details in their performance of various works he helped me hear new things in the works themselves—in many cases introduced me to those works. Similar things happened with the Budapest String Quartet, and Balanchine's *Apollo*, and the quality of Bix Beiderbecke's cornet tone.

I began to read Haggin in graduate school, when I was also reading F. R. Leavis's literary criticism. Both Haggin and Leavis insisted on giving and taking away, on ranking artists and their works (in *Music on Records* Haggin divided Sibelius into The Good Works, The Lesser Works, The Poor Works, and The Worst Works). Both were heady, exhilarating fare for someone trying to get his intellectual and aesthetic bearings. Both had eventually to be resisted, and though they insisted that disagreement about a poem or a piece of music was legitimate, even necessary, it was hard to disagree with them. Soon after I met Haggin I tried to argue with his low opinion of Bach's Concerto for Violin and Oboe, but didn't get far. Just two years ago, when I wrote him about enjoying Christopher Hogwood's recordings of Mozart symphonies, he shot back with the strong suggestion that it must have been Mozart, not Hogwood, I was enjoying.

Like Leavis he was notoriously "difficult" as a person, invariably quarreling with the magazines he wrote for and intransigent about his principles. When I invited him, years ago, to lecture at Amherst, the title of his talk was, characteristically, "The Approach to Music" (not "An Approach"). And when after it a student asked whether perhaps musicology might in some cases be of some use as far as listening went, Haggin told him brusquely that no, it was not, ever. Afterward, at a carefully arranged party (once, at another party, a reckless guest had insisted on singing Puccini to him, with disastrous results), one of my colleagues praised a performance of Furtwängler's. On the way back to the inn Haggin said what a nice party it had been, but how very strange it was that this seemingly nice colleague of mine had praised the Furtwängler performance. It was the capacity for making good or bad art a personal matter that made Haggin difficult to deal with and a critic of the highest order. Randall Jarrell, whose friendship with him was one of the pleasing events in recent cultural history, once spoke of Haggin's "clear, troubled, rapturous spirit," and charged him with having "the shameless honesty of the true critic—he couldn't lie to you if he tried." The *Times* obituary stated bluntly that "there are no survivors." True indeed, and that was the way Haggin wanted it.

New Republic, July 6, 1987

The Old Buffer

Since the death of Sir William Empson in 1984, in his seventy-eighth year, various collections of his essays have appeared, the first of which, *Using Biography* (1984), he had assembled before his death. This was followed, two years later, by *Essays on Shakespeare* (edited by David Pirie) and, just last year, by three further books: *The Royal Beasts* and *Argufying* (both edited by John Haffenden) and *Faustus and the Censor* (edited by John Henry Jones), a study of Marlowe's play. I haven't the scholarly expertise to pronounce on the *Faustus* book, but, with the exception of some essays in *Using Biography,* there is little in the posthumous collections that will add significantly to Empson's critical reputation. The two books considered here are both edited by his official biographer, who has written lengthy introductions to each. *The Royal Beasts* contains early unpublished and uncollected poems and fragments, a "fable" ("The Royal Beasts"), a "plan for a ballet" ("The Elephant and the Birds"), and three stories (termed a "one-act melodrama"). Mr. Haffenden's biographical account of Empson at Cambridge—where he was dismissed after a college servant discovered contraceptives in his room and noted the visit late at night of a young woman—is of more note than the Empson items that the account is supposed to illumine. *Argufying* proves more substantial, and it is good to have these scattered pieces collected. But *Argufying* reveals, to my eyes, less of Empson the great literary critic than of a man eccentric to the point of, not madness, perhaps, but maddeningness certainly.

Of course the eccentricity was there from the outset when Empson, as a brilliant twenty-four-year-old student of I. A. Richards, brought out *Seven Types of Ambiguity,* a book which (as Hugh Kenner said in a sentence that both gives and takes away) "reduced the passivity before poetry of hundreds of readers without imposing—or proposing—a single critical judgment of any salience." *Seven Types* is still a wonderful book to read (or to read parts of) with undergraduates who haven't yet quite seen what the language of poetry is

The Royal Beasts and Other Works, by William Empson, edited by John Heffenden. University of Iowa Press, 1988, and *Argufying: Essay on Literature and Culture,* by William Empson, edited by John Heffenden. University of Iowa Pres, 1987.

capable of. If Empson never knew when to stop in talking about a line of poetry—reticence or tact were virtues he cared little for—he was engagingly willing to admit that perhaps he might have gone too far in the specific instance. Consider some remarks about Macbeth's lines (from Act 3, scene 2) "Light thickens, and the Crow / Makes Wing to the Rookie Wood":

> Various similar sound effects or associations may be noted; there is a suggestion of witches' broth, or curdling blood, about *thickens*, which the vowel sounds of *light*, coming next to it, with the movement of stirring treacle, and the cluck of the k-sounds, intensify—a suggestion, too, of harsh, limpid echo, and, under careful feet of poachers, an abrupt crackling of sticks. The vowel sounds at the end make an increasing darkness as the *crow* goes forward.

If one didn't think about these things (and which of us did?), Empson's next sentence offered some reassurance—"But, after all, one would be very surprised if two people got the same result from putting a sound-effect into words in this way." And he proceeds to expatiate blithely on the difference between those rooks and crows that Macbeth sees through the window (Empson has him looking out of a window). Then in the second edition of *Seven Types* a footnote apologizes for the whole business he has stirred up: "It was stupid of me to present this example as a sort of test case, with a tidy solution drawn from the names of birds. Obviously the passage is still impressive if you have no opinions at all about the difference between crows and rooks. But it is at least a good example of a heavy Atmosphere, and I don't think my treatment of it was wrong as far as it went." With such a disclaimer, so vaguely put—how far *did* the treatment go, anyway?—who would bother to make a fuss about the overall oddity, if not irrelevance, of much of his commentary on Shakespeare's lines?

Still, I am extremely fond of these remarks about Macbeth's observation. Empson's commentary, whatever its truth—or its lack of a "critical judgment of any salience"—makes me pay more attention to Shakespeare's language, and it does so in part by acting as if it were legitimate, even necessary, to try out different ways of reading and listening. There is much of that kind of stimulation in *Seven Types*; at the same time one can't dwell very long on any page without losing—if one picked it up at all—the thread of argument. As I read paragraphs in this and indeed in any Empson book, my mind is constantly hazing over. What *is* he going on about? *Where* can he possibly be

The Old Buffer

headed? *How* did he ever get *that* out of those lines? And yet his criticism—as he himself said about the experience of reading poetry—is "a taste in the head" that is unique.

My purpose here is not to consider the deficiencies in Empson's theoretical account of meaning and poetry (in this connection Elder Olson's rather devastating attack on it in *Modern Philology,* May 1950, is still worth looking up), nor to appreciate—as such critics as Christopher Ricks, Roger Sale, and Paul Alpers have done—the audacity and originality of his operations in the books that followed *Seven Types* (*Some Versions of Pastoral, The Structure of Complex Words, Milton's God*). I want instead, taking my examples from *Argufying,* to show how an essential Empson—for me, I'm afraid, *the* essential Empson—is continuous with the young man who quoted "Light thickens, and the Crow / Makes Wing to the Rookie Wood" and went on enthusiastically about curdling blood, stirring treacle, the careful feet of poachers, and the abrupt crackling of sticks (not to mention the differences between rooks and crows).

You might call this literary character Wild Bill Empson, the man who would say anything as long as it seemed an amusing, possibly shocking thing to say at the time. In later life he liked to refer to himself as an old fogy or buffer: "When I was young I did not mind this . . . but I find now I have become one of the old buffers who are made fretful by it." But even as a young buffer, at age twenty-two, he published in the Cambridge magazine *Granta* a short review of George Rylands's *Words and Poetry* that concluded with the following paragraph:

> There is a charming introduction by Lytton Strachey, about Poetry being written with words, but it is a tiresome dogma; he would at once see through something a trifle more sophisticated, and there seems to be nobody who is teased when it is brought forward. In fact, all the bad poetry of the moment is written with words; I believe myself poetry is written with the sort of joke you find in hymns.

Surely this is the style of the buffer *terrible,* baiting Strachey with "the sort of joke you find in hymns," as if everyone knew what that was, or as if Strachey knew how to deal with hymns. There is as well the quiet bullying of *tiresome,* a word Empson grew increasingly fond of wielding against opponents. (Another favorite word was *suspect,* a verb that is used to usher in most extraordinary utterances, as if when one merely "suspects" something, anything is permissible: "Milton, one may suspect, was for most of his life what he was then called, a shallow-pated young puppy." We are unlikely to investigate whether or for how long Milton was really like that, when the "that" is so sensationally named—how wickedly amusing to think of the author of "Lycidas" as a "shallow-pated young puppy."

"The kind of criticism that most interests me, verbal analysis or whatever one calls it, is concerned to examine what goes on already in the mind of a fit reader." The proclamation sounds eminently sensible, except that what goes on in Empson's mind, as he reads literature and other minds, seems rather more spectacular than is suggested by the modesty of "fit." Often the result is delightful, as when, in a review of some Robert Graves lectures, Empson takes on The White Goddess:

> I remember noticing in my twenties, when my mental eyes were peeping open, a rather curious tone about love taken at times by Peter Quennell and Edgell Rickword as well as Graves, authors unlike in every other way. They wanted to combat a fashion for male homosexuality among intellectuals, a thing which was becoming tiresome for the boys as well as the girls, and they did this by saying it was sentimental to love other young men (because so reliably agreeable and comforting) whereas any man worth the name would take on a woman (because she would be certain to crucify him after stripping him of all his goods). This has always seemed to me a farcical way to recommend normal life.

But surely the farce here—and a very amusing one indeed—is the work of Empson's style as it reduces Graves's sacred mythology to a strategy for dealing with a "tiresome" situation involving the boys and the girls. Without batting an eye, Empson puts himself forward as the sensible fellow with a purchase on "normal life," surrounded by very strange people recommending odd and abnormal practices.

Empson rides a number of hobbyhorses in *Argufying,* among which are his conviction that literary studies are falling prey to neo-Christian principles (there is much about this, of course, in *Milton's God*); that Imagism is nonsense, since it's good to argue (or argufy) in poems; that good poetry originates in mixed feelings; and that, in order to talk well, a critic doesn't need to theorize but rather to follow his nose. And Empson takes every occasion to express his annoyance at the critical doctrine that deemed it illicit or unnecessary to inquire into the motives behind a work of art. Here W. K. Wimsatt, with his "intentional fallacy" (which Empson calls, perversely, "The Fallacy of Intentionalism"), was the villain. As a Christian, Wimsatt was suspect on two grounds, but I'm not convinced he deserves the following salute from Empson's 1955 review of *The Verbal Icon:*

> I have long felt uneasy about Mr Wimsatt's drive against what he calls the Fallacy of Intentionalism; it seems almost a behavioristic position and I am not reassured by the photograph he has put on the dustcover of this collection. He looks like a mastodon rising with dripping fangs from a primeval swamp. A generation or two ago he would have made as much effort to look winning and sympathetic, and really, considering what people in our profession undertake to do, that was a more sensible fashion.

Even for Empson this is extreme and, unless you are more dispassionate than I, you may find it difficult to proceed beyond his picture of the fanged mastodon and the joke (what is it exactly?) about "people in our profession," so as to assess objectively the merits and demerits of the issue at stake. Empson has opted for farce, and if I had been Wimsatt (who was indeed very tall) I would not have felt justly dealt with, even if Empson's following remarks had been more telling than they appear to me to be.

A principal objection to Empson's handling of poetry in *Seven Types* was that—in dealing with a line or lines—too many associations were brought in without regard to "context" and with a sort of more-the-merrier attitude. An especially egregious instance of piling up ambiguities was his commentary on Shakespeare's line from the seventy-third sonnet, "Bare ruined choirs, where late the sweet birds sang." In 1961 Empson returned to that line in the course of a puzzling discussion of prosody in a lecture delivered to the British Society of Aesthetics ("Rhythm and Imagery in English Poetry"). While making a point about what he calls "jammed stress," which calls for a more "emotive" reading when it occurs at the beginning of a line, he noted about "Bare ruined choirs":

> If we make it emotive, that is, if we make Shakespeare at the age of thirty squealingly indignant with the stealing clutches of time: "Why, but I can't be friends with an exciting young lord, like you; I'm a shambling old man, with no *teeth*"—then, whether it began as a joke or not, the two syllables become practically one noise:
> BEARRU ined-choirs where-late the sweet-birds sang.

Without trying here to assess the validity of the prosodic point as Empson so oddly diagrammed it, I would suggest that the reader has been effectively diverted from coming to any decision about prosody, since he's thinking instead—or perhaps laughing aloud, as I did—about this shambling thirty-year-old, acting like an old-fashioned poof whose "Bare ruined choirs" turn out to be empty gums. Those of sterner cast may be able to read this sequence, admit that Empson's paraphrase is perhaps slightly overdone, but keep their minds focused on the prosodic question. For me, the farcical poetry of the performance obliterates any plausible argument.

A related situation arises in his discussion of Cleanth Brooks's *Well-Wrought Urn* in which we are diverted away from Empson's "points" by his continually referring to Keats's famous Attic shape as a "pot." Assertions like the following crop up: "We turn back to the pot with a painful ecstasy in the final stanza. . . ." "And while we are in this peculiar condition is clearly the time for the pot to identify truth and beauty. . . ." "But we cannot suppose that the aphorism is merely dramatic, in the sense of being a suitable remark for a silent pot. . . ." "He wanted us to feel, I think, that the wise pot means a good deal more by its aphorism." Empson effectively demystifies the poem even as he sounds somewhat like the comedian Steve Martin or John Candy imitating a literary critic.

In so insistently making my point about Empson's excessiveness, I have been insufficiently appreciative of a number of fine things in *Argufying*. As always he writes wonderfully about Spenser; the *Ancient Mariner* essay has salient judgments about Coleridge; and my favorite piece in the volume is a BBC talk on Cowper's "The Castaway" where Empson proceeds stanza by stanza through that remarkable poem and identifies its profundity—"that somehow in the nature of things this is true about everybody, we are all in the same boat." That view of the poem never occurred to me, yet, once heard, seems inevitable. But my closing piece of Empsonian rascality—an especially outrageous, but also pleasing, example of old bufferism—surfaces in a letter quoted by Mr. Haffenden in his introduction to *Argufying*. One has noted a hospitality in deconstructionist circles to Empson's criticism, since unlike other New Critics he licenses multi-interpretive readings and likes to subvert and tease all orderly, "orthodox" accounts of poems and critical principles. A few years ago the English deconstructionist Christopher Norris (who went on to write a not very helpful book on Empson's "philosophy of literary criticism") wrote to Empson, encouraging him to read Derrida's works—to which Empson replied:

> I feel very bad not to have answered you for so long, and not to have read all those horrible Frenchmen you posted to me. I did go through the first one, in translation, Jaques Nerrida, and nosed about in several others, but

they seem to me so very disgusting, in a simple moral or social way, that I cannot stomach them.

"Nerrida" and the others, Empson felt, "use enormously fussy language, always pretending to be plumbing the very depths, and never putting your toe into the water. Please tell me I am wrong." Wrong? One hopes Norris saved his breath and didn't even attempt to refine Empson's spelling of the Great Jacques's two names. If it is a distortion to say we read Empson for moments like these, they should nevertheless be recognized for their prominency, their frequency, and the singular satisfactions they provide.

American Scholar, Autumn 1989

Helen Vendler

To begin with a judgment widely shared, if not a truth universally acknowledged: Helen Vendler is the best poetry reviewer in America. Her virtues are a rigorous attending to verbal structure and texture; the ability to quote appositely and economically; a sure though a not too-exclusive taste; above all, the ability to do the poem one better by putting into words the relevant responses we might have had if we'd been smarter and more feeling. These virtues have been evident in her writing over the past decade; we have looked forward to what she would say about the latest volume by a Lowell or a Merrill, and inevitably she has brought aid and comfort. Of course to call her our best reviewer of poetry is hardly a full enough labeling, since she has published full-length critical studies of Yeats, Stevens, and George Herbert (as well as writing on Keats and Wordsworth), and since her operations as a practical critic are everywhere displayed in the essays and reviews which make up this new volume.

What makes Vendler special may be suggested by a sentence from the foreword to this book where she tells how her career as a reviewer began in 1966 when she was asked to do an omnibus review of the year's poetry: "It seemed to me then a windfall, and seems no less to me now, as books arrive in the mail carrying the one form of writing that is to me the most immediate, natural, and accessible." I read this sentence as one through whose own hands a fair number of slim volumes have passed during the same decade, and realized how unlikely that I should ever speak about poetry, especially contemporary poetry, in such a way. There is in all Vendler's dealings with poetry (and she seldom has written about prose fiction) the pressure of an appetite, a feeling, and a love which—as it must do in her classroom teaching—renders her immune to academic or professional vices. Nothing is more obvious and natural to her than wanting and needing to share with others the "news" brought by important new poets, and by older ones whose voices one may have had difficulty hearing.

Part of Nature, Part of Us: Modern American Poets, by Helen Vendler. Harvard University Press, 1980.

208

Helen Vendler

The unreticent forcefulness of Vendler's judgments and preferences invites argument, and I shall engage in a bit of that presently. But first let me name the pieces in this collection that are indispensable criticism, required reading in the years to come for anyone who cares about poetry. These are the reviews of Randall Jarrell's *Complete Poems* and Elizabeth Bishop's *Geography III;* the long appreciation of Frank O'Hara's collected poems, and the short one of A. R. Ammons's; the wonderful essay on Marianne Moore which obliges us to see her freshly; and the passionately argued case for Adrienne Rich's work, which would convince me if anything could (and it can't) that she is a splendid poet. Most centrally there are the intrepid confrontations with difficult new books by Robert Lowell and James Merrill which appeared in the 1970s: with Lowell's books of sonnets, his *Selected Poems,* and *Day By Day;* with Merrill's *Braving the Elements, Divine Comedies,* and *Mirabell: Books of Number.*

Taken together, her writings about these last two poets seem to me the most distinguished work in the whole volume. The fifty or so pages on Lowell make an unqualified claim for the greatness of his later work, finding the life in the *Notebook* sonnets (now divided into separate volumes) to lie in "lawless free associations of the rocked and dangerous mind." Vendler sees Lowell's preceding books (*Near the Ocean* and *For the Union Dead*) as relatively less "fertile" than the sonnets (I'm not sure I can agree with any demotion of *For the Union Dead,* even relatively), which she says "contain the first legitimate continuance of Shakespeare's sonnets since Keats." Lowell's "free association, irritating at first, hovering always dangerously toward the point where unpleasure replaces pleasure, nonetheless becomes bearable, and then even deeply satisfying, on repeated readings." This judgment seems to me daringly made and also true, even more so when we encounter it framed and illustrated by quotations like this one from the poems:

> . . . I'm for and with myself in my otherness,
> in the eternal return of earth's fairer children,
> the lily, the rose, the sun on brick at dusk,
> the loved, the lover, and their fear of life,
> the unconquered flux, insensate oneness. . . .

While *Day by Day,* which she calls "a stern and touching volume," reveals Lowell finally as a writer "of disarming openness, exposing shame and uncertainty, offering almost no purchase to interpretation" whose last poems acknowledge exhaustion and expect death. As for the thirty pages on Merrill, here is a single sentence wonderfully describing the way his narratives are autobiographical but not "confessional":

> These poems are gripping because they are quiet and conversational: it is as though a curtain had been drawn aside, and we were permitted a glimpse of the life inside the house, a life that goes on unconscious of us, with the narrator so perfectly an actor in his own drama that his presence as narrator is rendered transparent, invisible.

If the pieces on Lowell and Merrill are the indispensable heart of the volume, Vendler's opening ones on Stevens (two of them independent essays) seem less so, perhaps because she already has had a full and definitive say about him. As the book's title suggests, Stevens is the presiding spirit of *Part of Nature, Part of Us*, perhaps a little too much so since—as with Kermode, Bloom, Hartman, and other hardcore Stevensians—Vendler constantly weaves phrases and lines from his poems into her own argument dedicated to showing their excellence. In "Apollo's Harsher Songs," for example, she aims to show that Stevens's poems are often "brutal" in their handling of experience, and she focuses on the violence felt in a poem titled "Chaos in Motion and Not in Motion" ("Oh, that this lashing wind was something more / Than the spirit of Ludwig Richter . . ."). But her sentences about how humanly moving the poem really is refer us more to the verbal maze created by other Stevens poems than to "life": "As self and beloved alike become, with greater or lesser velocity, the final dwarfs of themselves . . . the poet sees dream, hope, love, and trust—those activities of the most august imagination—crippled, contradicted, dissolved, called into question, embittered." And soon afterward this interestingly argued brief for Stevens as a "poet of human misery" has recourse to another allusion, when she says his poems express "the late plural of the subject, whose early candor of desire reposes further down the page." The knowledgeable reader will have caught three references to other poems by Stevens which, taken together, don't make one feel more deeply about the humanness of "Chaos in Motion . . ." and its invoking of "Ludwig Richter, turbulent Schlemihl." Vendler's quotings here, untypically, make me feel that Stevens's poems reinforce themselves more as arcane textures of cross references than as moving gestures at real troubles in a human world. He seems to me still, even after her insistence that his poems contain great "amplitude of human vision," a chillier, more academic poet than she is willing to admit.

There may be a relation between Vendler's extreme admiration for these late poems (in which by "an incorporation of the imperfect and the tragic Stevens discovers the sublime") and her denigration of the later Eliot. In her review of *The Waste Land* manuscript she compares the "late work"—what must be *Four Quartets*, though she doesn't mention them by name—to Wordsworth's "Ecclesiastical Sonnets," and gives a friendly nod to Harold Bloom's "mischievous" remark that Pound and Eliot may turn out to be the Cleveland and the Cowley of our age. By contrast Stevens's late work is all "sublime," and that magic word (especially magical in New Haven) is almost compulsively summoned up by Vendler to turn what I had always thought a delicate piece of minor Stevens ("Not Ideas About the Thing But the Thing Itself") into something much deeper: "The scrawny cry [a phrase from the poem] of its emergent birth . . . represents Stevens's utmost sublime. It is a sublime of denuded language, a sublime of indicative effort . . . [a] transparently beautiful poem." And this is the same reader who, evidently, is untouched by the gloomy hills of London, the vast waters of petrel and porpoise, the river, the fishermen, and the children in the apple tree who populate Eliot's long poem. I would give up even the *true* sublime ("Sunday Morning," one of my all-time sublime hits, gets less than high marks from Vendler since it represents a "false sublime") in exchange for the sadness, the lifelikeness I find in *Four Quartets*.

She can provoke disagreement, and that is all to the good. The essay on Rich's poetry, with its comparisons to Herbert and Stevens, convinced me less that Rich is comparable to them than that Helen Vendler has been preoccupied with Herbert and Stevens. I don't see myself as one of the "crippled creatures" Vendler says Rich sees us all as; nor have I seen any indication in any of Vendler's writings that she sees herself as such a crippled creature. I finished the essay surmising that the "new generosity and new self-forgetfulness" prophesied for Rich's future poetry was really a whistling in the dark. And I was gratified then to read, in the next essay, a fine, unsentimental analysis of Rich's "rhetoric of violence" . . . accompanied by a rhetoric of sentimentality" which Vendler found in the prose of Rich's book on motherhood, *Of Women Born.* To admire the poems yet to say this about the prose seems to me an impressive instance of critical integrity.

In conclusion, there is Vendler's humor, only occasionally indulged; but anybody who can say that W. S. Merwin "has been maintaining his starved and mute stance so long that one has a relentless social-worker urge to ask him to eat something, anything, to cure his anemia" gets an assent from me. *Part of*

Nature, Part of Us belongs on the shelf (from where it will be taken down often) just to the right of *Language as Gesture* and *Poetry and the Age,* since in her brilliant fusion of reviewing and criticism Helen Vendler is the legitimate successor to R. P. Blackmur and Randall Jarrell.

New Republic, March 29, 1980

Polemics

Polemic: Of or pertaining to controversy; controversial, dis-
putatious (*OED*). The next three pieces disputatiously take aim at
critical procedures that seem to me perverse or insufficiently critical. "The Hermeneutical Mafia," written almost twenty years ago
and in response to which I got a lot of mail, takes up the work of
Harold Bloom and Geoffrey Hartman and suggests that—along
with J. Hillis Miller and Paul deMan—these men constituted
something like a Yale school of theoretical writing. Since then,
deMan has died, Miller has moved to California, and Bloom has
taken to excoriating deconstructive practices as spawned by his
Yalie comrades—so the mafia no longer operates. "Salvos from the
Gender Wars" shows disinclination for gender talk applied to poetry, certainly as practiced by Sandra Gilbert and Susan Gubar.
"Love Story" sends up what struck me as a pompous book by the
prolific historian Peter Gay.

The Hermeneutical Mafia or,
After Strange Gods at Yale

Twenty and more years ago William F. Buckley burst upon the scene with a book telling the world how Yale professors were Godless and Keynesian, believed in neither religion nor the further rise of capitalism. At present we observe, in the same academic sanctuary, comparable attempts to frisk students of their principles as naive or enthusiastic readers by proposing new, it may well be revolutionary, ways of reading poetry and criticism. In their New Haven precincts at least, literary study is no longer the relaxed appreciating of good books à la William Lyon Phelps or William DeVane (author of *A Browning Handbook*); nor the devoted explications of irony and paradox by Cleanth Brooks or Maynard Mack. The titles of these recent books by Geoffrey H. Hartman and Harold Bloom suggest that very big game is being stalked, nothing less than the fate of reading, literature, the agonizingly problematical nature of poetry and its interpretation. Since the most common adjective used to describe their work is "brilliant," I shall accept that term as fair enough. But I propose here to look at a few of the brilliant sentences and paragraphs that make up their latest as well as earlier books, then to draw some conclusions about the world they invite us to enter and the style through which they engage it.

In reviewing Hartman's new book, Richard Poirier (*New York Times Book Review*, April 20, 1975) advised us that, along with his previous ones, particularly the essays collected in *Beyond Formalism* (1970), it asks to be "taken as part of a community enterprise meant to constitute the most significant challenge to literary studies since Northrop Frye and, before that, I. A. Richards." Besides Hartman's colleague Harold Bloom, the most prominent members of that community enterprise are two other colleagues, Paul deMan and J. Hillis Miller, whose works are equally well known and who are often to be found giving papers and addresses at meetings of the M.L.A., the English

The Fate of Reading, by Geoffrey H. Hartman. University of Chicago Press, 1975. *A Map of Misreading*, by Harold Bloom. Oxford University Press, 1975.

Polemics

Institute, and other professional organizations. When Poirier at one point in his review asks who the imagined audience is for Hartman's book, one barely suppresses the thought that members of this community seem to be writing and speaking above all to each other.[1] This is understandable: they share a passion for comparative literature and Continental philosophical, psychological and literary speculation; they read Derrida, Poulet, Lacan, and Blanchot; structuralism is mother's milk to them; eristics, hermeneutics, and propadeutics no more than ordinary language at ordinary evenings in New Haven. And except for deMan, about whose preference I'm not sure, the supreme modern poet, the last word on all things visible and invisible is their necessary angel, Wallace Stevens.

Yet, and to confine things for the moment to Hartman's essays, this reader often feels desperate, wondering how he could possibly remake his life so as seriously to be touched by the problems the critic sees as troubling and exciting. In his lead essay ("The Interpreter") to the new book Hartman provides us with paragraphs about the excitements and dangers of "interrupting" a "text" (the Yale people always deal with texts, never mere books) and then discusses the "alternate" or "*déjà lu*" theory of describing our responses to individual works. Interpretation as "interruption" can be understood as "a shadowy double of the work of art," or, in the alternate theory

> act and shadow are considered of equal dignity. Both, that is, reflect the possibility of a Heavenly City of Mutual Discourse. At the same time, the reactive or *a posteriori* character of interpretation, which includes its dependence on source texts, is questioned. The hermeneutic universe now envisaged is no longer a closed system, with Classics at the center, spin-off works as satellites, and the critic-interpreter either encouraging such spin-offs by denying exhaustive centrality to certain books (and so keeping the system expanding) or discouraging them (and inviting closure). "The stubborn center must / Be scattered . . ." (Shelley).

1. *Beyond Formalism* was dedicated to Bloom; Bloom's collection of essays *The Ringers in the Tower*, to Hartman. Hartman's new collection contains a review of Bloom's *Anxiety of Influence* ("this dense, eloquent and experiential brooding") while his previous one had a backcover blurb from Hillis Miller ("this admirable book, a subtle and long-mediated vision of literary history"). Paul deMan, the subtlest analyst and best writer of the community, publishes relatively little compared to the others. Particularly unforgettable are moments in which one of the giants confronts another; I remember an English Institute meeting at Columbia when, in the discussion period following Bloom's talk, Miller rose to ask a question and was recognized by Bloom in some such terms as "my great antagonist" (or was it "mighty opposite"?). At such moments other academics in the room felt kind of humble and kind of proud.

The Hermeneutical Mafia

There are disadvantages too, in terms of literary-critical *praxis*. (I do not try to judge the theory except in this light.) By diminishing the book-centeredness of literary discourse you bring it closer to philosophical discourse and run the risk of homogenizing it. True, you may still have "texts" rather than "books"—but what constitutes a text is a slippery thing to define, and the tendency of Heidegger to excerpt freely, of Derrida to use a highly repetitive or snippety canon, and of Lacan to meld everything into his prose by inner quotation produces an intensely frustrating *clair-obscur*. Theology also fragmented scripture into proof-texts, yet the literal text remained, and the discrepancy between letter and figurative development was the very space of revisionary shock or "hermeneutic reversal." Now, however, the *facticity* of a book or, the *force* of a "dialectical lyric" like Hölderlin's "Der Rhein" or Shelley's "Mont Blanc" or Kierkegaard's *Fear and Trembling* may be lost.

Hartman has just referred, in his preface, to a certain group of critics that "justifies everything by the pragmatic test of the classroom, as if the world had to pass through that needle's eye, or as if a pedagogy accommodated to the pressures of a particular community were the best we could hope for." Nobody wants to be a miserable pragmatist, but I think the test of the classroom—of a good classroom that is, since they vary—would be less of a needle's eye than the aperture Hartman has constructed for us to get through in the above paragraphs. That is to say, anyone who spends any time in class with students is aware that whether you call the thing in front of you (or wherever it is) a "book" or a "text," you will be dealing with a slippery thing, and you will find it wise not to "define" it for more than a minute or two lest someone should interrupt you to say, no that is not it at all. We learned this pretty early along, as teachers or students, just as we learned that words are not things, art not life, the "unmediated vision" (the title of Hartman's first book) what isn't around to be had, or is to be had only in a world of abstraction. Hartman's abstracting is off-putting because of the style in which it's conducted: reactive spin-offs on the one hand, hermeneutics and closure on the other (or is it the same hand?) with a line from Shelley vainly stabbing at uniting them. To say nothing of *praxis* (practice?) and *clair-obscur* and *facticity* (equaled only by Bloom's favorite, *rhetoricity*). Taken together these, like other and even more striking overreachings in Hartman's style make up *clair-obscurs* that are intensely frustrating. Stop for a moment and ask yourself who in the world of readers—classroom or otherwise—"may" ever lose the facticity of Hölderlin's or Shelley's poems. Who ever had the facticity of Kierkegaard's difficult meditation to lose anyway? But we refer now to ordinary readers rather than these extraordinary troubled men of Yale.

Perhaps not all that troubled. Most of the time Hartman seems the opposite of anguished and not overburdened with, as he calls it, the fate of reading. *Beyond Formalism* contained a thick swatch of overwhelmingly learned essays on aspects of poetic language in Milton, Marvell, Blake, Wordsworth, Hopkins; the new book continues these interpretative performances with ones on Smart, Keats, Goethe, and Valéry. I respect, and at times receive, genuine pleasure and illumination from such essays, even though I find them written in never much less than a daunting style, and though the level at which they operate is refined perhaps beyond the point not merely of desirable but of civilized practice, in or out of the classroom. Still, such essays have a specifiable audience, one of academics whose favorite magazines are *New Literary History, ELH* and others less well known to me. In this league, and it is a big enough league, Hartman is one of the very best players of the interpretive game; although if you are going to play it with him you must prepare yourself to read a footnote like the following to an essay on Akenside's "Ode to the Evening Star":

> The preposition "to" in st. 1 foregrounds itself so strongly that, to subordinate it, one is tempted to read it on the pattern of "to-night" (i.e., proclitically) and so bring it closer to the bonded preposition "sub" in *supply, suppliant* (a near pun, anticipating the reversal mentioned above) and even *suffer*. Compare the syntax of st. 6; also the "prefer" of l. 19 which makes "vows" both its direct and indirect object. It draws attention once more not only to the prepositional but also to the syntactical bonding of one verse-line with another. All this fosters a sense of the discontinuous or precarious path followed by the verses' "feet." It is interesting that in Christopher Smart's *Song to David* (1763) the problem of hierarchy, subordination (hypotaxis), and prepositional-syntactical bonding reaches an acute stage.

This is not quite a grammarian's funeral but it sounds like it, and Hartman's most strenuous engagements with verbal matters (his earlier essay "The Voice of the Shuttle" shows them at their best) are forbiddingly couched so as to resist all but the most devoted reader—and of Dr. Mark Akenside to boot. And so when, in the title essay to *The Fate of Reading*, Hartman announces things like the following—"This indifference, an apathy or arbitrariness of emotional reaction, or an orgasmic shuttle of both together, remains a complex phenomenon"—the reader may very well conclude he'd rather be in Philadelphia. Whose indifferent apathy or arbitrary emotional reaction combined into which orgasmic shuttle is he supposed to care about? In case you accuse me of quoting out of context, be assured that the reference is to, in the preceding paragraph, "the activist potential of articulated or publicized thought, in whatever form."

In his review Poirier refers to Hartman's "sometimes gleeful unintelligibility," and the other review I've seen (Denis Donoghue's in *T.L.S.*, August 29, 1975) also admits to unhappiness with the critic's style. Both of them, though, are more forgiving of these lapses and more generous in their appreciation of Hartman's virtues than I can find myself to be; and neither reviewer evidently finds more than trivial faults, since neither mentions them, Hartman's misquoting of lines and his heavyhanded attempts at lightness of touch. "I admit to a variable style, which consists mainly of a playful dissolving of terms and abstractions . . ." he winks at us; but without systematic checking of his quotations my ear caught the following dissolvings of lines originally written otherwise. The examples are from his two books of essays, and I specify the poet misquoted: "As flies to wanton boys, so are we to the gods" (Shakespeare); "The forward Youth that would appear / Must forsake his muses dear" (Marvell); "blanket of the night" (Shakespeare); "a road not taken" (Frost); "The best lack all conviction, and the worst are full of passionate intensity" (Yeats); "Soldier, there is a war between the mind and the sky" (Stevens); plus the invention of Stevens-titles like "The Snowman" and "L'Esthetique du Mal." I don't mean to claim that Hartman is in Stephen Spender's league in the misquoting stakes (see the latter's *Love-Hate Relations* for the champion book in this respect) but what these errors suggest to me is that his ear for the rhythm and tone of individual lines of poetry is a good deal less secure than his formidable ability to spin words around them. He gives us the ritual or Continental business about how "complex" it is "to decide where a text ends or begins," then seems to find it similarly complex to decide whether accurate quotation is worthwhile.

His "playful" style is even more bothersome: "Is criticism a yea, yea, nay nay affair, best conducted in as dry a prose as possible?" No, professor, it is not, but the alternative to dryness needn't be the following bit of liveliness from "History Writing as Answerable Style": "Our hearts are sad at the culture supermarket; packaged historical reminiscences meet us everywhere; the Beatles' *Yellow Submarine* is a moving toyshop of topoi." Hartman's invoking of 1960s pop has the effect of too-eagerly assuring us that an erudite fellow like him can relax too. And like pop like feminism: "It is proper to recall here Pope's wittily sexist observation that 'Women have no character at all.'" But of course it is highly improper, because Pope never wrote a line close to the one Hartman invents, nor did the author of "Epistle to a Lady" make (like Johnny Carson, say) "wittily sexist" remarks. "But let me damp my superciliousness" he nervously intrudes into his essay "On the Theory of Romanticism," and in the acknowledgments to *The Fate of Reading* salutes his wife who "occasionally tried to chasten my style." Mrs. Hartman must have desisted or nodded during the title essay when her spouse got on to the following conceit: "The point is . . . that sexuality is simply a pointing. If you don't get the point, there is little one can do. You fear castration, and you hover compulsively, emptily, near that point. 'Omne tulit punctum' said horny Horace. A promiscuous metaphor is better than a faceless literalism. So Freud moves on, winning his point." Such depressing high jinks are, I'm convinced, a consequence of Hartman's desire to expatiate on all sorts of nonsubjects (like The Fate of Reading) we can well live without investigating. At any rate the playful style has its grim corollary in the unanswerable one, as when the historical space between Hegel and Greece "is less the space of mystery than of interpretation: it is hermeneutic as well as pneumatic. Hegel stands here on the threshold of the passage from *Gesitergeschichte* to *Gesitesgeschichte*." "No man is an island (except some Englishmen)" he wittily remarks at one point, and I rejoin, standing there on the threshold with the abominable Hegel and his hermeneutics, Give me Leavis, nay give me Grigson, nay give me Clive James even. Or just give me an American like William James who said in 1882 that "Hegel's philosophy mingles mountain-loads of corruption with its scanty merits."

But let us turn instead to Harold Bloom, introducing him through Hartman's summary of Bloom's argument in *The Anxiety of Influence* (1973). Since I do not believe, as Bloom claims in his dedication, that the new *A Map of Misreading* should be understood as "an antithetical completion" to the earlier book, I take Hartman's description to be still accurate:

> [Each essay from] . . . this dense, eloquent and experiential brooding . . . defines what is called a "revisionary ratio," that is, a specific type of "misreading" which helps poets to overcome the influence of previous poets. Influence is understood as dangerously preemptive (hence the anxiety), as an in-flowing that tends to become a flooding, so that for the later poet to survive means to wilfully revise (euphemistically, "correct") his precur-

sor. . . . Bloom seeks "a wholly different practical criticism" which would transfigure source-study by revealing in each poem, or in the poet's corpus as a whole, echoings of a precursor, imitations as complex as those by which the child wrests his life-space from parents.

Assuming most readers of this magazine will by now be somewhat familiar with this argument, at least in its compressed form, and because the bypaths Bloom pursues can't be adequately paraphrased or charted (is he not, in his own terms, a Strong Poet?), I shall inquire instead whether Bloom's "wholly different practical criticism," as practiced by himself, delivers the goods so loudly promised by his theoretical performance.

First though, it is silly to pretend that anyone comes to Bloom's work with a wholly open mind, ready somehow objectively to weigh the evidence, then "agree" or "disagree." From the beginning of his productions as a critic he has made no pretense to open-mindedness or fairness. Like Robert Graves in only one respect (Graves who was reprimanded by his Oxford tutor for preferring some books to others) Bloom has from the start been polemical, even pugilistic. My own reading of him began with *Shelley's Mythmaking* (1959), an intemperate, exaggerated defense of Shelley against which I had to examine my inert received notions (received from Leavis, alas) of how Shelley's poetry would not do at all. More recently Bloom's book on Yeats energetically combated received opinion about the Yeats canon and his status as a great poet. And *The Ringers in the Tower* (1971) contained strongly argued essays on Keats, Shelley, appreciations of Ruskin and Pater as literary men, good accounts of Robinson, Hart Crane, and an extremely useful one of Stevens's "Notes Toward a Supreme Fiction."

On the basis of his published work then, Bloom seems most himself and most engaging as a proselytizer for neglected, misvalued or imperfectly understood creative work—mainly poetry—produced by English and American writers—mainly since 1800. As a provocative spokesman he needs constantly to be argued with, but this is good for a reader's faculties and provides an experience different in kind from most academic assays. And there are passages in Bloom's latest books where he indulges in sweeping annoyances which seem to me to make for health and life—as when in *Anxiety of Influence* he excoriates "the anti-humanistic plain dreariness of all these developments in European criticism that have yet to demonstrate that they can aid in reading any one poem by any one poet whatsoever." He is also, at moments, less than absolute for his own theory, suggesting at the beginning of *Map of Misreading* that the theory's truth may be irrelevant to its usefulness for practical criticism; though perhaps this disclaimer permits him all the more to be extravagant in unqualifiedly setting forth the reader's situation: "Reading, despite all humanist traditions of education, is very nearly impossible, for every reader's relation to every poem is governed by a figuration of belatedness." Is there any point in saying that some of us old-fashioned humanists thought coming late to the poem—sometime well after it was written—was what made reading *possible* as well as necessary? But with "very nearly impossible," the bold formulation takes itself back just enough for safety's sake.

Of course one feels less than magnanimous in asking such commonsense questions since, as Bloom has said in *Anxiety,* "strong poets can only read themselves. For them, to be judicious is to be weak, and to compare, exactly and fairly, is to be not elect." From his writing, I presume Bloom has taken this admonition to heart, and that strong critics also must abjure these weaker virtues. How it applies to style is revealed through his quoting, of all people, the Elizabethan rhetorician George Puttenham on the "far-fetcher" trope— "as when we had rather fetch a word a great way off than to use one nearer hand to express the matter aswel and plainer . . . so . . . leaping over the heads of a great many words, we take one that is furdest off, to utter our matter by. . . ." An example from the new book, in which Bloom proposes to consider "a Post-Enlightenment crisis-lyric of major ambitions and rare achievement, wholly in the abstract," must suffice to illustrate how faithfully he has followed up Puttenham's tip:

> Applying the Lurianic dialectics to my own litany of evasions, one could say that a breaking-of-the-vessels always intervenes between every *primary* (limiting) and every *antithetical* (representing) movement that a latecomer's poem makes in relation to a precursor's text. When the latecomer initially swerves (clinamen) from his poetic father, he brings about a contraction or withdrawal of meaning from the father, and makes/breaks his own false creation (fresh wandering or error-about-poetry). The answering movement, *antithetical* to this *primary,* is the link called *tessera,* a completion that is also an opposition, or restorer of some of the degrees-of-difference between ancestral text and the new poem. This is the Lurianic pattern of *Zimzum→Shevirath ha-kelim→Tikhun,* and is enacted again (in finer tone) in the next dialectical pair of ratios, *kenosis* (or undoing as discontinuity) and *daemonization* (the breakthrough to a personalized Counter-Sublime).

The Hermeneutical Mafia

The paragraph (and the "analysis") goes on, but I cease to quote, only admitting that Bloom in one of his many maddening incorporations of Wallace Stevens's lines into his own prose calls what he is doing here "the accomplishment of an extremist in an exercise." Hartman finds these terms "exuberantly eclectic," and I suppose one might revel in the high spirits of such extremity since there is certainly no point in objecting to what looks like deliberate devilishness. Yet when later on Bloom confides (to whom? the elect?) that "I will try to remember that the common reader cares little to be taught to notice tropes or defenses," it may well be hazarded that this common reader, not necessarily to be despised, would more willingly submit to such instruction if it were expressed in English.

When Bloom gets round to considering post-Enlightenment crisis-lyrics in the concrete they still sound pretty abstract. An important exhibit is Wordsworth's Immortality Ode and its relation to the precursor, Milton. Here is a sample from Bloom's commentary on stanzas I–IV of the poem:

> The first part begins with images of absence, the realm of "there was a time." There is an *illusio* here, for though Wordsworth actually fears that a Glory has passed away from himself, he says it has passed from the earth. As a defense, this reaction-formation wards off instinctual impulses by means of that mode of self-distrust that creates the superego. Poetically, instinctual impulses are internalized influences from a precursor-fixation, and Wordsworth's selfdistrust reacts therefore to Milton's strength. "Intimations" in the title means something very like "signs" or "tokens" and the title therefore suggests that the poem is a searching for evidences, almost a quest for election. The precursor poem, in a deep sense, is Milton's *Lycidas,* and Wordsworth's Ode also is intended primarily to be a dedication to the poet's higher powers, a prolepsis of the great epic he hoped still to write. But that intention, though it will determine the poem's final attempt at a transumptive stand towards Milton, seems largely negated by much of the poem's first two movements.

This writing veers uneasily from loose, "ordinary" language—Wordsworth "reacting" to Milton, the poem "almost" a quest for election (all Romantic poems are of course, for Bloom, Quests), *Lycidas* being the precursor "in a deep sense"—to psychoanalytic paraphrase, for which the ideal reader is clearly Vladimir Nabokov, and finally to the shiny terms wheeled out for inspection—transumption and prolepsis and more to follow. But there is precious little about the "movements" of Wordsworth's poem at the level of voice and diction, and nothing about them at the level of sound, pace, rhythm— the level at which everything is heard. The "strong" way of writing about poems is often a barbarous and sometimes a bathetic way. "I am myself an uneasy quester after lost meanings" says the on-stage troubled critic, sinking as he speaks.

Moreover, to be strong is to bully, and especially there to be bullied is that common reader who needs to be told who is better than whom. For example: Browning, we learn from Bloom's headnote in the *Oxford Anthology of English Literature,* surpasses not only his rival Tennyson but all modern poets "including even Yeats, Hardy, and Wallace Stevens, let alone the fashionable modernists whose reputations are now rightly in rapid decline." What must be said to this is Nonsense, Eliot's reputation is in decline of no sort, except in Bloom's head; and nonsense it is too to talk about Browning's "surpassing" the other moderns we care most about and whose work helped us shuck off Browning. (This is heresy, I am aware; I have also read Browning recently with some care, and he surpasses neither these modern poets nor Tennyson.) But at the least such big talk should be backed up by practical criticism of Browning's work; instead Bloom offers us in the new book yet a further analysis of "Childe Roland"—he had analyzed it twice before, once in *Ringers,* once in *Anxiety*—proving once more to his own satisfaction that it is a great quest poem.

The large-mannered motions Bloom makes in the directions of poems often seem not very practical criticism at all, indeed not very critical. I could not begin to quote the numbers of times lines or phrases from Wallace Stevens are woven into Bloom's sentences, as they are into Hartman's, the allusions never ironic (as in the one I committed just above) but rather celebratory and reverential. Though not quite as "great" as Browning, Stevens now seems to be beyond any attention other than devoted construing and quoting as "proof" of the critic's high argument. So even a minor, pleasant little poem like "The Rabbit as King of the Ghosts" becomes (in *Anxiety*) an example of poetic *askesis* which "compensates for the poet's involuntary shock at his own daemonic expansiveness. Without askesis, the strong poet, like Stevens, is fated to become the rabbit as king of the ghosts." And after quoting some lines which end with "You become a self that fills the four corners of night," Bloom adds "Humped high, humped up, the poet will become a carving in space unless he can wound himself *without further emptying himself of his inspiration.* He cannot afford another *kenosis.*" Proceeding in this vein, Bloom turns what I as common reader had thought was Stevens's indulgence of the rabbit's momentary grandeur into (it turns out to be instead) a cautionary tale for the modern strong poet who needs a good dose of askesis to counteract his kenosis. In the process, not only has the individual poem been ransacked, its pleasantly odd language ("Humped high, humped up") wrenched out of the poet's context into the critic's (the word "carving," which doesn't occur in the Rabbit poem, may have been borrowed for the occasion from "The Auroras of Autumn" where "The necklace is a carving, not a kiss") and the whole business humped very high indeed.

Space forbids my pursuing further examples of what strikes me as huffing and puffing rather than demonstration. But I will refer to an instance of such in *Misreading* when Hardy's final book, *Winter Words,* is put forth as a "superb volume" to which "few books of twentieth-century verse . . . compare . . . in greatness." This would be marvelous if true, and I can only ask the student of Hardy's verse to read through *Winter Words* and see if with the best of intentions and loving respect for the old poet he can find Bloom's statement to be more than hyperbolic and misleading (misreading, if he'd prefer). But, and again, no practical criticism of the poems is provided; rather Bloom has his eyes on the precursor Shelley, on "The Return of the Dead" [Apophrades], on "the chastened return of High Romantic Idealism." If you accept Bloom's systematic theorizing it *does* makes a difference after all, for whether or not it's true you will begin to see the last poems of Hardy to which it's applied become portentous, exemplary, and therefore great.

As for his taste with regard to contemporary writers, Bloom finds Robert Lowell "anything but a permanent poet . . . mostly a maker of period-pieces from his origins until now." John Ashbery, however, because he expresses the American Counter-Sublime and follows on from the deified Stevens, is a "radiant" poet ("an inevitable comfort in our current darkness," says Bloom, darkly, elsewhere). "Radiance" is one of Bloom's favorite good words, and I am not able quite to fathom what richnesses it portends. A. R. Ammons is also extremely radiant, but Norman Mailer is extremely flawed, while Saul Bellow really isn't all that satisfactory, and Bloom prefers Pynchon to Mailer, but. . . . At which point someone says, don't you see that he is a *romantic?* to which I answer, yes and I see also why he should have spent much energy in castigating T. S. Eliot and the "churchwardenly critics" (Bloom's phrase, proving he himself is no sissy) who were supposedly crippled by their priest. For Eliot pointed out in *The Sacred Wood,* apropos George Wyndham, that "Romanticism is a short cut to the strangeness without the reality" and that Wyndham employed it "to complete the varied features of the world he made for him-self." So, Eliot concluded, the only cure for Romanticism was to analyze it. To be cured of his own Romanticism Bloom, and Hartman too, would need to draw upon modes of self-irony, possibilities for a comic perspective on things (and here they could take a lesson from their admired Kenneth Burke) which they are surely not about to do. Listen to Bloom on Blake's Tyger: "Hartman acutely points out that 'fearful symmetry in *The Tyger* should be read as 'fearful ratio,' since *The Tyger's* speaker is the ephebe and the Tyger's maker the precursor. The Tyger, as Hartman suggests, is thus a Spectre or Covering Cherub, imposed by the late-comer imagination upon itself." Let it be pointed out then that there are, still are, other people listening to, reading, reading Yale professors in hopes of extending their literary-critical imaginations, but they may not find it in them to stay much longer at this exclusive hermeneutical shindig.

Hudson Review 28, no. 4 (Winter 1976). Copyright © 1976 by the Hudson Review, Inc. Reprinted by permission.

Salvos from the Gender War

If you haven't heard about it, you haven't been hanging around the academy lately: gender is *in*. Not sex, what with all the current worries about social diseases, but gender most definitely. Whether it's the poetry of Torquato Tasso or Alexander Pope, the novels of Samuel Richardson or Ernest Hemingway, the plays of Shakespeare or Shaw, you had better not plan on making a critical reputation these days by concerning yourself merely with their language or "literary" value. For in the prefatory words to a recent collection of essays titled *The Poetics of Gender* ("poetics" incidentally is another rave favorite in the academy, applied to any and all subjects, gender to ketchup), "Feminist criticism has shown that the social construction of sexual difference plays a constitutive role in the production, reception, and history of literature."[1] These critics ask "what it might mean to read and write through the prism of gender," and they have not been behindhand in coming up with answers.

The most influential and confident of such answerers have been two academics, Sandra M. Gilbert and Susan Gubar, whose survey of nineteenth-century women writers, *The Madwoman in the Attic* (1979), found this madwoman (the prototype is Bertha Mason Rochester in *Jane Eyre*) in every woman writer's attic, even Jane Austen's, which hitherto we had thought clean and tidy. (I still do think it's pretty bare of unseemly people, but no matter.) In 700-odd pages, Gilbert and Gubar thoroughly explained and interpreted novels by Jane Austen, the Brontës, Mary Shelley, George Eliot, and the poems of Christina Rossetti and Emily Dickinson. Their chapter titles bore sensationally promising invitations to the stories told therein: "Emily Brontë's Bible of Hell"; "George Eliot as the Angel of Destruction"; "Strength in Agony: Nineteenth-Century Poetry by Women." Their model of conflict between the writer, her society, and her precursors was at least as agonistic as Harold Bloom's, from whose lexicon they borrowed terms, refashioning them so as to accommodate the other gender. Although *Madwoman* was relatively untheo-

No Man's Land: The Place of the Woman Writer in the Twentieth Century, volume 1: *The War of the Words,* by Sandra M. Gilbert and Susan Gubar. Yale University Press, 1988.

1. *The Poetics of Gender,* ed. Nancy K. Miller (New York, 1986).

retical (feminists who groove on Luce Irigaray and Hélène Cixous find Gilbert and Gubar somewhat too unFrenchily down-home in their approach to "texts"), the book became a basic reference-point for teachers and critics who deal with gender issues in classic nineteenth-century novels and poems.

Now this team (hereafter G&G) has brought out the first of three volumes dealing with the woman writer in our century.[2] *The War of the Words* is described as "an overview of social, literary, and linguistic interactions between men and women from the middle of the nineteenth century to the present," and G&G promise to "theorize about the ways in which modernism, because of the distinctive social and cultural changes to which it responds, is differently inflected for male and female writers." In their preface they warn us that, back in the bad old days of New Criticism (though the culprit is not so named), "a number of literary critics dealt with texts as if they were autonomous and universal monuments of unaging intellect." It was this practice that distorted understanding of the modern period: "Privileging certain works as purely aesthetic or philosophic objects and repressing significant aspects of the history in which the authors . . . were engaged, many readers and teachers failed to perceive the sexual struggle" lying beneath them. No such naivete for these clear-eyed perceivers of that struggle:

> Once we reimagine the author as a gendered human being whose text reflects key cultural conditions, we can conflate and collate individual literary narratives, so that they constitute one possible metastory, a story of stories about gender strife in this period.

In other words, what Kenneth Burke or Cleanth Brooks was doing when he analyzed monuments of unaging intellect like "Sailing to Byzantium" or "Among School Children," was not merely ignoring "history" but—for G&G—the only history that matters, sexual politics. In Robert Graves's memorable lines, "There is one story and one story only / That will prove worth your telling."

Volume One of *No Man's Land* has already been praised by a reviewer for the clarity of its prose, and it's true that compared to some feminist theorists G&G lack obscurity and pretentiousness. Still, the ease with which they em-

---

2. The book's preface concludes with a wall-to-wall acknowledging of the authors' familial debts, first to their respective husbands, one of whom was so supportive as to help make compatible their two systems of word-processing; then to their five children; then their mothers, still alive, who have bequeathed them "fierce survival instincts"; finally their fathers, both dead, who taught them to "love men" and to whom they dedicate the book. My critical spirit was almost disarmed.

brace the going academic-critical jargon isn't cause for satisfaction. To speak of "privileging" the individual work and "repressing" history makes to my ears a drearily predictable start; to have a "text reflect[s] key cultural conditions" is not to improve the terms of discourse—especially if one doesn't read books to see key cultural conditions reflected in them. As we move on through conflating and collating and constituting "one possible metastory," it all begins to sound thoroughly departmental, further and further away from those old, "autonomous," wrongly privileged poems and stories and novels we admired as works of imagination. This is the language of professional litsociology as spoken in the late 1980s, and it brought to mind the wistful question Randall Jarrell asked thirty-five years ago in "The Age of Criticism": "Critics exist simply to help us with works of art—isn't that true?"

What happens when these critics go to work on particular works of art? They apologize in the preface for the brevity of their "readings," since this introductory volume must deal with so much material; and they promise later on to analyze major texts in detail, devoting "entire chapters to key figures." But it may not be *lengthier* readings we need from them—at least I had doubts after reading their first chapter, titled "The Battle of the Sexes." Its opening questions are wholly rhetorical: "Is a pen a metaphorical pistol? Are words weapons with which the sexes have fought over territory and authority?" Better believe it if you're going to turn out a three-volumed work on the subject, so away we go with sex-warrior Ted Hughes in a typically lurid bit from *Crow* ("His looks were bullets daggers of revenge / Her glances were ghosts in the corner with horrible secrets / His whispers were whips and jackboots / Her kisses were lawyers steadily writing"). No matter that this isn't a very good poem, it gets G&G started on a tour of some major battlefields of the sex war: Tennyson's "The Princess" and Gilbert and Sullivan's rewriting of it; *The Blithedale Romance; The Bostonians;* Swinburne, Prufrock, Yeats, Lawrence, Faulkner, Nathanael West, *Paterson, An American Dream,* and many others.

Poems and stories thus exist to demonstrate or "prove" G&G's point that "the consciousness of sex warfare" pervades modern literature. At one point early along they take on a relatively minor instance of that warfare, T. S. Eliot's "Cousin Nancy" (quoted here to jog the reader's memory):

Miss Nancy Ellicott
Strode across the hills and broke them,
Rode across the hills and broke them—
The barren New England hills—

Riding to hounds
Over the cow-pasture.

Miss Nancy Ellicott smoked
And danced all the modern dances;
And her aunts were not quite sure how they felt about it,
But they knew it was modern.

Upon the glazen shelves kept watch
Matthew and Waldo, guardians of the faith,
The army of unalterable law.

This cynical squib in the Poundian manner (see Pound's "Les Millwins") is equally satiric of Nancy and her aunts, Arnold and Emerson ("guardians of the faith" indeed!), and it now feels to us as thoroughly "period" as does Cousin Nancy. But hear G&G get down to business:

> "Cousin Nancy" . . . frankly satirizes the specious modernity of the liberated Miss Nancy Ellicott, who not only "smoked / And danced all the modern dances" but also, as if to destroy the earth itself, "Strode across the hills and *broke* them" (emphasis ours). Even the poem's allusive conclusion implicitly censures this aggressive protoflapper. . . . Though Eliot presents Matthew (Arnold) and Waldo (Emerson) ironically, as fragile "guardians of the faith," the fact that they are identified with the "army of unalterable law" which defeats "Prince Lucifer" in Meredith's "Lucifer in Starlight" suggests that Eliot sees the rebellious Nancy as a diabolical upstart whose breaking of nature (the hills) also threatens to break the grounds of culture.

Nancy, they go on to say—using the New English Academic's most favorite word—is "problematic."

I have never deeply cared for or bothered much with "Cousin Nancy," but now, seeing the havoc wreaked upon it by such "analysis," I begin to grow fond of it. G&G try hard to show that the poem is a major male putdown of Nancy, but they do this by foisting their own terminology on Eliot's presentation of her ("a diabolical upstart whose breaking of nature . . . also threatens to break the grounds of culture") as if that's what the poem in fact says. It never occurs to them, evidently, that the ringing line from Meredith might be used just as ironically as the poem's other materials, everything being grist for Eliot's satiric mill. For G&G are interested in "Cousin Nancy" only as an item to throw into the hopper, adding further to their point about the battle of the sexes. If the poem gets a bit ground up in the process, so be it.

The other notable instance of heavy artillery aggressively manned (as it were) by G&G is their gloss on a line from W. D. Snodgrass's "April Inventory." In that poem (from *Heart's Needle*) Snodgrass—perhaps too satisfiedly—congratulates himself on the few things he's learned recently, one of which, *mirabile dictu,* was "to ease my woman till she came." Actually this line is followed by "To ease an old man who was dying," putting a little play on the word "ease." But G&G care only about the first easing, in fact it throws them into a fit of knowing solemnity:

> On the surface, of course, Snodgrass's desire to "ease" his woman "so she came" seems notably generous. But actually such a construction of female desire ultimately implies female dependency: if a man does not "ease" her, Snodgrass suggests, the woman cannot come.

In the twinkling of an eye, we are launched into very deep and exciting waters indeed:

> In this regard, Freud's theory of woman as a "castrated" man was useful, for it implied a valorization of the implemental (sexual) utility of the penis (as opposed to the clitoris or vagina) which intensified a widespread cultural assumption of female passivity.

On we go to a lecture about further bad assumptions directed at "nymphomaniac" or "frigid" women who must be punished by "the penis . . . on the verge of turning from a therapeutic instrument in the domestication of desire" into "a penis as pistol, an instrument of rape or revenge." All that from Snodgrass's little boast, now pressed into service of the "metastory." Two pages later we have moved on to *A Streetcar Named Desire,* of which G&G seem to approve, not as far as I can see for anything in its language or artistic construction but for the way "the homosexual author . . . simultaneously records, rationalizes, and critiques the use of the penis as a weapon. . . ." "Critiquing" the penis (and how much more official sounding than merely criticizing it) clearly wins old Tennessee a raft of points, all the ones lost by Snodgrass.

Gilbert and Gubar are lively, but mainly humorless; they have no time for comedy since there are so many examples to be run through. But they do go into stitches, relatively speaking, over "an exceptionally funny short fantasy" by a science fiction writer named William Tenn who (in 1965) wrote "The Masculinist Revolt," in which angry men revive their virility by bringing back the codpiece. The hero, named P. Edward Pollyglow (also known as "Old Pep"), advertises his codpieces with the following slogan:

MEN ARE DIFFERENT FROM WOMEN!
Dress *differently*
Dress *masculinist!*
Wear Pollyglow Men's Jumpers
With the *Special Pollyglow Codpiece!*
And join the masculinist club!

G&G think this hilarious but see nothing the least bit funny in a poem ("Letter from Chicago") written by May Sarton in 1953 about what Virginia Woolf's death had meant to her: "Here where you never were, they said, / 'Virginia Woolf is dead' / The city died. I died in the city," Sarton writes, and proceeds to note that "yesterday I found you," "I speak to you and meet my own," and "I send you love forward into the past." The point about these sadly inept lines, if we hadn't already guessed, is that "Sarton's gesture of amorous salutation is an exemplary one for many modernist women of letters" who want to throw themselves "into the arms of powerfully aesthetic foremothers." It matters not a whit that there's nothing the least "modernist"—not to say aesthetic—about Sarton's attempt at a poem, so long as it can provide another exemplary block in the metastory.

A voice from within now accuses me of fussiness, nit-picking, of neglecting the book's larger argument in favor of local disagreements; of being insufficiently appreciative of the way (in J. Hillis Miller's cover blurb) it "rewrite[s] the history of modernism." That argument, or overview, emphasizes the violence twentieth-century male writers directed at women and how the women fought back, looked for their foremothers, made the historic effort (in G&G's words) "to come to terms with the urgent need for female literary authority through fantasies about the possession of a mother tongue." In fact, I don't at all object to the "overview" as a provocative and—on inspection of much evidence dug out of the works themselves—a justifiable line to take. Gender strife is the real thing and, insofar as it motivates or enlivens the "organized violence upon language" Frost said made up poetry, is even the real right thing. After all, nothing exciting happens in literature when amity, mutual respect, and peaceful commerce obtain between the sexes—as if literature were someone's liberal ideal of a coeducational college campus.

Another cover blurb, this one from Joyce Carol Oates, warns me that "Male readers and critics will ignore it at their own peril." As far as I can tell, I am not taking a negative line about the enterprise because of my identity as a *male* reader and critic; it's rather that as a male *reader and critic* I'm unhappy with what, too often, these female critics make of their chosen texts. For whenever the language of the work in question is delicate and complicated in its figure, that work—often a poem—suffers from their treatment. Pound's quite distinctive "Portrait d'une Femme," we are told,

> implies that woman is herself botched. Asserting that "Your mind and you are our Sargasso Sea," he defines her as both the debris and the destroyer of a shipwrecked civilization: her "Ideas, old gossip, oddments of all things, / Strange spars of knowledge" are not fragments she has shored against her ruins; rather, they represent the ruinousness of a mind replete with "Nothing that's quite [her] own."

I can only say in response to this that it is hopelessly mangling of the poem's tone and atmosphere, and that the *Waste Land* allusion is no help. Among other things, Pound's portrait is witty and slightly rueful, not to say rhythmically interesting; but "rhythm" is not something these metastorytellers care overmuch about.

Rather, their aggressive eagerness as readers propels them into claims you wish they would reconsider, like this one about the end of Elizabeth Bishop's "Invitation to Miss Marianne Moore":

> Come like a light in the white mackerel sky,
> come like a daytime comet
> with a long unnebulous train of words,
> from Brooklyn, over the Brooklyn Bridge, on this fine morning,
> please come flying.

One may be charmed or not so charmed by the poem, but have you thought of it in such terms as G&G propose?

> Indeed, the consummation Bishop devoutly wishes to achieve in her confrontation with this woman artist seems not only erotic but also apocalyptic: erotic because Bishop envisions Moore "com[ing]" and "mounting" the "white mackerel sky / . . . like a daytime comet," apocalyptic because Moore's "com[ing]" and "mounting" herald what Adrienne Rich calls "a whole new poetry beginning here."

I won't comment on this except to say that to "envision" Marianne Moore in this erotic/apocalyptic way may be something Adrienne Rich might do, or approve of, but surely ruins the fairy-tale whimsy of Bishop's concluding plea to her mentor.

This first volume of the trilogy shows incontestably that Gilbert and Gubar know exactly what they want to demonstrate about the battle of the sexes in our century and that there is nothing likely to stand in their way of demonstrating it. Certainly not literature, which can be beaten into shape, its rough edges or ambiguous tones ironed out through rewordings into a metastory such as we have here. The question is whether such rewordings are strenuously to be avoided. John Carey, for one, thought so when in his inaugural lecture as Merton Professor of Literature at Oxford (titled "The Critic as Vandal") he called it "a paramount duty of the literary critic not merely not to reword himself, but to contest and discredit all rewordings fabricated by other critics, demonstrating their inadequacy and destructiveness."[3] If this is being, in effect, an anti-critic, it will at least—in Carey's further words—"bear witness to the fact that literature is irreplaceable, irreducible and irrefutable, and quite distinct in its mode of being from literary criticism." But I suspect this is a fact over which the authors of *No Man's Land* aren't going to lose much sleep.

Hudson Review 40, no. 2 (Summer 1988). Copyright ©1988 by the Hudson Review, Inc. Reprinted by permission.

3. John Carey, "The Critic as Vandal," *New Statesman,* August 6, 1978.

Love Story

Peter Gay's general introduction to what will be a five-volume study of—in his words—"the bourgeois experience" explained that the first volume, *Education of the Senses* (1984), would examine "the bourgeois sensual life" while the volume to follow would

> explore theories of love; the cultural fantasies that the fiction of the age enshrined; the disguises that erotic desire could assume in the so-called higher realms of culture; the forms of loving that divines called sinful and psychiatrists perverse; and the price that bourgeois constraints on sexuality exacted, or were thought to exact from the middle classes.

Since in his view the bourgeois experience from Victoria to Freud demanded nothing less than a "symphonic" treatment, Mr. Gay sees himself as, above all else, an orchestrator who needs enormous space and leisure adequately to shape the "rich material" so variously illustrated by the lives and writings of Western European, English and American men and women over the course, more or less, of a century.

The presiding genius of the whole enterprise is Freud, and in *Freud for Historians* (1985), a smaller book (a mere 252 pages) sandwiched between the first two large volumes of *The Bourgeois Experience,* Mr. Gay reveals that ten years ago he entered the Western New England Institute for Psychoanalysis as a "research candidate." This "fascinating" experience only made him more professionally aware of how useful Freud could be—and was not being permitted to be—for his brothers and sisters in the historical profession. *Freud for Historians* argued for a more thoughtful canvassing of the uses of psychoanalysis in the individual historian's project; it is "history informed by psychoanalysis," rather than "psychohistory," that Gay sees himself as writing in his massive work in progress. At times Freud's legacy "informs" Gay's history in a familiar, perhaps too-familiar way, as when (in *Education of the Senses*) a nineteenth-century American diarist, Lester Ward, racked with unconsummated desires toward his fiancée, notes that "I strained to push my steel pen

The Bourgeois Experience: Victoria to Freud, volume 2: *The Tender Passion,* by Peter Gay. Oxford University Press, 1984.

into my pencil case a moment ago, and it became stuck so that I broke my pencil case to get it loose." Comments Mr. Gay: "The steel pen was obviously not the only pointed object that Ward wanted to activate, the pencil case not the only thing he wanted to break." Heh-heh. There are a few such too-knowing moments in the history when one wishes for the presence of a commentator named, say, Vladimir Nabokov.[1] But compared to some of his predecessors in the mode, Gay is discreet and humane in his analyses.

A more essential and immediate problem for the reader is what to *do* with all the rich detail Mr. Gay is concerned to orchestrate. Taking the "symphonic" analogy seriously, we love and admire the skill, in Haydn or Brahms or Tchaikovsky, with which themes are treated and developed through individual sequences of movements and through the succession of movements which is the entire symphony. With Bruckner, by contrast (and unless one is Winthrop Sargeant), we may grumble and shut off the radio or phonograph: the material has been pushed around at too great a length in too portentous a manner. Peter Gay is a case of the writer who cannot bear to omit anything, and his sequences within individual volumes and from one volume to the next are difficult to tease out. In one of the few really critical reviews *Education of the Senses* received, Paul Johnson (*Commentary*, June 1984) admitted that Gay's manner was engaging and that he had a sharp eye for good quotations and examples, but went on to say that "Nevertheless, at bottom this book is a lot of miscellaneous information chasing a subject." I do not think he would revise his estimate in the light of this successor volume.

Paul Johnson also pointed out that Gay's method of writing history, which derives in part from the French *Annales* school of "total history" (Marc Bloch is the distinguished progenitor), has in some of its practitioners, such as Fernand Braudel, been "characterized by pretentiousness and flatulence." "Its greatest weakness," Johnson argued, at the risk of seeming pedantic, is "the lack of a chronological framework. History without chronology tends to degenerate into fuzzy anecdotage." Peter Gay is seldom pretentious, and only occasionally flatulent; but the lack of chronology means that one never really knows what is going to come next. (The first volume begins with the erotic life of Mabel Loomis Todd, c. the 1880s in America; the second, in its first chapter, considers early-nineteenth-century "treatises" on love by Stendhal and Balzac,

---

1. "Freudism and all it has tainted with its grotesque implications and methods appears to me to be one of the vilest deceits practiced by people on themselves and on others. I reject it utterly, along with a few other medieval items still adored by the ignorant, the conventional, or the very sick" (Vladimir Nabokov, *Strong Opinions*, 1973).

Love Story

in 1820s France.) This refusal to honor chronology may have something to do with Gay's preference for the symphonic treatment, but it does run the risk of anecdotage, anecdotes too often told at too great length.

An example from the first volume is Mabel Todd, whose journals provide the basis for almost forty pages of treatment. It may be that, as a resident of Amherst, indeed an owner of a house that Mrs. Todd built and stored her mahogany furniture in, I am peculiarly resistant to the lady's charms. But when in a chapter well along in the new volume, titled "Stratagems of Sensuality" (in which Gay goes about showing how such stratagems as music, food, and nature served as substitutes for sexual expression among the bourgeoisie), Mabel Todd comes back for another turn on the boards, I found my heart sinking. "There is happiness amounting to ecstasy in being on the long white beach, with lines of breakers rolling up in foam, the sun glittering on the little waves out to sea and the blessed east wind blowing health into one's face, an ecstasy which I have never experienced under any other circumstances, but which is faintly suggested to me by seeing white steam come out of a pipe or chimney against the blue sky." Immediately Mr. Gay, Detector of Symbols, goes to work: "her unconscious phallic fantasies breaking through with her association to pipes and chimneys emitting steam, hint at the sexual charge that participating in the world of nature and machines gave her." Well, O.K., if you must. But there is more, much more of the diarist: "Do you hear the crickets, *our* crickets, my beloved, at twilight? And when you hear them do you think of me? I sat on the east piazza last evening listening to them, and again in front of the house, until it seems to me you *must* be with me. Do you hear them sweetheart?" Those crickets, Mr. Gay tells us, are "emblems of bliss remembered and hopes betrayed": and Mabel Todd's "erotic mode of assimilating nature . . . explodes, with little rocket showers of joy and pathos" in the course of her love affair with Emily Dickinson's brother. The historian of the bourgeois experience loves Mrs. Todd, because he can use her as contradictory evidence to the cliché about how all Victorians, especially women, suffered from repression: here was a woman, likely one of many men and women, who actively enjoyed and cultivated, through "stratagems of sensuality" and through the thing itself, an erotic life. The trouble is that Mr. Gay doesn't imagine the possibility of looking at the whole Mabel Loomis Todd story with something less than reverence; that a little of it goes a very long way; that a reader of Evelyn Waugh, not to say Terry Southern, might be less than captivated by the whole throbbing affair.

It may sound arrogant, obtuse, or both to complain that a historian's tone is not ironic enough about its subject and subjects. (By irony I do not mean the too-knowing Freudian reading of the steel pen-and-pencil case moment quoted earlier from Lester Ward's diary.) But Mr. Gay has invested so much energy in being, always, a sympathetic reader of every diarist or letter writer, man or woman, from W. E. Gladstone at the helm of empire, to Mabel Burrows at St. Margaret's School in Waterbury, Connecticut, in love with her schoolmate Mary Dennison—that for fear of scoring off his subjects through irony (perhaps with the contrary example of Lytton Strachey in mind), he becomes overprotective of them. Eros in all its manifestations is thus regarded with too much reverence. So his final plea in this second volume is that we "once again learn to read them [the Victorian middle classes] if we wish to recapture that particular mixture of sensuality and shy reticence, and the subtle, poignant compromises between drives and defenses with which they regulated their loves in imagination and in life." Granted there is always a swell in any book's final sentence, but this one seems to me "overdetermined" (a favorite Freudian word of Gay's), with its "subtle," its "poignant," its "drives and defenses." Strachey was less warm hearted, and a better writer.

As a practitioner of "total history"—if it is fair to saddle him with the phrase—Mr. Gay has to be ready, calmly, to handle everything: there is nothing that is not grist for his mill. Perhaps the most important form of expression he deals with in *The Tender Passion* is the novel, and not only in England. In his approach to novels he sounds quite aware of what he is and is not doing, noting at the beginning of his chapter "The Work of Fiction" that he is "writing neither literary criticism nor literary history, neither appraising style nor assigning merit." Rather, he is "solely concerned here with the portrayal of love in nineteenth-century fiction." Does he realize how that seemingly innocuous claim is bound to set the literary critic's teeth on edge, brought up to distrust such presumed neutrality—to style, treatment, merit—as the refuge of a sociologist or something worse? His assumption, it soon becomes clear, is that he is as free to characterize the erotic life of someone in a novel as he is when the someone is a real person writing in her journal, or in a letter to a beloved. Sometimes, it seems, freer. His inclination is to believe that the written record of bourgeois erotic life "is far different, in fact, far more tepid, than that experience itself." Yet he can't get inside the bedroom to ascertain whether Walter and Eliza Bagehot had a really satisfactory relationship. (They had plenty of intellectual companionship but also frequent headaches, so "whether they enjoyed one another's bodies as they enjoyed one another's minds must remain a question.") But with Edward Casaubon, that memorable figure in George Eliot's *Middlemarch*, Mr. Gay is ready to give us the whole scoop on the man's lack of sexual contact with his (in Eliot's word) "ardent" young wife, Dorothea. For Mr. Gay, Casaubon is a "disastrous first husband, the sterile pedant . . . who seems to have been quite as impotent in bed as he was at his desk." *Seems?* . . . I know not *seems*. Has it occurred to Gay that behind George Eliot's words there *is* no bedroom in which Casaubon did not perform? By talking this way about literary character, he shows how not doing "literary criticism" is disabling to his credibility as a describer of Eliot's portrayal of love or its absence.

Often in the chapter on fiction, as elsewhere, Gay's passion for getting everything in, using every one of his notecards, makes for the kind of omnibus one doesn't much want to ride on. A paragraph informs us that "Serious nineteenth-century fiction . . . undertook critical, pointed investigation of society" (so what else is new?), quotes Henry James on the Novel's virtue being its "air of reality (solidity of specification)," and says that "love" is a principal ingredient in that reality (again, who would disagree?). He then "proves" his point by citing titles from Balzac, Zola, de Maupassant, then says it wasn't only the French who recognized this: "Henry James's *Wings of the Dove* and Trollope's *Phineas Finn* show lovemaking to be essentially a political game and, conversely, politics often an erotic sport—for high stakes." There is no "politics" in *The Wings of the Dove*, unless I missed it, and I don't see why these totally different novels should be jammed together. The paragraph rolls along, embracing Eça de Queiros, Mrs. Gaskell, Melville, and Twain, but adds up to no more than what Paul Johnson accused Gay's earlier volume of being—"a lot of miscellaneous information chasing a subject." And some of the individual bits of "information"—as with the yoking of James and Trollope—stand up to close inspection in only the most superficial way.

At one point, apropos of Thomas Bridgeman's *Florist Guide*, a book designed for the "softer sex" which concludes with a postscript comparing marriage to a "garden," Mr. Gay says: "It may seem heavy-handed to read this largely irrelevant postscript to a sensible guide as an extended metaphor for sexual intercourse or sexual panic." In fact, as he shows by extended quotation from the florid document, his reading is perfectly justified and entertaining as well. Where the heavy-handedness comes in is in description like the following of what reading fiction involves. The full battery of Freudian terms is hauled out:

The work of reading calls upon all the principal institutions of the mind: it teases the id by counterfeiting instinctual satisfactions, flatters the ego with formal beauties, soothes the superego in enlisting the reader in an invisible moral community where the wicked and the innocent receive their due . . . or where suffering comes to all as man's lot.

Isn't this faculty psychology, come back with a vengeance, conjuring up an experience so abstract, so remote from anyone's reading of an actual novel, that it seems merely perverse, or merely an example of the theorist's cleverness? When a particular novel, and a great one, comes under the Freudian glass, the results are even more painful:

Anna Karenina's suicide, a pathetic mixture of despair and revenge, of obedience to a punitive superego, and rebellion against intolerable narcissistic injuries, was the final act of a transgression in the realm, and under the impulsion, of Eros.

So *that's* what it was! we are invited to breathe. Anna's suicide of course brings the railroad to Mr. Gay's mind, so this "favorite actor in the theater of libido" takes a bow, first in something called *Auch Einer* by Friedrich Theodor Vischer, then in Dickens, whose writing about Mr. Dombey on the train ("Away, with a shriek, and a roar, and a rattle," etc.) has, predictably, "something erotic about it." We are even treated to Freud's hoary old thing from *Three Essays on Sexuality* about how "every boy, at least, has at some time in his life wanted to be an engine driver or a coachman." (I never wanted to be an engine driver, and I never even thought of being a coachman—or am I repressing something?) Once again, Nabokov's is the voice one yearns for here.

As with the earlier volume, *The Tender Passion* concludes with a "Biographical Essay," forty-six pages long, mentioning every book, article, and person Mr. Gay has consulted, and telling us what he thinks of each item.[2] Like the index, the book itself is an enormous Chinese dinner (except that it doesn't taste so good piece by piece) after completing which the reader soon wonders where it all went, what substance it left behind. Perhaps no more than what we knew already, that—in the book's truest sentence—"It all depended."

Hudson Review 28, no. 3 (Autumn 1976). Copyright © 1976 by the Hudson Review, Inc. Reprinted by permission.

2. This produces some very odd couplings indeed: "William Empson's *Seven Types of Ambiguity* (1931), and the perceptive study of Walter Muschg, *Psychoanalyse und Literaturwissenschaft* (1930) retain much of their authority." Frequently Gay uses the word "magisterial" to describe someone else's book, and would probably welcome its application to *The Bourgeois Experience.*

Personal Disclosures

The disclosures are three in number and don't exactly add up to a major soul baring. But the subject of each continues to occupy me. "West of Boston: Robert Frost" is a short memoir of a poet whose name is spread all over this volume and whose influence on my sense of life and art is incalculable. "The Scholar and the Soap" tells the tale of my brief involvement with the New York media world in an attempt to keep "Search For Tomorrow," a beloved soap opera threatened with cancellation, on my local channel. "Search" lingered awhile longer, then died, and I have successfully switched my affection to ABC's "Loving" at the same time of day. "Nasty Reviews: Easy to Give, Hard to Take" seemed a sensible way to end a book full of reviews, not all of them nasty.

West of Boston: Robert Frost

I encountered him first when I was a sophomore at Amherst College in the fall of 1950—not at one of the public readings he gave each year to overflow crowds in Johnson Chapel, but in the living room of a fraternity to which I'd recently become pledged. Accompanied by a member of the English department, Robert Frost came to spend a couple of hours with the brothers of Phi Alpha Psi, who turned out for the occasion dressed up in their gray flannel slacks, scuffed white bucks, button-down collars, and striped ties (*de rigueur*). He read poems to us for a while and talked about them and life generally. I can't remember anything he said, probably because I had in mind a question to put to him. When it came time for such, I asked him about his poem "Bereft," which we had studied that fall in an introductory course in critical reading. "Where had I heard this wind before / Change like this to a deeper roar?" it began, and concluded this way:

> Word I was in the house alone
> Somehow must have gotten abroad,
> Word I was in my life alone,
> Word I had no one left but God.

Fresh from Johnson City, New York, and beginning to have doubts about my confident Episcopalian faith, I asked the poet just how much that "God" of the poem's final line amounted to. "Where are you when you have no one left but God?" I said, imitating a member of the English department who had suggested that in such a situation you were more or less nowhere.

Frost didn't answer the question but rather gave me a little lecture, kind but firm, about how poets draw a line over which they won't step, and how my question was the sort of one that invited him to step over that line, and how he wasn't going to step over it. I subsided, aware that I had been taken down a bit, though not scolded too severely. But later one of my fraternity mates—a rather pompous fellow, I thought—took me to task: hadn't I realized that we were *not* supposed to ask Mr. Frost direct questions about what lines from his poetry did or didn't mean? How could I have been so crass?

After that I remember almost nothing about Frost during my undergraduate years at Amherst. (I do remember one evening at another fraternity where the assembled students asked him too much about baseball—they had been clued in that he was in favor of baseball.) He made himself available at the Lord Jeffery Inn during certain hours for individual visits, but I would never have dared go. I didn't think of myself (and quite rightly) as a poet; indeed, I was majoring in philosophy rather than English. But when I left Amherst for graduate school I carried along the green volume of *Complete Poems* (1949) and grew as much or more attached to them as to those of any poet, ancient or modern. Eventually I undertook a doctoral dissertation on him and decided— since I was then at Harvard and Frost had a residence on Brewster Street in Cambridge—to write and request a private chat. With much fussing and twisting I penned the letter, posted it, and never received a reply. So I reminded myself, a bit ruefully, that the important thing about a poet was his poetry and that Frost was a public figure with better things to do than answer letters from eager graduate students.

Little did I expect that I would soon have that public figure on my hands during one of his two-week biyearly stays at Amherst College. I had accepted a job in the English department there and was asked, the fall that I arrived, to take charge of Frost's social schedule—to see that he knew with whom he was having lunch or dinner on each particular day, field any requests or complaints, and generally check in on him in the mornings to talk over the night before and the shape of the new day. (Was I not writing a dissertation on his poetry? Who better to do these things?) Our first meeting was agreeable enough. Though he teased me a bit about writing on him, he didn't seem annoyed by the fact ("I don't read criticism," he insisted more than once). The moment that remains vividly in memory, though, came at the end of an evening when my wife and I had been invited to have dinner with him and one or two others at the home of the widow of a professor (George Frisbie Whicher) with whom Frost had been friends. We had a drink or so before dinner and Frost asked for some rum, into which he put sugar, explaining that sugar was good for you and also that there was a colonial air about the beverage that he approved of. Dinner and the talk afterward—mostly by him—were pleasant enough (I got him to talk a bit about Santayana), and as things drew to a close Frost suggested we walk back to the inn.

It was a splendid October night, leaves most satisfyingly in evidence, and as we crunched through them up Amity Street—which felt at that moment like the most beautiful street in the world—poetry was the subject. Somehow we got on Browning, a poet I'd had a terrible time reading in graduate school and was pretty sure was Browning's fault. Suddenly Frost began to quote some verses I had never before heard:

> The fancy I had to-day,
>   Fancy which turned a fear!
> I swam far out in the bay,
>   Since waves laughed warm and clear.
>
> I lay and looked at the sun,
>   The noon-sun looked at me:
> Between us two, no one
>   Live creature, that I could see.

He went on quoting and I could follow well enough to register the arrival of a live creature, indeed a butterfly:

> A handbreadth over head!
>   All of the sea my own,
> It owned the sky instead;
>   Both of us were alone.

There was something thrilling about the way he said that line "Both of us were alone." What was it—an early poem of Frost's I'd never read? No, he said, it was Browning. But what poem, I wanted to know. He suggested I look it up, perhaps because he couldn't remember the title, perhaps because he wanted to make me earn it.

By this time we had come to the inn and I prepared to see him to the door and continue on my way toward what was sometimes referred to as "the compound," a college housing project in which young instructors resided. I didn't know then that Frost would initiate his ritual of prolonging the evening: "I'll walk a ways with you in your direction," he offered, and we rounded the Beta corner and continued on to Chi Phi. "Do you want to go back?—I'll walk you back," I offered, and we headed toward the inn. There were at least one or two more shorter turns, and by the time the talk was over and I got home, it was late. Frost liked to stay up until 2 A.M. or so, especially if he had someone to talk to. I, on the other hand, was teaching two sections of Freshman Composition which met every day, Monday through Saturday, and with a set of papers to be graded and handed back for each class. A slight conflict of interest there, and if my interest in Frost prevailed I still had to get the papers back on time. When I got home I looked for the Browning, couldn't find it, then discovered it next day in a complete edition of his poetry under the title "Amphibian," prologue to a late, lengthy, and not appealing operation called, of all things, *Fifine at the Fair*. As I read "Amphibian" through, I discovered a later stanza Frost hadn't quoted:

> Emancipate through passion
>   And thought, with sea for sky,
> We substitute, in a fashion,
>   For Heaven—poetry.

It hit home, since substituting poetry for Heaven was what, in a fashion, I had been trying to do for years. As was later the case with James Shirley's "The glories of our blood and state," or William Collins's "How Sleep the Brave," or Edwin Arlington Robinson's "The Sheaves," Browning's little poem meant and means a lot to me largely because it was Frost who literally passed along the word—something more sustaining than the "Word I had no one left but God."

Looking back from the vantage point of almost thirty years, those evenings and readings blend into the undifferentiated, though I rarely remember being bored or wishing I were anywhere else. I do remember things about food and drink—for example, that we tended to serve him chicken or beef when he came to supper at our house. We didn't offer him rum, but he would have a bourbon and water with some added sugar (sugar is good for you). When he gave his public reading in the chapel he ate nothing before; afterward, in the kitchen of the president's house, he had scrambled eggs, toast, and milk. At one point I even became aware that not everybody in the world, even in Amherst, loved Mr. Frost—at least didn't love to have him around in all situations. At the English department cocktail party, a yearly institution to which Frost was once brought by a senior faculty member, a younger, rather unruly colleague who had (like the rest of us) had a few, felt constrained by his presence and growled at me, "Get that old man out of here." Frost must have felt somewhat out of place, not enough the center of attention, because on leaving rather early he cast his eye about us all and said rather threateningly to the professor who had brought him, "Get rid of them all! Fire 'em!" We assured ourselves, after he left, that he had just been teasing and wouldn't decide to push the suggestion further. Anyway, I survived.

A couple of additional pictures, the first of them remaining fondly in the mind's eye. My infant son was brought in to be introduced to the old man.

West of Boston

Frost was eighty-six years old and my son about three weeks old; the poet kindly paid him some attention, taking one of his tiny hands in his hoary one, playing with the fingers for a few seconds. Words don't get the picture into very good focus. The last time I saw him was after he had been ill with pneumonia. He said he was tired, and the business manager of the college (who had come along with Frost to our house after a reception) suggested to him loudly—Frost being selectively deaf—that he might move to Amherst and settle down for good. "Why, you could live in this house," he offered, as my wife and I shared a moment of concern. But the most vivid recollection, along with that late walk up Amity Street, comes from the time when, at the end of his annual spring visit, he suddenly decided he wanted to go back to Cambridge. I volunteered to drive him, even canceled a composition class to do it, while to my wife fell the uneasy task of calling up the people with whom he was to have had dinner that night and explaining to them why Frost wouldn't be showing up. At that time we owned a 1952 Dodge that was on its last legs and burned oil like crazy. To save money I carried along a can of oil in the car and was always prepared, should smoke begin to issue freely from the exhaust, to step out on Route 2, raise the hood, and pour it in. So was I also prepared to change a tire. But I was prepared neither to change a tire nor to pour in oil with America's first poet looking on in amusement or dismay from the front seat. Crossing my fingers, I checked the oil, kicked the tires, and we proceeded without incident to Cambridge.

As I drove along I told him that I hoped to turn my recently finished dissertation into a book about his poetry, and that a commercial publisher had shown interest (that was all they showed). Frost was less than enthusiastic about the idea: "Keep it around," he advised. "Deepen it." At the time it was just what I didn't want to hear, though of course he was right. When we got to Cambridge he suggested lunch at a restaurant. Where should we go? Why, to the Commander Hotel, a Cambridge spot somewhat out of the graduate student run of things. We were seated in fine style. Shouldn't we have a cocktail, he said, and shouldn't it be a daiquiri? One of my less favorite drinks, but I accepted with pleasure and agreed that sugar was a good thing. Afterward we proceeded to his house, and though I had always looked down on autograph seekers, I asked him to write something in my old copy of *Complete Poems*. There was no index to this edition, as he found out while trying to locate a particular poem. So the inscription, when he slowly and laboriously finished it, read "To William Pritchard: Thanks for sight of this old edition without index of titles and first lines." He signed and dated it, then added underneath, as if in afterthought, "And for the ride from Amherst to Cambridge he made pleasant." Driving home I felt about as pleasant as I've ever managed to feel.

Yale Review, Spring 1987

The Scholar and the Soap

Eight years ago, when others had begun to jog, to correct their corrupt diets, to engage—it was rumored—in affairs of various sorts, I had a different response to creeping middle age. A spry forty-four, I was well settled as a creature of routine—teaching literature classes at the same hours each term, usually in the morning; always finishing essays and reviews before rather than after they were due; eating interesting mixtures of canned soups, plus a ham sandwich with mayonnaise, for lunch; making a habit of gin and vermouth before dinner; taking a half-hour nap each day, and so forth. A suitable addition to this routine, I felt, might be the cultivation of a less sublime literary form than I held forth about in my classes, so I decided to find a soap opera to watch, preferably one occurring in the middle of the day while I was eating the ham sandwich, and preferably of the half-hour rather than full-hour brand. It was thus I settled on CBS's venerable "Search for Tomorrow."

This show (hereafter referred to as "Search") had been running since 1951 and became the oldest living soap when its competitor, "Love of Life," fell by the wayside. It boasted an actress, Mary Stuart (she plays the heroine, Joanne, and has had many different last names as men have come and gone), who had graced "Search" since its inception. It concerned itself mainly with the small-town scene: hospitals, marriage and divorce, gossip and rumor, worry, worry, worry. As in every good soap, financial ruin or incipient brain tumors were on the horizon for every member of the cast. Yet somehow the contemplation of these and many other daily disasters makes us, the viewers, feel good. A sonnet by David Slavitt concisely accounts, I think, for this paradox; it ends this way:

> Stupid, I used to think, and partly still
> do, deploring the style, the mawkishness.
> And yet, I watch. I cannot get my fill
> of lives as dumb as mine. Pine Valley's mess
> is comforting. I need not wish them ill.
> I watch, and I delight in their distress.

As the years went by, I would from time to time compile lists of characters, all the ones I could remember, present and past. More often than not at the family supper table I would recount, to a not always enraptured wife and children, the depredations that had occurred earlier in the day. My third son began to watch it with me, during vacations and other times off from school, and if, occasionally, I had to be out of town for a few days, he would be waiting at my return, ready to read off his notes on those productions I'd missed. And even though "Search" didn't do much in the ratings and had nowhere near the popularity of such shows as "General Hospital" or "All My Children," it managed just barely to survive. At one point, in the spring of 1982, it moved from CBS to NBC and for a time occupied a slot at 2:30 in the afternoon. This ordinarily would have been an awkward time for me to view it; luckily I was on sabbatical, so I adjusted my schedule, came home later to lunch, and arrived back at the office at the relaxed hour of 3 P.M.

Then one Thursday afternoon last April, just before the beginning of "Search," a local broadcaster on WWLP, the NBC affiliate in Springfield, Massachusetts, announced that beginning the following Monday her talk show would be switched to 12:30 P.M. (the "Search" slot). It took a moment to penetrate before I began frantically scanning next week's *TV Guide* and, indeed, saw no listing for "Search" on WWLP. The Boston NBC channel had already disdained to carry it; two other stations that still broadcast it could not, to my knowledge, be received on my tube. I watched the show that day and the next, thoroughly distracted by the thought that this might very possibly be the end of the line for me and "Search."

The next morning I fired off letters: one to the station manager, deploring the decision to cancel and urging a reconsideration; one to the college newspaper, asking students to write and protest; a final one to the *Hampshire Gazette*, where my wife was employed. The station manager responded immediately, informing me that "Search" had been, in his words, "fledgling for a long time on the network" and adding, self-righteously, that NBC itself had been thinking of discontinuing it. I wrote back to point out that I understood a fledgling to be a baby bird just learning to use its wings, and that "Search" had been flying for more than thirty years until (I concluded dramatically) "you shot it down." But clearly I was wasting my words—no reconsideration was in the offing.

Meanwhile my wife had mentioned my loss to a reporter at the local *Gazette*, who called up for an interview, then ran a clever piece about the distraught professor who didn't know what to do with himself in the middle of the day, having been deprived of his pleasure. Suddenly, the next morning, things began to move. The wire services had picked up the story and phone calls began. One came from the offending affiliate in Springfield, wanting to do an interview, another from CBS in Hartford, which showed up with the cameras and was to stick with the story through its life. The exciting question seemed to be, as *USA Today* put it, why this "mild-mannered professor" was also an "addict." "And just why should this English scholar, who teaches poetry, fiction, and criticism, be a 'Search' junkie?" they asked, barely staying for an answer.

My mail improved mightily, both at home and in the office. Most of the letters were from women in the western Massachusetts area who commiserated with me, or wanted me to know how outraged they were and that they had written the station manager. And as the wire services beamed the story to various farther-flung localities, letters arrived from California and Washington (state), Bethany, Pennsylvania, and Gadsden, Alabama, Route 2, Box 61, where a Mrs. Arlene Gregg had an interesting proposal. She would tape two weeks' worth of shows, and send them along to me for viewing. Then I would send the tape back to her, at which point she would have a further two-week batch ready for me. I wrote Mrs. Gregg that I would be happy to receive the first two weeks' worth.

The plot thickened a couple of days later when a call came from someone at NBC, inviting me to fly down to New York City, meet the cast of "Search," and in fact play a bit part on that day's show. Let me think this over, I said, and call you back. Five minutes later I called back to accept, asking only that my wife be permitted to accompany me. (Her reportorial skills would be invaluable; she would remain cool and perceptive while I became flushed and excited.) Accordingly we were put up for the night at an East Side hotel, the Berkshire (I could have dinner *free* in the dining room if I wished), and called for by an NBC publicity person early the next morning.

At the studio it was all bewildering, fast moves from one person to the next, and the sudden disconcerting appearance of tube idols in less than heroic identities. For example, I didn't recognize that female having her hair put up in curlers across the makeup room. Introduced to me, she chirped out a "Hi, William, welcome to the show." It took some time before I registered that the figure being worked over was Marcia McCabe, or more significantly, "Sunny Adamson," tireless investigative reporter fresh from subduing a rapist intent on working his will on her and others. And there was the star herself, the venerable Mary Stuart, who was not in the taping that day but who had come over to the studio at lunchtime to say hello and, as it turned out, share some of my Zabar's corned-beef sandwich.

It was time for the rehearsals of different scenes—a hospital bed, a cabin where the kidnapped teenager was tied to a post and trying to escape, another cabin where pregnant Suzi Wyatt suddenly went into premature labor, and, for me most salient, Bigelow's Bar, where my brief moment would come to fulfillment. I was to precede one of the regulars into "Big's" and for a few seconds, until they moved the cameras to her and forgot me forever, it was all mine. No lines, merely an opening and closing of the saloon door, a couple of steps to the bar, a firm, friendly handshake with "Big" the bartender, and an indication that I needed a beer. And lo, there was the beer, a real one, which I proceeded to sip, while knocking back some real potato sticks. The heavy cameras quickly rolled away from me toward Sunny Adamson. While members of the cast fluffed their lines, cursed things out, or made jokes about the dialogue, my own take was boringly perfect. There was evidently no way my ten-second journey from door to bar could be improved.

My episode didn't appear on the air until about nine days later, and I spent some time figuring out how to arrange a viewing for myself of myself. We had talked about renting a motel room near Hartford, say, someplace where we could pick up the show, but then a number of people in the area called or wrote to tell me that I might be able to see it on my own set from a channel in New Britain, Connecticut. So I purchased an ancient, secondhand outdoor antenna and had it installed on the upstairs porch outside the bedroom. The day of my appearance, however, the reception was worse than average, and the viewing was further complicated by the presence of the faithful Hartford TV crew come to film the professor watching himself.

"Prof lathers in the soaps" ran the lead to the AP account in a Rochester newspaper someone sent along. At about that same time I received my first crank call, from a strange, unidentified voice who said he'd been an "activist" all his life (evidently thinking, because of the letter I'd written to the station, that I too was an activist). He was inviting me to address a "Sexual Liberty meeting" that he was organizing for the Fourth of July. I was to put what he called my "Shakespearean mind" to work and give a speech on, oh, perhaps a nuclear freeze, or some topic related to sexual freedom. I quickly declined. More letters poured in, and radio talk-show hosts from Canada to Delaware issued me invitations to join them on the air. (I finally turned down one station that wanted me to arise for a 6:20 A.M. interview.)

Within the space of two weeks I had gone from a private man who cultivated his habit for half an hour a day, five days a week, to someone to whom such gratification was first denied, then to whom unexpected gratifications came in a flurry. Robert Frost liked to muse about his own career that, as with a wedding, "it begins in felicity and ends in publicity." And then, thinking of marriages that go wrong, Frost would add, "And maybe really *ends* there." But my own bit of publicity was felicitous because I knew it would end, fickle creatures that the media have proved themselves to be. So I was eager to squeeze whatever further experiences I could out of the whole affair.

It turned out that I didn't have to do much squeezing, since about a week after the first New York venture at the "Search" studio, courtesy of NBC, CBS called to suggest I might like to come down and occupy a spot on their "Morning News" program, presided over by Bill Kurtis and Diane Sawyer. My classes had just ended, and CBS's offer to pick me up and bring me back in a limousine was irresistible. (CBS puts up its guests at the Essex House, Central Park South, and my room contained a faulty shower and no telephone book.)

I was slotted to appear at approximately 7:50 A.M., and as I arrived at the CBS studio the next morning Cyrus Vance and Strobe Talbott were being ushered out, having concluded their bit of chat about nuclear arms. In fact this was a big mixed-bag day on "CBS Morning News." The English romance novelist Barbara Cartland was to be interviewed (by Bill Kurtis) and so was the redoubtable Louis Farrakhan. Farrakhan was supposed to precede your humble soap-watcher, who was to be the subject of Diane Sawyer's ministrations, but it was almost 7:30 and the minister had not arrived. While anxious phone calls were being made, suddenly in he swept, flanked by a retinue of well-suited (in a sort of Baptist undertaker-ish way), tie-clasped, highly groomed aides (disciples? bodyguards?). Farrakhan shook hands all round, including the professor's, though conversation did not flow freely between the two of us as we proceeded, in our makeup, to the studio.

Mr. Farrakhan's interview went on for quite a while, indeed was judged to be so important that he was let run overtime. As the clock moved toward 7:55, I began to wonder how I was to be gotten on and off in time for the news at eight. A legitimate wonder, for just as I was directed to occupy the throne, another order came through: "Professor, we're *terribly* sorry about this but there's no time to interview you before the news and (we're *really* sorry about this) there's no time during the second hour of the show either—everything is totally scheduled, filled up." I can still feel the pain. Diane Sawyer came over, sympathetically concerned, telling me how much she'd really wanted to do this story—but her sympathy was powerless against the inexorabilities of scheduling.

There was nothing for it, so it seemed, but to head back to Amherst, dragging my tail behind me. How to describe the mixture of feelings—wounded pride, annoyance at the silly waste of time, rage at CBS, at the intolerable Farrakhan, and at Kurtis for letting him go on, then a glimmer of ironic acceptance of the whole thing as somehow my just deserts ("You *will* move out of your accustomed sphere, will you!"). "Would you like to have your makeup removed?" asked my host for the morning, and I told her never mind, figuring I could wear it back to Amherst. A hasty good-bye and I was at curbside, hand out to open the door of the waiting limousine—when suddenly voices were calling to me to come back, come back, they had canceled some boring bit of consumer research in the next hour and were going to slot me in instead.

After such a victory, snatched from total defeat in the nick of time, the interview itself felt a bit anticlimactic. Diane Sawyer was friendly and enthusiastic, but she must have thought she had a queer bird on her hands, this "professor" who watched a soap, and she asked me with a rather heavily underlined facetiousness whether I watched it for its "high literary value." I allowed as how she was teasing me, but then obligingly went on to suggest possible reasons why a literary person might be interested in a narrative that is all talk and that never concludes itself, unless forced to by a sponsor. Almost before it began, my moment was over, with Miss Sawyer—under her own steam or that of a clever assistant—concluding that, in the words of Yeats (which poet the professor taught), some people ate "a crazy salad with their meat." It was then time for me to depart, truly depart, and, I assumed, to conclude my career as a mild-mannered media event.

One last but very pleasant gasp came at the end of the summer when I received a call from a friend congratulating me on the restoration of "Search" to WWLP Springfield. "Restoration?" was my surprised response, but indeed it had been restored, without my eagle eye catching it in *TV Guide*. My loyal retinue regrouped: the wire services, two or three radio stations, and faithful CBS Hartford called for an interview, asking me—once more—how did I feel *now?* "Ecstatic," was about all I could muster. The station manager of NBC

The Scholar and the Soap

Springfield was quoted in the paper as wondering why, now that the program had been restored, he had heard nothing from me. I wrote him explaining that I thought it was no more than my due, and that usually I wrote such letters only to complain about something.

New Republic, September 9, 1985

Nasty Reviews: Easy to Give, Hard to Take

Some years ago, when *Books Do Furnish a Room*—the tenth novel in Anthony Powell's twelve-volume sequence, *A Dance to the Music of Time*—was published, an American reviewer, Marvin Mudrick, addressed himself in no uncertain terms to the limitations of the novel and of the sequence. "Powell's method of getting on with the story must be the most ponderously inefficient of all time," Mudrick sweepingly began, noting that when a character is introduced, Powell's narrator spends three or four pages speculating on the probable nature of this figure, who, it may be, "is blond, has small ears, and wears a black overcoat." Later in the novel, when "the overcoat turns up," our narrator seizes on new bits of evidence which, at further length, confirm or change his expectations of the character.

According to Mudrick, such a narrative method is less method than "a spreading tumor of speculation," appropriate only to "the most interminable soap-opera since Australopithecus." Powell, Mudrick decided, suffered from "an elephantiasis of the will, making harrumphing preparations for something that never happens." As if such charges weren't enough to sink the book, Mudrick went on to call it " 'a pedestal without a statue,' as Tchaikovsky remarked of some of Brahms's music" (evidently to be compared to Brahms was the last indignity). It must have been only with difficulty that the reviewer refrained from further disparagement and ridicule; possessed by the animus, he found it irresistible.

As a lover of Mr. Powell's work, I found myself, perhaps oddly, enjoying Mudrick's mockery of it as well. So I was pleased to come across recently two small compendiums of reviewer animus titled *Rotten Reviews* and *Rotten Reviews II* edited by Bill Henderson. They are dedicated to "all writers who spent years, if not a lifetime, writing a book and then had it dismissed by a rotten review," and they contain, in alphabetical order, various writers whose books and names are still alive today, to each of which is appended a sentence or paragraph from a reviewer or critic who tried, more or less, to kill them dead on the spot. When Samuel Johnson, in his life of Milton, came to treat "Lycidas," he didn't think it a "rotten" poem exactly, nor was he reviewing it;

still, the words quoted from Johnson are enough to establish him as no friend of "Lycidas": "The diction is harsh, the rhymes uncertain, and the numbers unpleasing. . . . Its form is that of a pastoral—easy, vulgar and therefore disgusting." Then there is H. C. Harwood, whoever he or she may have been, writing about Virginia Woolf's novel *The Waves:* "This chamber music, this closet fiction, is executed behind too firmly closed windows. . . . The book is dull." I revere Samuel Johnson, but his judgment on Milton's poem is famously, certainly, most wrong; H. C. Harwood I never heard of, but as a judgment of Woolf's novel it seems to be dead on. Which may mean nothing more than that I too would be willing to give *The Waves* a rotten review, and that I might turn out to be certainly wrong, if not—like Dr. Johnson—famously so.

Mr. Henderson doesn't have any righteous moral purpose in making these collections; in fact, he says in his editorial note to the first one that in putting them together he was impressed "by the balance, intelligence and fairness of most reviewers," and that he found truly malicious reviews to be rare. But it was with a double take in which things suddenly blurred together slightly that I discovered, in one of the collections, my very own name next to a sarcastic comment about Kenneth Gangemi's short novel *Olt.* Actually, my words bore on the novel only insofar as I facetiously observed that its publicity copy, telling us that Mr. Gangemi had been born in Scarsdale and attended the Rensselaer Polytechnic Institute, was more interesting than anything in the novel itself. Wincing at this bit of airy dismissiveness (admittedly it was two decades ago, before I had "matured"), and also noting that Mr. Gangemi was thanked in the introduction as one of the novelists and poets who had sent in "meanest" notices of their work, I began to think more personally and autobiographically about the strange phenomenon of reviewing and being reviewed.

Since I am neither novelist, poet, nor dramatist—merely an academic who reads a lot—there are those who would claim I'm debarred from producing relevant and sympathetic criticism of novels, poems, and plays. Yet at least I know what it feels like to have been given a rotten review, and at a time—on the publication of a first book—when perhaps the author being reviewed may be most hurt. I had written a study of the English novelist and painter Wyndham Lewis, and while spending a sabbatical year in London decided to publicize the book by sending it to some potentially responsive English reviewers.

One of them—Martin Seymour-Smith—immediately (from Bexhill-on-Sea) acknowledged receipt of my book and said he was looking forward with great interest to reading it.

Not until later did I recognize the clever trick of promptly acknowledging a book someone has sent you before you read it; for a few months later, in the weekly *Spectator,* there appeared a review by the very Seymour-Smith which cast a cold eye indeed on my work. The reviewer found my "academic (albeit) American" approach to be "timid, donnish, obtuse" and on occasion "sneeringly dismissive." My critiques of two Lewis novels were "inept, sixth-form condensations, shyly tinctured with tiny Aristotelian 'objections,'" and admirers of Lewis were to be warned that obtuse dons (albeit American) were moving in on him. Strong stuff, and this rotten review made me feel, well, *rotten.* But after I brushed away the tears, consolations began to present themselves. My book had, at any rate, been reviewed, in a respectable English paper, by a well-known critic, and all publicity was good publicity, so a friend assured me. I thickened my skin to the extent that some years later when another Brit reviewer—the notorious Auberon (son of Evelyn) Waugh—referred to a later effort of mine as "an idiotic little book," I managed something close to a smile.

On the basis then of my own experience I conclude that, far from ignoring and throwing away rotten reviews, their recipients never forget, indeed preserve and treasure them all their days. This persistence in memory, often in the review's exact terms, has not merely to do with the personal bruising suffered but with our tendency to remember the sharp-tongued putdown more than the gentle pat. The language of praise is often gaseous and employs words like "brilliant," "absorbing," "authentic," "deeply moving" (a favorite of some years back), all of which can be plucked from the back of any dust jacket and are absolutely capable of being recycled.

There is an old literary formula about how the novelist may be excellent at creating vicious or "bad" characters (Charles Dickens's Quilp, Jane Austen's Mary Crawford) but has trouble making virtuous ones convincing or interesting (Austen's Fanny Price, Dickens's Esther Summerson). The first time I reviewed a number of poets together (an "omnibus" chronicle for the *Hudson Review*), I struck off, justly or unjustly, some pretty lively sentences about poets whose work seemed of less than star quality; my "rotten" reviewing self, back in those days, felt limber and full of mischief. But when it came to a work I wanted to purchase—in this case Louis MacNeice's *Collected Poems*—my language disintegrated, became soft and squishy as I began to throw around words like "ironic intelligence," "seriousness," "wit," and "incomparable." Early in the reviewing game I found that it was easier to carve up an inferior poem or poet than find terms for praising a superior one, and that the art of encomiastic criticism was indeed an art.

But what is the point, anyway, in castigating the bad poem? Why summon chapter and verse by way of citing the fatuity of someone's first (or tenth) novel? Who breaks a butterfly upon a wheel? And what happens when the person doing the breaking is himself broken by a bad review? One such person, James Atlas, having published a novel which was duly kicked around by reviewers, promised a change in his own attitude toward reviewing. Although he would continue to tell the truth about a book he didn't like, he would tell it "in a gingerly way and with genuine remorse," since "they think we can take it, but we can't."

Yet Mr. Atlas's reminder of the artist's vulnerability is not often at the front of the artist's young reviewer's mind as he sits there, banging away at his typewriter, defending the cause of good art (so he thinks) by pillorying the bad as cleverly as he can. Nor does he think about Henry James's distinction between the good novel and the bad one: "The bad is swept with all the daubed canvases and spoiled marble into some unvisited limbo, or infinite rubbish-yard beneath the back-windows of the world, and the good subsists and emits its light and stimulates our desire for perfection." How assiduous the reviewer needs to be about helping out with the sweeping is, at the least, an open question. Probably not as much as he would like to think.

Having received rough treatment by reviewers, at least James Atlas has resolved to change his own reviewing ways somewhat. But think of the rough treatment critics routinely put themselves in the way of by speaking harshly of an artist's work. In his introduction to the first volume of *Rotten Reviews,* the critic Anthony Brandt tells how, after committing such a review, he met a mutual friend (fictitiously named Don) of the novelist under fire and received a "long, hard stare" from Don, followed by an "Ah . . . it's the Reviewer"—after which Don never again spoke to Mr. Brandt. In fact, as Mr. Brandt goes on to point out, it could have been worse—there have been threats by the injured party of physical assault, even an instance in which one author threw his reviewer down a flight of stairs.

I can't claim anything quite so exciting, though the friend of a poet I had reviewed adversely promised, so the word was passed along, to do something like punch me in the lip. And I have received threatening letters, the most abusive of which, in response to something I'd said about Amy Lowell (herself not even *alive!*), began with the chilling salutation "Sir," and went on to say I had degraded myself and my calling by taking "cheap shots" at the deceased. Of course (the letter continued) I lived in a world so "small, provincial, narrow" (could she have had Amherst, Massachusetts, in mind?) that I would be unable to appreciate Lowell's artistry. After further ascriptions to me of bigotry and narrowness, the letter concluded with a single-paragraph sentence: "Shame on you, shame." That was nine years ago, but I still take out the letter and periodically reread it. Like rotten reviews, rotten retaliations maintain their hold over us.

A scarier experience than mere threats and abuse, however, is the social situation in which one is thrown together with a writer one has slightingly written about. My most embarrassing moment, as the phrase goes, surely came the evening I was invited out to dinner and upon entering the front door of the house noted, already in the living room, The Poet, he of whom I had written, and obviously—like me—an invited guest for dinner. The look of horror and despair which came over my face must have been powerful, at least enough for the concerned hostess to ask had I forgotten something. No, just remembered it. It was not in the least a disastrous evening, for The Poet was all charm, acting as if he'd never read a thing I'd written. Perhaps he hadn't; more likely it was a fine performance in noblesse oblige. There are of course no precautions, short of solitary confinement, to be taken against such chance meetings. But one could predict trouble might be in store for someone like me when I did a one-night stand at the Bread Loaf Writers' Conference, with all those resident poets and novelists I had reviewed, some of them rottenly. Nothing bad happened to me at Bread Loaf either, though it took some joint maneuvering between me and Another Poet to manage not to meet, not even to be introduced. Both of us emerged the better for it (or the lack of it), I am convinced.

One of this country's foremost producers of rotten reviews, composed while he was a young man making his way in the trade, was Randall Jarrell, so gifted at hitting off the masterly short dismissal that even victims of it marveled at his skill. Reviewing several poets he began, by saying of a forgotten book of verse, "If I were a dust jacket, I should call *Farewell to Walden* 'sonnets of love and social protest'; being what I am, I can say only that they are all Italian, all regular, and all bad." Two paragraphs later, Archibald MacLeish's "America Was Promises"—which Jarrell pretended was a "malicious parody of Mac-Leish's public-speaking period"—fell under scrutiny: "Here on the platform, huge against the leaves, the sea, the night (courtesy of Maxfield Parrish); flanked by Freedom, Truth, Justice, stiff in their collapsible chairs, a nominating committee to be periodically apostrophized; stands the declaiming 'I': he speaks for Man." A moment later, Kenneth Patchen met his doom: "His poetry has a big violet streak of original Swinburne-with-a-dead-baby; and his detailed version of 'Sex is *wonderful*' gets much worse than Swinburne's 'It's *wicked.*'" Could Jarrell top that? He went on to try with Frederick Prokosch, whose poems "pour out like sausages, automatic, voluptuous, and essentially indistinguishable." This response, incidentally, prompted Mr. Prokosch to write to the *New Republic* and declare that "I shall publish no further verses in America, where they have met with [such] vituperation."

In other words, Mr. Prokosch was not amused to have his poems compared to sausages—his aesthetic detachment failed him. Karl Shapiro, on the other hand, although reviewed dismissively by Jarrell (who once called a poem of Shapiro's "a sort of bobby-soxer's *Mauberley*"), testified later that he felt as if he had been run over but not hurt. Yet about a decade after he made those crushing remarks about Prokosch, MacLeish, and the others, Jarrell repented of the whole reviewing scene, notifying Margaret Marshall at the *Nation* that, having written another rotten review of MacLeish, "I just couldn't bear to publish it—it would depress and vex the poor guy and do no *good* at all. . . . It's all the truth, but the whole thing would be like digging up a corpse to tell it it wasn't any good when it was alive." Soon after, and on the same subject, he wrote Robert Lowell that since they lived in a "reviewing criticizing age that doesn't give a damn for works of art, mostly—why should I help it along? I'll write articles occasionally about what I *like* and all the rest can just die quietly without any help from me."

Jarrell was almost as good as his word, proceeding to compose his invaluable appreciations of Whitman, Frost, William Carlos Williams, and others. But once in a while, when the occasion demanded it, he slipped back into the older style of damning—though now with the faintest praise: "Stephen Spender is, I think, an open, awkward, emotional, conscientiously well-intentioned, and simple-minded poet. To like his poems as much as we shouldn't, we need to respond to what they are meant to be—not to what they are—and it is surprisingly easy to do this." It almost sounds complimentary.

My impression is that as reviewers age, they tend not to write so many rotten reviews. The nice word for what happens to us is "mellowing"; but it's also likely that we're going soft, not necessarily in the most attractive sense. There may, however, be a practical explanation that accounts in part for the tendency toward more appreciative reviewing, since age does bring, for the reviewer, the likelihood that he'll have more opportunities to write about books he really cares for. If I'm in the position to request a new novel or book of poems by someone whose previous work I've admired, it's unlikely I'll find the book destitute of all taste and competence. Or—as with Jarrell when confronted by new work by MacLeish or Spender—the effort at one more castigation just doesn't seem worth making. Yet perhaps the fiercest and most entertaining American reviewer (mainly of novels during the last few decades), the aforementioned Marvin Mudrick, never lost the zest with which he denounced the latest miserable piece of fiction or criticism to fall his way.

As with respect to other complicated human activities, one can't make up rules for proper reviewing behavior, or for criticism generally. Jarrell writes of how the latter "demands of the critic a terrible nakedness: a real critic has no one but himself to depend on. He can never forget that all he has to go by, finally, is his own response, the self that makes and is made up of such responses—and yet he must regard that self as no more than the instrument through which the work of art is seen, so that the work of art will seem everything and his own self nothing."

Can anyone live up to such purity of aspiration and intention? Should one always try to? The "work of art" one is confronted with often seems a good deal less than "everything," sometimes quite a bit less than a work of art, and one's "own self" refuses to submit to it. My own self, says the reviewer, is more interesting than the one I've met with here—and sometimes the reviewer is right. Nor is it possible to control the impulse to pan a book by reminding oneself that mere "critical" work is subordinate or inferior to "creative" work. And, as Orwell reminds us, the first motive out of which one writes any prose is "sheer egoism. Desire to seem clever, to be talked about, to be remembered after death." Most reviewers don't expect to be remembered after death, but while alive they wouldn't mind being talked about, even being perceived— rightly or wrongly—as clever. It serves us right, then, when the morning mail brings a shocker like the anonymous postcard recently informing me that something I had published was "Absolute gibberish. You can't *write!* Absolute rubbish!"

We may conclude that the reviewer lives, or keeps going, by holding extremes together in his mind; when he's down he may quote Henry James to himself about how "art lives upon discussion . . . upon the exchange of views and the comparison of standpoints," and he may fancy that he is contributing, however modestly, to that discussion. And when he becomes too flushed with virtue, making bold to think of himself as a guardian of culture, a servant of the truth, Orwell is there to provide the corrective terms: "Sheer egoism. Desire to seem clever, to be talked about." If our reviewer is also a professor of literature—and there are a good many such in this country—he may fancy that some of his colleagues in the profession think of him, if at all, as a Literary Hack, willing to sell his soul for the production of a few thousand, or hundred, words on most any book or topic. On the other hand, the Hack may reply that at least he's not despoiling the environment with further reflections on currently hot academic topics like Canonicity, or The Problematics of Gender-Related Theory.

One of the great English literary hacks of this century was Geoffrey Grigson, who died a few years ago and who must have reviewed thousands of titles, more often than not with acerbity and unconcealed displeasure. A self-styled "reviewer with a bill-hook," Grigson believed, in his later years at least, that one shouldn't review books unless one wished strongly to promote them, and he opined that he would like to check in himself "an ardent wish to demote, now and then." Looking back on his career he generalized from it that "One starts reviewing books when young for the vanity of being asked to review them and of seeing one's name on the review, one continues it for money, one persists in it as a way of acquiring books one wants very much which are too expensive to buy." Reviewing, he summed up, was a disease, or at least a compulsive habit. Yet Grigson never kicked the habit and lived with the disease until a respectably advanced age, even writing a few more rotten reviews in the process. We should all be so lucky until called at last before the great tribunal, there to answer for our crimes.

New York Times Book Review, May 7, 1989

Name Index

Acheson, Dean, 36
Ackroyd, Peter, 28
Adams, Henry, 30, 34
Agee, James, 58
Aiken, Conrad, 27–28
Akenside, Mark, 218
Aldington, Richard, 33
Alger, Horatio, 148
Alpers, Paul, 213
Alvarez, A., 70
Amis, Kingsley, 14, 20–21, 61, 75–83, 136, 174,
    195
Amis, Martin, 131
Ammons, A. R., 209, 225
Annan, Noel, 196
Aristotle, 27, 176, 258
Arnold, Matthew, 138, 145, 172–73, 198, 230
Ashbery, John, 21, 73, 98–102, 225
Ashkenazy, Vladimir, 199
Astaire, Fred, 63
Atlas, James, 259
Auden, W. H., 46, 48, 51, 57, 60, 66, 76, 104, 195
Austen, Jane, 13–14, 116–17, 155–56, 159, 173,
    227, 258

Babbitt, Irving, 185
Bach, Johann Sebastian, 191, 198–200
Bagehot, Eliza, 239
Bagehot, Walter, 239
Baird, Theodore, 3–4, 6
Balanchine, George, 199
Balzac, Honoré de, 172, 236, 239
Barth, John, 165
Barthelme, Donald, 165
Baskin, Leonard, 89
Bate, W. J., 73
Baudelaire, Charles, 172
Bayley, John, 60–61, 76
Beethoven, Ludwig van, 199
Beiderbecke, Bix, 199
Bell, Clive, 182
Bellow, Saul, 17, 225
Bennett, Arnold, 122–23, 195
Bennett, William, 128

Berlioz, Hector, 199
Berryman, John, 51
Betjeman, John, 60, 75, 136
Bidart, Frank, 19
Bishop, Elizabeth, 72, 209, 233
Bishop, John Peale, 38
Blackmur, R. P., 40, 193, 212
Blake, William, 174, 218, 226
Blanchot, Maurice, 216
Bloch, Marc, 236
Bloom, Harold, 37, 100, 210–11, 213, 215, 217,
    220–27
Blotner, Joseph, 147, 149
Bodenheim, Maxwell, 30
Borrow, George, 171
Boswell, James, 186
Boulez, Pierre, 48
Boulton, James, 119
Bowen, Elizabeth, 156
Bowra, Maurice, 82
Bradley, F. H., 183
Brahms, Johannes, 198–99, 236, 256
Brandt, Anthony, 259
Braudel, Fernand, 236
Brödel, Max, 188–89
Bromwich, David, 73
Brontë, Charlotte, 227
Brontë, Emily, 227
Brooks, Cleanth, 206, 215, 228
Brower, Reuben, xi, 3–4, 6, 10, 194
Browning, Robert, 69, 183, 194, 224, 244
Bruce, Lenny, 167
Bruckner, Anton, 236
Buckley, William F., 215
Bundy, MacGeorge, 36, 42, 44
Burke, Edmund, 174
Burke, Kenneth, 5, 193, 226, 228
Burrows, Louie, 119–22, 124
Burrows, Mabel, 238
Butler, Samuel, 31
Butscher, Edward, 93

Cage, John, 98
Calhern, Louis, 165

Name Index

Name Index

Name Index